# DEATHWATCH
# MARK OF THE XENOS

ROLEPLAYING IN THE GRIM
DARKNESS OF THE 41ST MILLENNIUM

# CREDITS

**LEAD DEVELOPER**
Ross Watson

**WRITTEN AND DEVELOPED BY**
Owen Barnes, Andy Chambers, Alex Davy, Andrea Gausman, Andy Hoare, Kevin Rubitsky, and Benn Williams

**ADDITIONAL WRITING**
Mack Martin

**EDITING**
Graham Davey

**PROOFREADING**
Paul King

**GRAPHIC DESIGN**
Kevin Childress

**ADDITIONAL GRAPHIC DESIGN**
Mark Raynor, Brian Schomberg, and Michael Silsby

**COVER ART**
Michael Phillippi

**INTERIOR ART**
Jacob Atienza, John Blanche, Alberto Bontempi, Joao Bosco, Alex Boyd, Matt Bradbury, Christopher Burdett, Kevin Childress, Paul Dainton, Wayne England, Mark Gibbons, Nikolaus Ingeneri, Karl Kopinski, Brandon Leach, David Lecossu, Damien Mammoliti, Hector Ortiz, Adrian Smith

**ART DIRECTION**
Zoë Robinson

**PRODUCTION MANAGER**
Eric Knight

**FFG LEAD GAME DESIGNER**
Corey Konieczka

**FFG LEAD GAME PRODUCER**
Michael Hurley

**PUBLISHER**
Christian T. Petersen

## GAMES WORKSHOP

**LICENSING MANAGER**
Owen Rees

**HEAD OF LICENSING**
Paul Lyons

**HEAD OF INTELLECTUAL PROPERTY**
Alan Merrett

**SPECIAL THANKS TO OUR PLAYTESTERS**
Matt Eustace, "Bring the Noise" James Savage with Davie Gallacher, Thomas S. Ryan, and Stewart Strong, "The Bolter and Chainsword Playtest Group" Ryan Powell with Matt Bogart, Jon Cox, Max Hardenbrook, Anders Lang, and Richard Sanders, "No Guts, No Glory" Sean Connor with Adam Lloyd, Stephen Pitson, Mark Smith, and Michael Thompson, "The Librarians" Pim Mauve with Keesjan Kleef, Jan-Cees Voogd, Joris Voogd, and Gerlof Woudstra

FANTASY FLIGHT GAMES

Fantasy Flight Games
1975 West County Road B2
Roseville, MN 55113
USA

ISBN: 978-1-58994-782-5  Product Code: DW05  Print ID: 958MAR11

Printed in China

For more information about the **DEATHWATCH** line, free downloads, answers to rule queries, or just to pass on greetings, visit us online at

**www.FantasyFlightGames.com**

# CONTENTS

**Introduction**     **5**
What's in this book?....................................5

**Chapter I: The Alien Threat**     **8**
The Tau Empire.........................................8
  Broadside Battlesuit.............................. 11
  Commander Flamewing ....................... 13
  Ethereal ............................................. 16
  The Kroot ........................................... 19
    Krootox ......................................... 23
    Knarloc ......................................... 25
    Great Knarloc ................................ 26
    Kroot Hound .................................. 28
  Tau Pathfinder .................................... 29
  Vespid Stingwing.................................. 31
Tyranids .................................................. 33
  New Tyranid Weapons .......................... 33
  Tyranid Psychic Powers ........................ 34
  Carnifex ............................................. 36
  Dagon Overlord .................................. 38
  Gargoyle ............................................ 41
  Lictor ................................................ 42
  Purestrain Genestealer ......................... 44
  Ravener ............................................. 46
  Ripper Swarm ..................................... 48
  Trygon .............................................. 50
  Tyranid Warrior Prime .......................... 52
  Tyrant Guard ...................................... 54
  Venomthrope ..................................... 56
  Zoanthrope ........................................ 58
Orks ....................................................... 60
  Ork Traits .......................................... 61
  Ork Boy ............................................. 62
  Ork Meganob ..................................... 62
  Ork Warboss ...................................... 63
  Big Mek Wurrzog ................................. 64
Other Xenos ............................................ 65
  Bruul Parasite ..................................... 65
  Crotalid ............................................. 67
  Diablodon .......................................... 69
  Lacrymole .......................................... 71
  Loxatl Mercenaries .............................. 73

**Chapter II: Radicals and Heretics**     **76**
Inquisitor Thaddeus Hakk ........................ 77
Apostate Cardinal .................................... 80
Pontifex Guard ........................................ 83
Magos Phayzarus ..................................... 85
Irradial Cogitator .................................... 88
Samech Redemption Servitors.................... 90
Slinnar War Machine ................................ 92
Spire Slayer ............................................. 94

**Chapter III: The Forces of Chaos**     **98**
Bloodthirster.......................................... 100
Great Unclean One .................................. 102
Keeper of Secrets.................................... 104
Lord of Change ...................................... 106

Kyrus the Chantleader............................. 108
Bloodletter ............................................ 109
Daemonette ........................................... 110
Pink Horror ........................................... 111
Plaguebearer ......................................... 112
Chaos Space Marine Sorcerers ................. 113
Khorne Berzerkers .................................. 115
Noise Marines ........................................ 117
Obliterators ........................................... 119
Plague Marines ...................................... 121
Possessed Chaos Space Marines ............... 123
Weapons of Chaos .................................. 125
  Noise Marine Weapons ........................ 125
  Plague Marine Weapons ....................... 126
  Other Weapons .................................. 126
Chaos Psychic Powers ............................. 127

**Chapter IV: Advanced Adversaries**     **130**
Using Hordes in Deathwatch ..................... 130
  New Horde Traits ................................ 133
Massed Battles ....................................... 137
  Running Massed Battles ....................... 138
Turning Points ....................................... 141
  Using Turning Points ........................... 141
  Example Turning Points ........................ 142

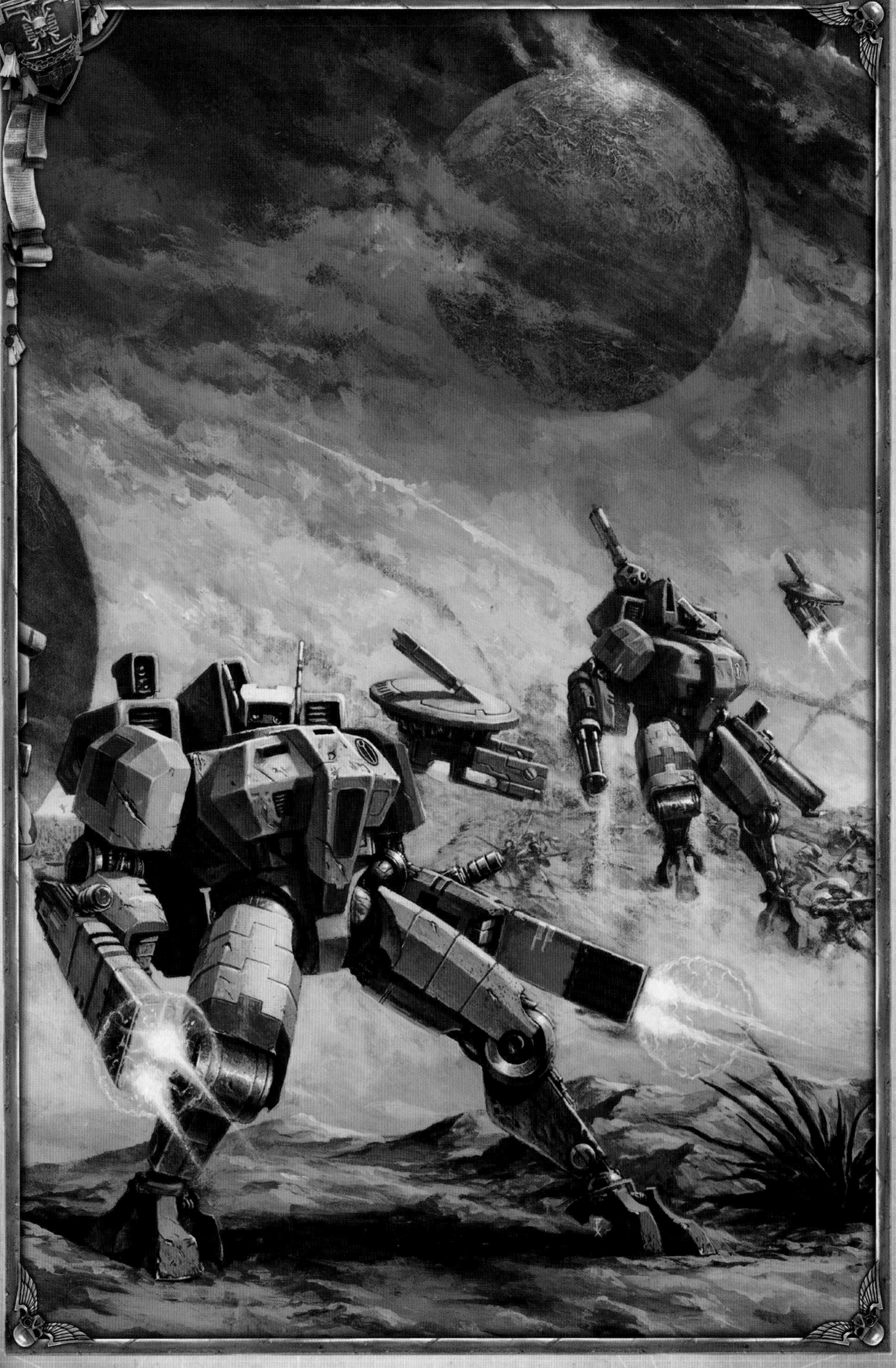

# INTRODUCTION

*To be Hunted...that is the Mark of the Xenos.*

*—From the Deathwatch's Catechism of the Xenos*

The Space Marines of the Deathwatch are legendary warriors, veterans of hundreds of battles, and heroes of the Imperium. Yet they are only a handful against the myriad threats that lay siege to the Imperium, from within, without, and beyond. The Deathwatch was founded to eliminate alien civilisations inimical to human life, and the eradication of such xenos is their main purpose. Yet, the Deathwatch does not shy from engaging the forces of heretics, daemons, or the Traitor Legions of Chaos Space Marines that emerge from the realms of Chaos, bent upon the destruction of man.

In the war-torn Jericho Reach, the Imperium struggles to re-conquer hundreds of lost, dark, and bitter worlds. The Achilus Crusade pushes ever-deeper into this region, facing horrific terrors on all fronts. Only the intervention of the Deathwatch Kill-teams can tip the balance, and the information collected in this book by Codicier Taelon of the White Scars Chapter places vital knowledge of their enemies into the hands of those warriors best suited to destroy any challenge to the Emperor's will.

## WHAT'S IN THIS BOOK?

MARK OF THE XENOS is a bestiary of the monstrous enemies that lurk within the Jericho Reach and strike back against the forces of the Achilus Crusade. This book includes commentaries, advice, and information from Codicier Taelon of the White Scars, a Deathwatch Librarian whose diligent work has gathered together information on the Deathwatch's greatest foes in the Jericho Reach into one place. Taelon put the resources of the Deathwatch, the Ordo Xenos, and the Chapters of the Space Marines to good use, gathering reports and notes from dozens of experts and first-hand accounts from across the Reach. Unfortunately, Taelon was among the fallen at the Battle of the Darkspire on the planet Ystobel, torn apart by a Hive Tyrant whilst keeping the creature at bay long enough for other Imperial forces to escape. His task remains incomplete, although his extensive notes have been highly praised by Inquisitors Ghraile and Quist of the Ordo Xenos, and many Watch Captains have taken heed of his wisdom in the decades since.

## MODIFYING ENEMIES

The enemies presented in this book can, and should, be modified by a Game Master to create the types of enemies he requires for his game. Some options and variations are presented as part of the enemy profiles but the possible variety of enemies far exceeds these, and a Game Master should feel free to make adjustments to them as he sees fit. If, for example, a game requires a group of Renegade Militia armed with missile launchers, they can be created by removing their autoguns, giving them missile launchers and the Heavy Weapon Training (Launcher) Talent.

The creatures listed in this book come with ready-made adventure hooks that a GM can use to drop the monsters directly into his Deathwatch campaign. Each of the following chapters focuses on a different breed of monster that the Kill-team may face in the course of their duties.

## CHAPTER I: THE ALIEN THREAT

The first chapter centres around the Enemy Without; alien races that exist within the Jericho Reach, and constitute the primary foes of the Deathwatch. The Tyranids of Hive Fleet Dagon and the Tau forces of the Velk'han Sept are presented in detail, accompanied by discussions of more minor (but no less dangerous) aliens such as the shapeshifting Lacrymole and the pernicious Bruul Parasite.

## CHAPTER II: RADICALS AND HERETICS

The second chapter focuses upon the heretics that abound within the cursed worlds of the Jericho Reach; recidivists misled by the rantings of Apostate Cardinals, the deadly machinations of a Radical Inquisitor, and the horrific constructs of tech-heresy are laid bare.

## CHAPTER III: THE FORCES OF CHAOS

Daemons, warpspawn, and Chaos Space Marines are but a few of the minions of the Ruinous Powers. The Hadex Anomaly spews forth armies of corruption into the Jericho Reach, a tide of evil that often clashes with Deathwatch Kill-teams.

## CHAPTER IV: ADVANCED ADVERSARIES

The fourth chapter of MARK OF THE XENOS presents new rules and guidelines for utilising adversaries in a Deathwatch campaign, including the proper use of Hordes and rules for scaling up to even larger conflicts.

## ENEMY PROFILE PRESENTATION

In all the entries presented in this book, the characteristics, movement values, and weapon damages have been presented with all modifications included. For example, a Chaos Space Marine's Strength includes the +20 increase from his Astartes Power Armour, and his Strength Bonus matches this and the effects of the Unnatural Strength Trait (and the Chaos Space Marine Sorcerer's force weapon includes his Psy Rating in its Damage and Penetration). Weapon damages include the effects of the enemy's Strength Bonus and Talents that always apply to damage such as the Crushing Blow Talent. Talents, Traits and Special rules that have a variable effect or will only apply in particular circumstances, such as the Hammer Blow Talent, have not been combined into the profiles presented here. It is also important to note that NPCs are not necessarily bound to follow the same strictures for their profiles as player characters.

To: Inquisitor Lord Hezika Carmillus
From: Codicier Taelon

The tome you see before you now is the result of our discussions regarding the myriad threats that our Kill-teams have faced amongst the worlds of the Jericho Reach. The entries within have been collected and researched from field reports, personal interviews, and data-vaults of ancient pedigree. A number of pertinent reports for this assignment are missing... I suspect the involvement of other Inquisitors or perhaps skilled heretical agents. Therefore, this tome is incomplete and not as comprehensive as I would like. Nevertheless, time grows short, and the lore of the reports herein will certainly benefit the commanders of the Achilus Crusade with proper clearances to view it.

Of particular note to your Ordo, honoured Inquisitor, is that a number of the threats detailed in this tome are not, in fact, alien in origin. Rather, these enemies are heretics, traitors, warpspawn, or worse. Some amongst your Ordo have questioned why such enemies are detailed alongside the others. The answer is simple... the Deathwatch may have been founded with the purpose of defeating the alien foe, but as Space Marines, we are honour-bound to oppose any threat to the Imperium of Man.

In the Jericho Reach, my Battle-Brothers and I have encountered bizarre daemonic entities, battled Traitor Space Marines, and destroyed heretic enclaves during the course of our duties for the Deathwatch. Many other Kill-teams have had similar experience. Thus, when I asked for the reports to create this tome, those reports included the threats that were judged worthy of the Deathwatch's interest in all aspects of war.

This book contains much knowledge and lore that must be placed under the highest ciphers, and I trust you and your fellow Inquisitors will know best how to disseminate it amongst the officers of the Achilus Crusade.

*-Codicier Taelon of the White Scars*
*Seconded to the Deathwatch*

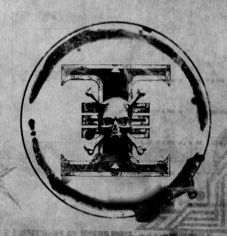

# The Alien Threat

The Tau Empire
·
Tyranids
·
Orks
·
Other Xenos

# CHAPTER I: THE ALIEN THREAT

*"The Deathwatch must remain ever vigilant against the xenos. The Enemy Within may tear at the Imperium's heart, and the Enemy Beyond may threaten the Imperium's soul, but the Enemy Without presents a unique danger; alien civilisations that stand in the way of the Imperium's destiny to conquer the galaxy."*

–Codicier Taelon, Deathwatch Librarian

No enemy is more central to the purpose of the Deathwatch than the numerous hostile alien races scattered throughout the galaxy and beyond. From the encroaching, remorseless hive fleets of the Tyranids to the technological and ideological danger represented by the Tau, the Deathwatch faces some of the deadliest foes in existence. They stand as a bulwark between the Imperium and the teeming hordes of aggressive xenos organisms. This Chapter details some of the better-known aliens in the Jericho Reach, often hunted by relentless Kill-teams of Deathwatch Space Marines.

# THE TAU EMPIRE

*"Wherever we have cast our gaze in this galaxy, we have seen only the dead and the dying, and those intent only upon casting themselves into burnings pyres of their own making. That is why we shall ultimately prevail, for we are different. We are united, we are determined, and we cannot fail but embrace the manifest destiny into which we are born."*

–Aun Talusi, Tau Ethereal and philosopher

Since the Tau Empire made its first incursions into the Jericho Reach, the Achilus Crusade's Departmento Tacticae has concentrated the efforts of several dozen Tacticae Primaris taskforces upon analysing their capabilities. Initial after-action reports submitted by the forces active along the Canis Salient tallied with the often confused and fragmentary accounts gathered in the aftermath of the Damocles Gulf Crusade, while more recent reports indicate that the xenos are committing assets not previously faced by the Imperium. During the Damocles Gulf Crusade, Imperial forces faced several classes of battlesuit as well as the most common Kroot forms. The Canis Salient has recently encountered more varieties of battlesuit, more extreme forms of Kroot, and a new type of foe entirely—the Vespid Stingwing.

The Departmento Tacticae is now busily engaged in consolidating gun-cam captures and interrogating Imperial troops that have faced these newly encountered foes on the field of battle. The Deathwatch has supplemented these findings with their own, though the Tacticae advisers remain convinced that Watch Fortress Erioch is withholding full disclosure, especially relating to the Vespid species, for some as yet undetermined reason. In truth, the ancient and vast cogitation stacks of Watch Fortress Erioch contain scant information relating to the Tau, for the species is young and its expansion so rapid that every battle the Deathwatch fight they learn something new. Several Kill-teams have become proficient in combating the alien tactics and technology of the Tau, and a standing order to take live prisoners where possible has been issued. Several specimens have already been interred in the secure chambers of Watch Fortress Erioch. The Ordo Xenos is especially interested in obtaining a live Vespid Strain Leader and several missions are being planned to bring this about.

Aside from the tactics used by the Tau against Imperial forces, the Departmento Tacticae seeks to unravel something of how the alien empire maintains control over the disparate species that serve it. Tau armies are mighty in themselves, but they are made even more so when the Fire Caste units are supplemented by warriors drawn from the many subject worlds ruled by the Empire. The most numerous of these auxiliary forces are the Kroot, savage and cunning carnivores that are infamous for their prodigious field craft and their horrible appetite for eating the corpses of those they have recently defeated. The Kroot themselves field a wide array of troops types, more of which are being encountered with every battle fought against them. Recently encountered Tau forces have been accompanied by the insectoid (for wont of a better term) Vespid Stingwings. These creatures are the product of a unique environment, having evolved amidst floating, lighter-than-air rock spires in the upper regions of their gas giant home world. Auxiliaries reported in other regions but yet to be encountered in the Jericho Reach include the space-borne Nicassar and other beings that may in fact be employed as mercenaries and not subject races at all.

Tau forces are organised in a very different manner to those of the Imperium, the warrior-philosophies and codes of the Fire Caste dictating a unique approach to war. The core grouping utilised by the Fire Caste is the Hunter Cadre, a group of Fire Warriors who serve together and are linked by unbreakable bonds of loyalty and duty. This in itself is not too different from the codes that bind such warriors as the Space Marines of the Adeptus Astartes, but it is a bond ingrained not by tradition or psycho-conditioning, but, apparently, by genetics. Fire Warriors possess an innate sense of their place within the Greater Good, which is magnified by the presence of a member of the Ethereal Caste to extraordinary levels. While Fire Warriors willingly sacrifice themselves for the greater cause, when led by an Ethereal they display levels of devotion unseen in any other sentient species.

Another point that makes the Tau military structure very different from that of the Imperium is the way in which it approaches specialisations. In the Imperial Guard for example, regiments are founded and organised according to well-established templates, such as infantry, armour, artillery, and so forth. Unless forced to downgrade by irrevocable losses, an Imperial Guard regiment maintains its role and specialisation, and is supported by a vast and rigid logistics train dedicated to its maintenance. A Tau Hunter Cadre is first and foremost a grouping of warriors, and, unlike an Imperial Guard regiment, is able to adapt its role to the strategic reality of war. Tau Hunter Cadres maintain large stocks of specialised equipment such as Devilfish troop carriers and Hammerhead tanks, and can switch roles from light infantry to mechanised assault very quickly. This is partly due to the short logistics train made possible by the dense nature of the Tau Empire, for even its frontline units are never far from a storage or manufacturing facility. However, it also has as much to do with the mindset of the Fire Caste. It is seen as a warrior's duty to master all forms of warfare and to advance in the service of the Greater Good. An experienced Fire Caste warrior will have started his career as line infantry and received cross training in the operation of every form of vehicle fielded by the Tau. He then progresses to serve first in a Pathfinder team, and next dons a stealth suit to complete his mastery of the arts of infiltration and ambush. The most skilled of warriors eventually join a battlesuit team, piloting one of the XV-8 "Crisis" Suits or one of its variants such as the XV-88 "Broadside." Of these elite veterans of service to the Greater Good, a small number progress to become leaders of their own Cadre, either replacing a fallen leader or taking command of a newly created formation.

This system renders the individual Fire Warrior far more skilled and versatile than the average Imperial Guardsman and affords the Fire Caste an unprecedented level of strategic flexibility. This is even more striking when the average lifespan of the Tau is taken into account. The Tau mature quickly, but their adult life rarely exceeds forty years. They only show signs of aging towards the very end of their lives, when infirmity comes quickly and death follows soon after. Some in the Ordo Xenos postulate that it is this cycle that drives the race forward with such energy, and that the Greater Good is founded on the notion that only the next generation will see the fruits of a Tau's labours. Most among the Imperium's upper echelons who know something of the Tau's collectivist philosophy despise it, regarding it as every bit as dangerous to the soul of Mankind as the threat posed by Chaos.

---

*To Codicier Taelon, by the hand of Plenipotentiary-Designate Ark: 387817.M41*

*I am recently returned from a contact negotiation with the Tau, and I am driven to commit my immediate thoughts to record. While maintaining the propriety that my station demands, I grow increasingly frustrated by the manner in which the Tau comport themselves. Indeed, I might go so far as to describe them as infuriating! Their Water Caste envoys maintain a mask of politeness and openness, yet they talk around every issue raised. I have come to understand that the Tau regard themselves as occupying some sort of moral high ground in everything they do. They condemn our actions, claiming our methods are excessive or unreasonable, yet have a justification for every one of their own, often equally extreme, deeds. When they hear that Imperial forces have decimated a rebellious world, they call us callous and state that such things could never occur under their beneficent rule. Yet, when they invade a world that refuses to submit to joining their empire, they at first deny all involvement, and then eventually cite the necessity of their vile collectivist creed. They preach equality and the value of every sentient being, yet they allow their auxiliary subjects to make sacrifices they rarely ask of their own kin.*

*I submit this observation to you in the hope that it may further your own studies into this particular xenos species. While my recent mission was undoubtedly trying, I have come away from it with a deeper understanding of the Tau, which I believe can serve us all. They do not seek to expand their empire for mere territorial or material gain, for their home region is bountiful in natural resources of every type. They expand because they must, just as we fight because we must. They believe it is their destiny to unite every sentient being in the galaxy under their rule. This, I believe shall be their undoing. By the time they discover the truth of the horrors that lurk between the stars, they will have fatally overstretched themselves, and then we can strike them down once and for all.*

*Perhaps, Emperor willing, the Jericho Reach is the place where they shall bite off more than they can chew. I pray this is so.*

*Yours in faith,*

*— Dragon Ark*

# TAU MARKERLIGHTS

Markerlights are laser designator devices, used to "paint" a target for other units to fire at. The device can be hand held, mounted on a weapon or carried by a drone. When activated, the Markerlight projects a beam of light at a target of the bearer's choosing, measuring the exact position of the target relative to the user. This targeting data is then transmitted to other units, who utilise it to guide their own fire. The most common and effective use of the Markerlight is to guide indirect or standoff fire, called in by the elite scouts of the Pathfinder teams. Utilising a concealed position, a Markerlight-equipped Pathfinder directs his device at an enemy target without the foe being aware of his presence. Seeker missiles carried by Tau armoured vehicles are then fed the targeting data captured by the Markerlight, and fired, often from some distance away or from behind intervening terrain features. The missile "rides the beam," which the Markerlight user must keep trained on the target until the missile strikes. Because Pathfinders are adept at working their way into flanking positions, they are often able to target the vulnerable sides and rear of their targets, destroying them with ruthless efficiency. The only downside of the device is that the beam, while invisible in normal conditions, becomes visible when it passes through dense airborne gas or vapour (such as smoke or fog) and in so doing risks giving away the user's position.

Markerlights normally take the form of a special sighting device mounted upon another weapon (often a Pulse Carbine), its operation slaved to the weapon's trigger, which is over-ridden by way of a simple toggle switch. Toggling between the main weapon and the Markerlight is a Free Action, and the Markerlight is "fired" in the same way as a ranged weapon. However, the Markerlight does not cause damage in itself, and is instead used to grant bonuses to other Tau units who subsequently fire upon the target that has been "marked." These benefits are as follows:

- +10 to all Ballistic Skill Tests to hit the target (these bonuses are cumulative)
- A seeker missile may be fired at the target with an effective Ballistic Skill of 80 (note that normally, seeker missiles may not be fired at targets that have not been hit by a markerlight)

A Markerlight hit remains in effect for one full round, or until the target is moved out of sight from the Markerlight beam (for instance, if the Space Marine hit by a Markerlight were to fall prone into a trench).

Markerlights do no damage and are considered to have unlimited ammunition. To avoid a Markerlight hit, the target must succeed at a **Hard (–20) Awareness Test** instead of a Dodge Test. Under conditions that include smoke or fog, this test becomes much easier, typically Challenging (+0) or Ordinary (+10). If the test is successful, the target is aware that he has being designated and avoids the hit.

## TABLE 1-1: TAU WEAPONS

| Name | Class | Range | ROF | Dam | Pen | Clip | Rld | Special |
|---|---|---|---|---|---|---|---|---|
| Airbursting Fragmentation Launcher† ‡ | Heavy | 60m | S/–/– | 1d10+5 X | 4 | — | — | Arm Weapon Mounting, Blast (5), Devastating (2) |
| Broadside Railgun | Heavy | 500m | S/–/– | 3d10+30 I | 15 | — | — | Mounted |
| Ion Cannon | Heavy | 200m | S/–/3 | 3d10+10 E | 9 | — | — | Mounted |
| Kroot Bolt Thrower | Heavy | 150m | S/–/– | 2d10+10 X | 2 | 20 | Full | Blast (3), Mounted |
| Kroot Bow | Basic | 40m | S/4/8 | 1d10+3 R | 3 | 20 | 2Full | Tearing, Toxic |
| Kroot Gun | Heavy | 150m | S/2/– | 3d10+8 I | 6 | 10 | Full | — |
| Kroot Rifle | Basic | 110m | S/2/– | 1d10+5 E | 1 | 6 | 2Full | — |
| Kroot Rifle (Melee) | Melee | — | — | 1d10 R | 0 | — | — | Balanced |
| Kroot Hunting Rifle | Basic | 150m | S/–/– | 1d10+5 E | 3 | 8 | Full | Accurate |
| Markerlight | Heavy | 150m | S/–/– | — | — | — | — | Mounted |
| Rail Rifle | Heavy | 150m | S/–/– | 2d10+10 I | 9 | 16 | Full | Devastating (1), Overheats |
| Seeker Missile‡ | Heavy | 500m | S/–/– | 3d10+10 X | 8 | — | — | Mounted |
| Smart Missile System‡ | Heavy | 90m | –/–/4 | 1d10+12 X | 4 | — | — | Arm Weapon Mounting |
| Vespid Neutron Blaster†† | Basic | 30m | S/–/– | 1d10+12 E | 8 | — | — | Toxic |

† Attacks from the Airbursting Fragmentation Launcher explode immediately above the target. As long as there is at least five metres of open space above the target, the weapon ignores the effects of cover.

†† Neutron Blasters only function when wielded by a Vespid.

‡ The bearer of these weapons need not be able to see his target to use them, but he must be aware of it. He does not suffer from the normal –30 penalty for firing at a target he cannot see, as the projectiles fired are self-guided.

# BROADSIDE BATTLESUIT

The Tau utilise a wide range of battlesuits for a myriad of tasks both on and off the battlefield. The most common by far is the XV-8 "Crisis" Suit, of which the Crusade's Departmento Tacticae has catalogued at least a dozen distinct variants. While the Crisis Suit is used as a utility unit and can be fielded in a range of weapon and sub-system configurations, its heaviest variant is a specialised sub-class codified by the Imperium as the "XV-88," or "Broadside."

The Broadside is equipped with the heaviest weapon systems it is possible to mount on an XV-8 battlesuit. Its structure is significantly upgraded to support the additional weight and power drain of the huge weapons it carries. The suit's design is a highly effective compromise between offensive firepower, defensive protection, and tactical manoeuvrability. Because of its static fire support role, the suit has been significantly up-armoured, making it one of the most well protected units in the Tau arsenal. During the Damocles Gulf Crusade, frontline Imperial forces submitted corroborated after-action reports of Broadside battlesuits surviving direct hits from autocannon and lascannon fire. The suits are rated as providing as much protection as a suit of Terminator Armour, but unlike the Imperium, the Tau are able to manufacture such heavy suits in huge quantities.

The primary weapon system carried by the Broadside is a twin railgun. This weapon is part of family that ranges from the man-portable rail rifle carried by some Pathfinders, up to the huge rail cannon mounted on the Hammerhead tank. Even larger versions are possible, but most are static or mounted on superheavy flyers or star ships. The basic principle of the technology is well known to the Adeptus Mechanicus, but the Imperium has never been able to utilise it in a worthwhile form due to the myriad issues inherent in the operation of the weapon. In essence, a small, solid conductive projectile is propelled by an electrical current between two charged rails, achieving staggering velocity before leaving the barrel. Because the projectile is capable of achieving a velocity of anywhere between six and ten times the speed of sound, it generates a tremendous force when it strikes its target, far more in fact than an explosive charge of the same size ever could. Because the projectiles are so small, huge numbers can be carried and they can be fired over a very long range. The limitations of such technology relate to the staggering amount of power required to propel the projectile along the rail, and the dissipation of the heat generated by the process. The Tau appear to have implemented solutions to these problems, and many heretical types amongst the Adeptus Mechanicus would very much like to understand how.

In addition to the twin railguns, Broadsides carry a range of secondary systems. They can be fitted with smart missiles systems or plasma rifles, affording point defence capability should enemy infantry compromise their position. Furthermore, Broadsides are often fielded with a support system selected to complement the role the Commander envisages them undertaking in upcoming missions.

Broadsides tend to be encountered supporting larger Tau formations, where one or more three-member teams are tasked with providing fire support for entire Hunter Cadres. Occasionally, a single Broadside is tasked with providing support for a smaller Tau force. Even individually, Broadsides are a formidable threat to a Deathwatch Kill-team, for their weapons are capable of utterly defeating even the most sanctified of power armour suits. The Deathwatch have learned to take advantage of the Broadside's relatively slow speed to outmanoeuvre them and silence them from behind. This tactic is rarely simple, however, because the Tau are adept at fielding mutually-supportive units well able to cover each other's vulnerabilities.

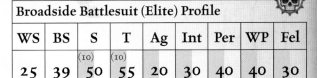

## Broadside Battlesuit (Elite) Profile

| WS | BS | S | T | Ag | Int | Per | WP | Fel |
|----|----|----|----|----|----|----|----|----|
| 25 | 39 | (10) 50 | (10) 55 | 20 | 30 | 40 | 40 | 30 |

**Movement:** 4/8/12/28      **Wounds:** 30

**Skills:** Awareness (Per), Common Lore (Tau Empire) (Int), Speak Language (Tau, Kroot) (Int).

**Traits:** Auto-Stabilised, Dark-sight, Unnatural Strength (x2), Size (Enormous), Unnatural Toughness (x2), Sturdy.

**Armour:** XV-88 Broadside Suit (All 12).

**Weapons:** Twin-linked Broadside Railgun (500m; S/–/–; 3d10+30 I; Pen 15; Mounted, Twin-linked) or Twin-linked Ion Cannon (200m; S/–/3; 3d10+10 E; Pen 9; Mounted, Twin-linked), Smart Missile System (90m; –/–/4; 1d10+12 X; Pen 4; Arm Weapon Mounting) or Twin-linked Plasma Rifle (90m; S/2/–; 2d10+9 E; Pen 10; Arm Weapon Mounting, Tearing, Twin-linked).

**Gear:** Broadside Battlesuit, micro-bead and xenos-crafted auspex. May be accompanied by one or two Shield Drones.

## ADVENTURE SEEDS

**The Greyhell Front:** Imperial forces battling the Tau on the Greyhell Front have recently reported a variant of the Broadside battlesuit that utilises not the normal Railgun weapon configuration, but shoulder-mounted Ion Cannons instead. Groups within both the Ordo Xenos and the Adeptus Mechanicus are keen to recover an example for further study, and so a plan to do so is conceived. A mass Imperial Guard assault is launched in the area where the variant suits were observed, under the cover of which the Kill-team will seek to disable, capture and recover a suit. As if this were not hard enough to achieve, the Adeptus Mechanicus have inserted their own group, consisting of a number of specialist Tech-Priests and their various combat servitors. This group seeks to recover the Tau's ion technology for itself, and is a rival of the Inquisition. The Kill-team has to face not only the Tau with their fearsome new weaponry, but heretical Tech-priests intent upon their own nefarious mission.

**Broadside Assault:** Broadsides are fearsomely destructive, and they always aim to engage their foe at extreme range. In fact, they have such long range that the first a Kill-team may know of the battlesuits' presence is when they come under fire from the powerful railguns. A single shot can slay even a mighty Space Marine, so the Kill-team will be forced to concentrate all of its efforts upon infiltrating the Tau's positions and outflanking any Broadsides present. While these battlesuits are relatively ineffective in close combat, they are still well armoured and more importantly, they are normally protected by other units, which the Kill-team must neutralise to be sure of mission success.

```
+++EXLOAD REQUEST GRANTED…COGITATING…COGITATING…
DISPLAY EXLOAD…SUBJECT: [TAU BATTLESUIT NOMENCLATURE]


EXTRACT A1: …and so this commission recommends the adoption of the attached system for
identifying and codifying the accursed machines of this foe. Initial interrogations of
Tau prisoners yielded the term "Her'ex'vre," which it was determined held the meaning
"Mantle of the Hero," the term by which the Tau designate their single-pilot battlesuits.
Her'ex'vre was transcribed phonetically as "XV," and thus forms the basis of the
designations that this commission sets out. XV shall henceforth identify the most common,
single-pilot suit.

Furthermore, we have identified a number of mass class and construction variations, which
shall be classified by way of one or two numerals placed after the XV codifier. The first
number shall be the suit's mass class. "1" shall indicate the lightest of suits, while "8"
shall identify the largest of the variants we have observed thus far.

Suits with a specific, confirmed function shall have a second designator, while what we
consider "utility" suits shall have only a single (mass class) numeral.

EXTRACT B3: The following roles have been identified and each assigned a numeric code.
This number shall be the second element of the suit's class designation. Note that it is
possible that a suit might have a secondary role, in which case a third numeral may be
included in its designation.

+++Suits believed to exist only as theoretical or developmental models shall be
designated "1."

+++Developmental suits that have progressed to field trials shall be designated "2."

+++Those suits that have not entered mass production but have been assigned permanently to
the pilot shall be designated "3."

+++Suits designed and approved for the command and control role shall be designated "4."

+++Those intended for use in the 'stealth' role we designate "5."

+++Air-space units are designated "6."

+++Those suits intended to facilitate infiltration shall be designated "7."

+++Fire support units shall be designated "8."

COGITATING EXAMPLE…

+++XV-8 single pilot heavy utility class…XV-88 single pilot heavy fire support unit…XV-15
single pilot ultra light stealth suit…XV-25 single pilot light stealth suit…XV-22 field
test prototype light stealth suit…


+++OVERSEER META-PROBE DETECTED…RETURN TO STATION…TERMINATING EXLOAD+++
```

# COMMANDER FLAMEWING

*"The Greater Good is more than a theory. It is more than a creed or a philosophy. It is a universal truth, and to deny it is as arrogant, foolhardy and ultimately futile as to deny the pull of gravity or the passage of time."*

–Commander Flamewing to the Second Emissary Council

Commander Shas'O Vior'la Suam Eldi, or to give him his contracted and more commonly used title "Commander Flamewing," is the leader of a Fire Caste Hunter Cadre currently operating on the outskirts of the Zurcon system. Flamewing is a comparatively young Commander, yet he has seen more combat in the last year than many of his rank expect to experience in a lifetime.

Flamewing hails from the Tau sept of Vior'la, a system in the Tau Empire renowned for the skill and potency of the Fire Caste warriors born there. The warriors of Vior'la are commonly held to be hot-blooded and ferocious, yet able to contain these traits and focus them towards the Greater Good. Commander Flamewing is typical of his peers in that he is possessed of a fearsome intensity that is made manifest in combat against the enemies of the Tau Empire. As a Fire Warrior, he defended the rimward frontier station of Hy'si against Dark Eldar raiders intent upon enslaving the Earth Caste scientists, earning much honour as well as many impressive scars. As a battlesuit pilot in a Crisis Team, Flamewing participated in the Defence of Sy'l'Kell on the sept world of Dal'yth Prime, where he gained three confirmed kills against the mighty Space Marines of the Imperium before wounds sustained in close combat forced his withdrawal from that action. After a period of convalescence, Flamewing took part in the actions that followed the Imperium's retreat from Tau space, fighting as part of Commander Farsight's force that swept into human space and took control of a number of colonies the humans had all but abandoned in their haste to re-deploy. With the foundation of the Velk'Han Sept, Flamewing was given command of a newly raised Hunter Cadre, which was tasked with opposing the advance of the recently discovered Tyranid hive fleet closing on the freshly established sept.

Sadly for Commander Flamewing and his Hunter Cadre, Tau high command massively misjudged the Tyranids' capabilities. Having already faced smaller tendrils of the larger enemy force that had arrived on the Eastern Fringe,

Flamewing was not naive as to their nature. He had studied every after-action report he could access and believed he had the measure of his foe. The problem was, the Tau's estimates of enemy numbers were grievously in error, and the Tau stumbled into a far more numerous and concentrated enemy than it could ever hope to defeat. Within days, dozens of Hunter Cadres were fighting for their very existence, cut off from support and massively outnumbered.

Flamewing found himself in command of an effort to effect a fighting withdrawal to a defensible position, a task that he executed with great skill and honour, saving the lives of many hundreds of Fire Warriors and their auxiliary troops. His Hunter Cadre exacted a fearsome toll as it fought across the burning sands of Zurcon Extremis, and Flamewing himself led a number of daring counter-attacks that accounted for a number of lynchpin Tyranid hive-node beasts. In one such encounter, Flamewing and his veteran Crisis Teams engaged a Zoanthrope, braving the horrors of its relentless psychic assaults to bring it down with concentrated plasma rifle fire. At length, Flamewing's Hunter Cadre established a defensive position high atop a wide, flat mesa, and stood unyielding as the Tyranid monstrosities broke around its base as a seething ocean battering a lone rocky isle. Flamewing and his warriors held the mesa for six days and nights, ever hopeful that the other Tau Hunter Cadres would be able to fight through and join them. They did not, and the Commander realised his cadre represented the last Tau presence on Zurcon Extremis.

On the seventh night of the battle, something strange occurred. Flamewing's warriors fell into a dark rage, one by one shedding the peerless discipline for which the Fire Caste is renowned and surrendering to something far more primal. Soon, the rage consumed Flamewing himself, and he observed his warriors growing surly and fractious. Shockingly, several brawls erupted in the ranks, a phenomenon that none had ever witnessed or experienced. Then the realisation of what was occurring came to the Commander, and dread filled his soul; the Fire Warriors were succumbing to the same barbaric urges that had set the castes against one another at the very outset of their history, a time of bloodshed that only the coming of the Ethereal Caste had put at an end. The fact that Flamewing's warriors were regressing to such an atavistic state could only mean that the last of the Ethereals on Zurcon Extremis had fallen to the Tyranids.

Realising his Hunter Cadre's position was all but lost and its fate too terrible to consider, Flamewing saw but one course of action. He determined that not a single Tau would fall at the hand of his own kin, and rallied his warriors for one last, glorious action. Flamewing's Hunter Cadre would sally forth from their position and sell their lives dear. If they were to fall, Flamewing promised, it would be for the glory of the Greater Good and they would serve the Empire by slaughtering its foes to the last.

Flamewing's words stirred his warriors into a righteous rage, and the entire Hunter Cadre launched itself at the foe, Flamewing at the head. The battle raged for the remainder of the night and well into the next day, and as the sun reached its zenith only Flamewing and his Crisis Team retinue were left standing, atop a small mountain of Tau and Tyranid corpses. The end was mere moments away, but suddenly, the survivors' rage lifted, to be replaced with a sudden sense of familiar, blessed calm. A moment later, the communications channels sang with transmissions and a huge, multi-Hunter Cadre force crashed into the rear of the Tyranid horde.

Within an hour it was all over. Commander Flamewing and his few surviving companions stood before the Ethereal Aun'O Tsualal, and gloried in the radiance of his sacred presence.

In the aftermath of Zurcon Extremis, Commander Flamewing entered a brief period of retreat and meditation. He had been grievously wounded, in body and in spirit, and has yet to fully recover. During his retreat, Flamewing conferred with and studied beneath the most learned of Fire Caste notables, Commanders who had faced and mastered the same inner turmoil he himself had suffered on Zurcon Extremis. He meditated on the deeper truths of the Greater Good, and emerged possessed of such inner knowledge that few of those who had known him took him for the same warrior. Donning his battlesuit once more, Commander Flamewing took command of a new Hunter Cadre built around the survivors of the old, and vowed to take the battle to the Tyranids anew, armed with his newly acquired wisdom.

Commander Flamewing is to be found wherever the Fire Caste faces the Tyranid menace, advising other Commanders or leading the charge in person. He greatly resents the waste of resources afforded by the need to fend off what he regards as petty attacks by the human Imperium, believing the two species should be working together against the overarching threat of the Tyranids. While the Commander has fought against human forces on several occasions, he has also cooperated with them and made several clandestine alliances amongst more open-minded factions within the Ordo Xenos and other groups. As yet, these alliances are tenuous at best, but Commander Flamewing is working towards a time when, he believes, Tau and human will stand together, united by common necessity, against a threat neither could survive alone.

## Commander Flamewing (Master) Profile

| WS | BS | S | T | Ag | Int | Per | WP | Fel |
|----|----|----|----|----|----|----|----|----|
| 41 | 57 | 50 (10) | 57 (10) | 48 | 52 | 55 | 65 | 44 |

**Movement:** 12/24/36/72  **Wounds:** 90

**Skills:** Acrobatic (Ag), Awareness (Per) +10, Command (Fel) +20, Common Lore (Tau Empire) (Int), Dodge (Ag), Forbidden Lore (Tyranids) (Int), Logic (Int), Speak Language (Tau, Kroot, Low Gothic) (Int).

**Talents:** Air of Authority, Fearless, Hatred (Tyranids), Iron Discipline, Litany of Hate, Meditation, Rapid Reaction, Sprint.

**Traits:** Auto-stabilised, Dark-sight, Flier (12), Size (Enormous), Unnatural Strength (x2), Unnatural Toughness (x2).

**Armour:** XV-8 Crisis Suit (All 9).

**Weapons:** Airbursting Fragmentation Launcher (60m; S/–/–; 1d10+5 X; Pen 4; Arm Weapon Mounting, Blast [5], Devastating [2]), missile pod (90m; S/2/–; 2d10+6 X; Pen 5; Mounted), plasma rifle (90m; S/2/–; 2d10+9 E; Pen 8; Arm Weapon Mounting, Tearing).

**Gear:** Crisis Battlesuit incorporating Command and Control Node, Experimental Battlesuit Shield Generator, Ejection System (see page 366 of the **DEATHWATCH** Rulebook), mirco-bead, xenos-crafted auspex.

## Special Rules

**Command and Control Node:** The Command and Control Node is a sophisticated drone intelligence communication system entering the final stages of development. The system provides the user with a totally immersive command interface and is wired directly into his central nervous system so that the data is fed directly to his subconscious mind and need not be interpreted or filtered by conscious awareness. The device instantly compiles the user's intentions into coherent orders, which are fired off by encrypted tight-burst transmission to all

## RITUAL OF THE TA'LISSERA

The Ta'lissera is a sacred undertaking made by the members of a single team. The ritual bonds the members together in a microcosm of the Greater Good wherein each individual sheds his individual identity in favour of his role in the group. Those who undertake the Ta'lissera are said to be "bonded," and the ritual is a solemn one indeed in which each Tau spills a portion of his own blood as a sign of his devotion to the whole. Those who are not bonded view those who are with awe, seeing them as the ultimate adherents of the Greater Good. The Ritual of the Ta'lissera is carried out in many areas of Tau society, but is most frequently undertaken amongst Fire Warrior teams, who enter the crucible of war together and often stand or fall by one another's deeds. The members of a bonded team will go to any length to aid one another, sacrificing their very lives if needed that the team might succeed in its mission. Members of a bonded team often carry ceremonial knifes, while those piloting battlesuits paint a stylised knife device on their armour.

Any Tau (not Kroot, Vespid, or other allied race) Horde or permanent grouping of Elites may be Bonded. This grants the Horde or group the Duty Unto Death Talent so long as the majority of the team members are still alive.

## Airbursting Fragmentation Launcher

This item of special issue equipment has been entrusted to a number of senior Fire Caste Commanders, and has undergone several improvements throughout its development. The weapon fires a proximity-fused explosive projectile, launched on a trajectory computed by an onboard drone intelligence. The warhead is fired at a high angle and explodes directly above the target, negating the effects of any cover the foe might be using. In Flamewing's hands the weapon has proved effective against swarms of Tyranids because it can be fired over the centre of the horde where the targets are most densely packed. It has also proved useful against the more stealthy types of Tyranid construct, especially those that make intelligent use of cover and those gifted of chameleonic qualities that are hard to pinpoint. Another major advantage of the weapon is that it can be targeted on an enemy even if the user does not have a direct line of sight to it, because of its indirect fire trajectory.

subordinate units. All Actions involving ordering or influencing other Tau units are Free Actions, so long as the target unit is equipped with a micro-bead or similar communication device.

**Experimental Battlesuit Shield Generator:** Commander Flamewing has been issued with a special issue shield generator designed to offer enhanced protection to the bearer, especially when fighting enemies like the Tyranids that utilise overwhelming swarm tactics. The generator features enhanced power storage and output systems. Rather than emitting enough energy to counteract incoming attacks, it shunts additional power through the contact point, potentially causing damage against foes who would engage the bearer in close combat. The shield has a Protection Rating of 50 and Overloads on a roll of 01–10 (it is still experimental after all). Any foe that hits Commander Flamewing in melee automatically suffers 2d10+3 E damage.

**The Patient Hunter:** (see page 366 of the DEATHWATCH Rulebook).

**Multi-Tracker:** Commander Flamewing's battlesuit is equipped with a sophisticated tracking system that lets him fire all of his weapons with the same action. For example, if he takes a Standard Attack action to fire a single shot with his plasma rifle, he can also fire a single shot from his missile pod and airbursting grenade launcher at the same time. The profiles of the weapons do not change; if he takes the Semi-auto Attack action, his plasma rifle and missile pod both fire using the Semi-auto Attack rules, but the airbursting fragmentation launcher still fires only once using the rules for a Standard Attack. When using the multi-tracker, all attacks must have the same target.

### Addendum by Codicier Taelon

Current intelligence suggests that Commander Flamewing is leading a Hunter Cadre of experienced Fire Warriors and other auxiliary fighters, and is engaged upon an unknown mission to the Death world of Mahir. Given that this planet has fallen to the Tyranids, his objective must be to strike some decisive blow against the Hive Mind or perhaps to attempt to deny or disrupt the Tyranids' consumption of Mahir's biomass. Our own, admittedly limited, reconnaissance of Mahir suggests that the Tyranids are struggling to subdue the world's fearsome flora and fauna, and my recommendation, ratified in Chamber, has been to allow the Tyranids to expend their energies in their attempt to consume a planet that appears to be just as determined to consume its invaders. I recommend the Tau force be observed lest it interfere with the delicate balance of power on Mahir.

## Adventure Seeds

**Escort:** The Player Characters are assigned as high-level escorts for an Imperial dignitary sent to meet with Commander Flamewing. The mission takes the group to an isolated world in space contested by the Imperium and the Tau Empire, an area rife with all manner of threats from void-lurking pirates to Tyranid vanguard organisms. When the meeting finally takes place, the dignitary is revealed as an agent of a Puritan faction intent upon slaying the xenos commander before his collectivist creed can infect other loyal servants of the Golden Throne. The Kill-team is forced to take sides, though Commander Flamewing is quite capable of looking after himself.

**Standoff:** The enemy of my enemy is my friend—the Kill-team crosses paths with Commander Flamewing whilst engaged on a mission against the Tyranids. The two forces might reach a compromise, fighting towards the same ends. Whether or not this arrangement is a formal one, brokered face-to-face, or an informal understanding to leave off killing one another until the mutual foe is neutralised, is up to the player characters.

### Using Commander Flamewing

Commander Flamewing can be used as both an enemy and an ally, depending on the sort of mission the Kill-team is undertaking. Keep in mind that he need not always be encountered in his battlesuit. Should the player characters encounter him off of the battlefield, he may well not be wearing it, though it will not be far away. To field Flamewing in this manner, simply disregard those Traits and other special rules that are obviously granted by the battlesuit, and give him Fire Warrior armour and a pulse pistol as a side arm.

# ETHEREAL

*"Those whose time is brief must surely strive all the harder, that the universe shall remember their deeds."*

–Aun O'Quva, Tau Ethereal

The Ethereals are the fifth caste of the Tau species, forming a ruling elite above the Fire, Earth, Air, and Water castes that make up the bulk of Tau population. Though their numbers are small compared to the other castes, Ethereals command total and utter authority over every other Tau. It is said that any Tau, from a recently birthed worker to a veteran Commander would slit his own throat at a single word from an Ethereal.

The Ethereals are as mysterious as they are powerful, especially to outsiders. Those Imperial dignitaries who have had contact with the species have invariably dealt with the Water Caste, which consists of ambassadors, traders, administrators and facilitators. They have rarely even glimpsed an Ethereal, yet their hidden hand is ever at work, guiding the Tau from afar. The caste first came into existence during the phase in the species' earliest history in which the four castes were at war with one another, the entire species apparently doomed to destroy itself in its own birth pangs. The Ethereals appeared as from nowhere, and ended the conflict with a single command. They have ruled ever since that time.

The rulers of the Tau Empire conduct themselves largely apart from their peoples, residing in great palaces within which they debate the course of their species and guide it forward for the Greater Good. The caste organises itself using the same system of ranks as do the other four, with the lowest formed into councils overseeing settlements, and the highest ruling over entire Septs—autonomous and self-sustaining colony systems. The species as a whole is guided by a body referred to as the Council of the Highest, consisting of all of the most senior Ethereals. No single individual heads this council, and it tends to be guided by the wisdom of whichever Ethereal is regarded by his peers as pre-eminent.

Some Ethereals have been known to accompany Tau forces into battle, and indeed they always accompany Tau colonisation and expansion forces. It has been theorised that Tau, especially those of the Fire Caste, not operating under the high level guidance of an Ethereal are likely to regress to the warlike state that so nearly destroyed their species at the dawn of its history. Needless to say, there are those amongst the Ordo Xenos keen to investigate this matter further, in the hope that targeted assassination of key Ethereals might bring about a favourable strategic situation. It is not necessary for Ethereals to participate in every conflict at the tactical level, and Fire Caste warriors are quite capable of operating without them being close at hand. It appears however that an Ethereal must be present at the operational or strategic level to ensure the stability of those under his command. When the Ethereals do participate in a battle, it is generally to provide inspirational leadership in order to push the warriors on to achieve otherwise impossible things in the name of the Greater Good. There is a downside to this however, for should the Ethereal fall in combat, the remaining Tau are likely to be consumed with maddening grief. Sometimes they collapse in total disarray, even if they could easily have won the engagement. Other times they become enraged and charge forward to avenge themselves on their foe. Either way, all cohesion is lost and the Fire Warriors lose all vestige of the disciplined and efficient warriors they ordinarily are.

The method by which the Ethereals maintain control over their species is unknown to the Imperium, and possibly even to those they rule. Several studies have been undertaken, and the Deathwatch is even in the possession of a low-ranked member of the caste having captured him as his vessel passed through an unclaimed system near Tau-controlled space. Prior to the capture of this specimen, it was assumed that the Ethereals must utilise some unidentified method of biological, psychic or even pheromone control over the Tau. The Ethereals sport an unidentified organ in the centre of their foreheads, a smaller version of which is possessed by other castes. It was assumed that this organ must be key to the control effect, yet the specimen captured has been extensively examined and no functioning system has been identified. Either the captured Ethereal is a deliberate attempt to misdirect the Imperium, or the matter is far more esoteric than had previously been thought. Investigations into this mystery are ongoing.

In temperament, Ethereals are enigmatic and studious, yet unfaltering in their authority and their drive to further the Greater Good. They are mystics and philosophers, possessed of knowledge and wisdom not shared by their more practical subjects. The origins of the Tau species are shrouded in mystery, and it is a great enigma that the Tau ascended from the status of primitive nomads to a highly developed, star-faring empire in less than six millennia. The Ethereals evidently had some part to play in this rapid development, and to this day guide their species in its dynamic expansion lest the castes revert to the savagery that once threatened to overwhelm it.

## Ethereal (Master) Profile

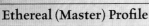

| WS | BS | S | T | Ag | Int | Per | WP | Fel |
|----|----|----|----|----|-----|-----|----|-----|
| 40 | 35 | 30 | 30 | 30 | 40 | 35 | 60 | 40 |

**Movement:** 3/6/9/18      **Wounds:** 20

**Skills:** Awareness (Per), Command (Fel) +20, Deceive (Fel), Evaluate (Int), Forbidden Lore (Tau) (Int), Inquiry (Fel), Literacy (Int), Logic (Int), Scrutiny (Per), Speak Language (Low Gothic, Tau) (Int).

**Talents:** Air of Authority, Chem Geld, Foresight, Iron Discipline, Inspire Wrath, Master Orator, Meditation, Orthoproxy.

**Armour:** None.

**Weapons:** Staff of office (1d10+3 I; Balanced; requires two hands) or Honour Blade (1d10+3 R; Pen 2; Balanced; requires two hands).

**Gear:** Ornate robes, various symbols of office, micro-bead.

### Special Rules

**Inspiring Presence:** Members of the Ethereal Caste exert a mysterious but palpable control over other Tau, an effect that has yet to be explained by the Imperium's biologis-savants. The Ethereal may make a **Challenging (+0) Fellowship Test** as a Free Action. If the test is passed, all of his Talents that effect his Tau Minions (not including Kroot or Vespid or other such allies) operate at an unlimited range.

**The Price of Failure:** The Tau revere their Ethereal leaders over all others, and the one thing that can reduce a disciplined Fire Warrior to unreasoning barbarity is the thought of one falling to their enemies. If an Ethereal is killed, every other Tau character and Horde (not Kroot, Vespid, and so forth) must take an immediate **Terrifying (–30) Fear Test**. If the test is passed, the character or Horde immediately gains the Frenzy Talent (without having to spend a Round fuelling the

anger). If the Test is failed, the character or Horde roll on the Shock Table (see page 277 in the **DEATHWATCH** Rulebook) as normal.

## DRONES

The Tau utilise drones for many different tasks, from menial maintenance tasks to jobs too dangerous for the Tau themselves to undertake. Drone is a broad category used to describe any "helper" drone that is assigned to a single owner and aids them in undertaking their duties. In battle, commonly fielded Drones include Shield Drones and Marker Drones. Many other types exist too, some very rare or still in the experimental phase of their development. Such Drones often possess an extremely loyal character, imparted to them by their creators to ensure they protect their masters with absolute loyalty.

## Drone Profile

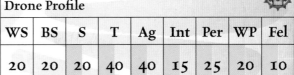

| WS | BS | S | T | Ag | Int | Per | WP | Fel |
|----|----|----|----|----|-----|-----|----|-----|
| 20 | 20 | 20 | 40 | 40 | 15 | 25 | 20 | 10 |

**Movement:** — (Flying 12)      **Wounds:** 15

**Skills:** Acrobatics (Ag), Awareness (Per), Dodge (Ag).

**Talents:** Fearless.

**Traits:** Flier (12), Machine (5).

**Gear:** One of the following: Tau Shield Projector†; Markerlight; long-range vox; Scanner; Injector and 5 doses of Pain Suppressant.

### Special Rules

**Slaved Devotion:** Drones are assigned to accompany a single individual and programmed to protect him at all costs. They will always remain within 2 metres of their owner. If the owner is killed another Tau equipped with a Drone Controller may attempt to take control of the Drone by passing a **Very Hard (–30) Tech Use Test**.

**†Tau Shield Projector:** The Shield Drone and all characters within two metres of it are protected by its shield projector from attacks originating from more than two metres away. The shield has a Protection Rating of 45 and Overloads on a roll of 01–10.

## DRONE CONTROLLER

A Drone Controller works as a micro-bead that allows the user to communicate his will to any Drone under his direct control. Most of the time the controller operates at a default level that simply keeps the Drone obeying its basic programming, but the owner can also use it to issue simple orders beyond the Drone's normal parameters. Team leaders and senior Tau (such as Battlesuit Commanders and Ethereals) may be assumed to be equipped with Drone Controllers at the GM's discretion. Doing so allows the bearer to control up to two Drones (these Drones may be of any kind, and need not be both of the same kind, i.e., one Shield Drone and one Gun Drone).

---

### HONOUR BLADE

Tau Ethereals utilise Honour Blades as symbols of office, ceremonial weapons, and (in an emergency) in self defence. While each weapon is custom-made and individual, they all feature a broad blade fitted to a long, lightweight metallic staff. Ethereals use the blades primarily to settle disputes, engaging in lengthy, highly stylised duels that are more coordinated co-meditation than combat. The combatants dance and weave as if in a trance, their weapons flashing past one another scant millimetres and microseconds from causing terrible damage. Yet somehow, the dance is always bloodless, as if the Ethereals are in total union with one another. In truth, the combatants are engaged in a deeply spiritual duel, conducted at a level which none outside of their caste can discern. Some Ethereals carry their Honour Blades on the field of battle, not expecting to have to use them, but prepared to make a last stand against their barbaric foes nonetheless.

## Addendum by Codicier Taelon

It is rare indeed that a Kill-team encounters one of these Ethereals, for they are inevitably found only in the company of significant numbers of their species. Their target rating is based not on their own combat potential, for this is relatively insignificant. Instead, they are dangerous for the morale-boosting and command-and-control benefits they confer to their underlings. In the presence of even a single Ethereal, ordinary Tau forces are transformed and become at once formidable and unpredictable. Tau Fire Warriors for example are disciplined and efficient in combat, but their battle doctrines call upon them to re-deploy in the face of overwhelming odds. When fighting alongside an Ethereal however, the Fire Warriors sometimes become dogged in their defence, redoubling their efforts to repulse their foe and to keep the Ethereal from harm at all costs. The Tau undoubtedly value the lives of their warriors, even those of their subject species, yet will make any sacrifice necessary to protect the life of a single Ethereal. This phenomenon was evident at the Battle for Bekrin V, where we fielded three entire Kill-teams in an effort to break through Tau lines and engage the Ethereal known as "Aun'O Bhi." The infiltration mission was carried out successfully, and Brother Umbra's team was closing on the compound in which the Ethereal was believed to be located. The instant the Tau became aware of our presence, and our proximity to their leader, the entire defence force re-deployed to oppose us. Three hundred and more Fire Warriors deserted their positions and raced for the compound, not in the usual disciplined manner but with visible fury. Force cohesion broke down as individuals yelled angry war cries and literally threw themselves onto our guns in an effort to keep us at bay.

It was a slaughter, and I can scarcely claim any pride in the estimated 1:500+ kill ratio recorded that day. By 0+3 hours our force was reduced to one tenth of issued ammunition and forced to engage in close assault against what had become a horde of ill-disciplined, yet uncharacteristically ferocious Fire Warriors. We became mired in the slaughter, until we saw the Ethereal's vessel launch from the compound and effect an escape. Their leader safe, the remaining Tau fought on with grim resolution, and we cut them down with ruthless efficiency. The compound was captured and the Tau's brief presence on Bekrin V was ended, but Aun'O Bhi escaped.

## ADVENTURE SEEDS

**Q-Ship:** Deep in the prison-vaults of Watch Fortress Erioch is held the single Ethereal that, to date, the Deathwatch have been able to capture, a low ranking individual called Aun'La Tsua'Malor Viorla. Although the taking of the prisoner was initially hailed as a great victory, doubts have since arisen that the operation to grab the Ethereal went too smoothly, and that too few Tau forces were present to guard such a valuable member of their caste. Recently, debate in the Chamber of Vigilance has raised the possibility that the prisoner is not all he appears to be, and that a mission to gather more intelligence should be undertaken. The player characters' Watch Captain decides to lay a trap. The Kill-team are to secrete themselves within a "q-ship," a merchant vessel heavily armed with hidden weapons. Word has been spread throughout a network of Inquisitorial assets along the Greyhell Front that the prisoner is to be moved from Watch Fortress Erioch to a hidden facility on the quarantined world of Argoth, a planet seething with Tau sympathizers and isolated by Ebongrave's decree from the Imperium at large. If the Ethereal is genuine, it is assumed that the Tau will make an attempt to recover him. If they do not, then it can be surmised that the prisoner is a ruse and of no value to the Tau. What if the Tau, via traitors or Radicals within the lower orders of the Inquisition get word of the scheme, and attempt to capture the Kill-team?

**Pariah:** An Inquisitor of the Ordo Xenos has come to Watch Fortress Erioch in the hope of recruiting the Deathwatch. He means to carry out an experiment to learn something of the process by which the Ethereals control the Tau. He is accompanied by an individual cursed as a "pariah"—someone who appears to have no presence in the warp at all and whose proximity is deeply unsettling to psykers. The Inquisitor intends to infiltrate an outlying Tau world where he believes an Ethereal to be operating, and observe the effect his pet pariah has on the Tau leader (if any). He believes that the pariah's presence, even if many kilometres from the Ethereal, should have some measurable effect which his contacts amongst the oppressed human population of the world could report back to him. The Chamber of Vigilance reluctantly agrees to the plan, and the player characters' Kill-team is tasked with accompanying the Inquisitor on his mission. Needless to say, the pariah has no effect upon the Ethereal, but the mission could prove interesting in many other ways. Perhaps the pariah's presence triggers a response in a number of latent psykers within the human population, betraying the Kill-team's mission and causing all manner of complications.

# THE KROOT

*"The Tribe of Seven Wings welcomes your offering. Let the warriors feast, and let the future take shape…"*

–Unnamed Kroot Shaper soon before the total defeat of the 309th Landrian Light Infantry

The Kroot are a species of almost limitless variety, having travelled countless evolutionary paths. While the form most associated with the species is referred to by the Imperium as the Kroot Carnivore, it is postulated that almost every single animal life form on their home world of Pech is related, albeit distantly, to the genus. Evolution in the Kroot has become a matter of rapid adaptation. The Kroot evolve so quickly that they are in danger of overtaking their own development and becoming so specialised that they are led down dead-end evolutionary paths. This has happened to many members of the genus, who have devolved into creatures only able to exist in a very specific environment or to eat only a particular prey. Even the slightest alteration in environmental factors can result in the extinction of these hyper-specialised sub-species.

Shapers are the leaders of Kroot Kindreds. They command their underlings on the field of battle and perform most of the functions associated with interaction with other groups such as the Tau. However, more significantly, they play a vital role within Kroot society which shapes the fate of the entire species.

For most of the species' development, this trait was uncontrolled, and caused by a unique feature. The Kroot have at some distant point in their past gained the ability to absorb the genetic characteristics of their prey, inheriting many of their features. This is achieved by way of the Kroot's unique DNA, which is able to store far more information than that of other species, allowing them to incorporate useful DNA strands into their own.

It is the task of the Shaper to oversee this process. At some point in the species' past, the riot of uncontrolled evolution must have produced the ancestors of the current incarnation, and they, uniquely amongst their entire genus, were sentient and capable of exerting some control over their own fate. Were they not, they would have been a short-lived passage in the species' history and would no doubt have succumbed to random evolution. When some quirk of evolution blessed the Kroot with sentience, they gained the ability to control their own destiny, and the Shapers are those in whom responsibility for this process is vested.

Shapers have the instinctive ability to sample and analyse the genetic characteristics of any creature they eat. They are able to isolate the prey's DNA so that it does not corrupt their own, and interpret which of its characteristics might be favourable to Kroot evolution and which might be detrimental. The Shaper then warns his Kindred against eating particular prey, and directs them towards others. By carefully guiding his Kindred's breeding, the Shaper can navigate the species' turbulent development. He is as much responsible for guarding against regression as he is for ensuring the development of new, favourable genetic traits.

Kroot are possessed of an overwhelming urge to consume the corpses of those they have slain in combat, a trait over which they have very little control and is a throwback to earlier stages in their evolution. The Shapers are the only Kroot capable of curtailing this instinct, and they can with a single hiss warn their

underlings away from consuming the flesh of an undesirable creature. Having determined that a particular prey is safe to consume, the Shapers invariably allow their Kindreds to obey their primal urges. Thus, Kroot will consume the bodies of fallen humans and other creatures if the Shapers have already determined that it is safe for them to do so.

There are three known types of creature that the Kroot will not prey upon, the Shapers having forbidden it. The first are Tyranids, who the Shapers have declared 'inedible' (the term has far worse connotations to a Kroot than to a human). Something in the function of Tyranid evolution causes utter revulsion in the Shapers, perhaps because Tyranids also modify the genetic inheritance of other species towards their own development, though in a very different manner. The second group the Kroot avoid preying upon are those humans who have turned to the worship of Chaos. This is a very hit and miss affair, for the Kroot are barely able to tell the followers of the Ruinous Powers from any other type of human. This proscription stems from an incident when the Kroot defeated a warband devoted to Slaanesh, and later developed a number of entirely undesirable mutations. The last group the Kroot are forbidden by the Shapers to feed upon are the Tau themselves. Even though the Kroot comport themselves as savage mercenaries and rely upon the Tau for material support in many matters, they are, as a species, deeply indebted and devoted to the Tau, for Pech would have fallen to Ork invasion were it not for the Tau's aid. To taste the flesh of the Tau is to earn the swift and deadly retribution of the Shapers.

## Kroot Carnivore (Troops) Profile

| WS | BS | S | T | Ag | Int | Per | WP | Fel |
|----|----|----|----|----|----|----|----|----|
| 42 | 33 | 45 (8) | 40 | 45 | 25 | 44 (8) | 30 | 18 |

**Movement:** 4/8/12/24      **Wounds:** 12

**Skills:** Acrobatics (Ag), Awareness (Per) +10, Barter (Fel), Climb (S) +10, Concealment (Ag) +20, Dodge (Ag) +10, Silent Move (Ag) +20, Speak Language (Low Gothic, Kroot, Tau) (Int), Tracking (Int) +10, Survival (Int) +20.

**Talents:** Basic Weapon Training (SP, Primitive), Exotic Weapon Training (Kroot Bolt Launcher, Kroot Bow, Kroot Gun, Kroot Hunting Rifle, Kroot Rifle) Furious Assault, Hyperactive Nymune Organ, Kroot Leap, Leap Up, Lightning Reflexes, Melee Weapon Training (Universal), Resistance (Fear), Swift Attack.

**Traits:** Eater of the Dead, Fieldcraft, Kroot Physiology, Natural Weapon (Beak), Overwhelming (Horde), Unnatural Perception (x2), Unnatural Strength (x2).

**Armour:** Hide Armour (Body 2; Primitive).

**Weapons:** Kroot Beak (1d5+8 R; Pen 0; Primitive), Kroot Rifle (110m; S/2/–; 1d10+5 E; Pen 1; Clip 6; Reload 2Full, [Melee] 1d10+8 R; Pen 2; Balanced).

**Gear:** Cut meat of varying freshness, bandolier of 30 charges for the Kroot Rifle, fetish pouch.

## Kroot Shaper (Master) Profile

| WS | BS | S | T | Ag | Int | Per | WP | Fel |
|----|----|----|----|----|----|----|----|----|
| 45 | 35 | 45 (8) | 45 | 50 | 30 | 45 (8) | 40 | 25 |

**Movement:** 5/10/15/30      **Wounds:** 35

**Skills:** Acrobatics (Ag) +10, Awareness (Per) +10, Barter (Fel), Climb (S) +10, Command (Fel) +10, Concealment (Ag) +20, Dodge (Ag) +10, Silent Move (Ag) +20, Scrutiny (Per), Speak Language (Low Gothic, Kroot, Tau) (Int), Tracking (Int) +10, Survival (Int) +20.

**Talents:** Basic Weapon Training (SP, Primitive), Combat Sense, Exotic Weapon Training (Kroot Rifle, Tau Pulse Weapons) Furious Assault, Hyperactive Nymune Organ, Kroot Leap, Leap Up, Lightning Attack, Lightning Reflexes, Melee Weapon Training (Universal), Resistance (Fear), Swift Attack, Touched by the Fates (2 Fate Points).

**Traits:** Eater of the Dead, Fieldcraft, Kroot Physiology, Natural Weapon (Beak), Shamanic Power (choose one) Unnatural Perception (x2), Unnatural Strength (x2).

**Armour:** Hide Armour (Body 2; Primitive).

**Weapons:** Kroot Beak (1d5+8 R; Pen 0; Primitive), Tau Pulse Rifle (150m; 1d10+12 E; Pen 4; Clip 36; Rld Half; Gryo-Stabiised), xenos-crafted hunting knife (1d10+8 R; Pen 2; Balanced).

**Gear:** Fetishes and talismans, 3 clips of Pulse Rifle ammunition.

## KROOT TRAITS AND TALENTS

The following Traits are common to all Kroot.

### EATERS OF THE DEAD

Kroot are infamous for their practice of devouring the corpses of their foes. If necessary, they will even turn cannibal and eat Kroot corpses. A Kroot who devours a fresh corpse (the GM has discretion to decide what qualifies as "fresh"—typically, the corpse must have been killed no more than 24 hours previously, and the corpse must be that of an organic creature; no daemons or machines!) gains a number of bonus Wounds equal to the unmodified Toughness Bonus that the corpse possessed when it was alive (typically three). These bonus Wounds may not exceed the Kroot's own Toughness Bonus and remain for a number of hours equal to the Kroot's Toughness Bonus or until they are lost, whichever comes first. Unlike normal Wounds, these bonus Wounds are removed when affected by the Damage of any successful attack, and are always removed first before applying Damage to the Kroot's normal Wounds. In addition, a Kroot who consumes a fresh corpse heals at twice the normal rate and adds one additional bonus Wound to any wounds healed through any other means (i.e., psychic healing, etc.) for a number of hours equal to his Toughness Bonus. A Kroot can only receive bonus Wounds from one consumed corpse at a time.

If a Kroot consumes a corpse while benefiting from bonus Wounds from a previous corpse, he loses the previous bonus Wounds and gains bonus Wounds from the new corpse instead.

### FIELDCRAFT

Kroot gain a +10 bonus to all Concealment, Shadowing, and Silent Move Tests. In addition, Kroot treat forests, jungles, and similar environments as open terrain.

### KROOT PHYSIOLOGY

Kroot are most comfortable wearing light armour or piecemeal protection scavenged from the battlefield. When a Kroot wears armour that provides more than 3 APs, he loses the benefits of the Unnatural Perception and Fieldcraft Traits.

### HYPERACTIVE NYMUNE ORGAN

The Kroot's nymune organs are hyperactive, storing great amounts of energy. The Kroot's metabolism is sped up, improving his raw muscle speed, reflexes, and reaction time. The Kroot gains one additional Reaction per round. When taking the Full Move Action, the Kroot may move an extra number of metres equal to his unmodified Agility Bonus. When taking the Run Action, he may double his movement for one Round. He gains one level of Fatigue if he uses this Talent in two consecutive Turns unless he passes a **Challenging (+0) Toughness Test**.

## Kroot Traits and Talents, Continued

The following Traits are common to all Kroot.

### Kroot Leap

Kroot are adept at using their long legs to jump, hop, and leap long distances. The Kroot has learned to use this advantage whilst rushing an enemy in close combat. When making a Charge action, the Kroot can ignore obstacles between him and his target by making a Running Vertical Jump (see page 207 of the DEATHWATCH Rulebook). This Talent may only be used if there is room for the Kroot to land next to his target and if there is enough overhead space for the Kroot to leap over the obstacles. For example, a wall that goes from floor to ceiling may not be leapt over, nor would something taller than the Kroot's vertical jump distance. If the Kroot successfully strikes his target whilst using this Talent, the Kroot may make a Knock-Down Action against the target (see page 241 of the DEATHWATCH Rulebook) as a Free Action.

## Kroot Shaper Traits

The following Traits are only for Kroot Shapers.

### Instinctual Understanding (Trait)

The Shaper may select one target that he can see. If the Shaper has previously devoured an example of the target's race, the Shaper may make a **Challenging (+0) Scrutiny Test** against the target as a Half Action. If successful, the Shaper may determine the number of Wounds that the target possesses, and may further determine a number of the target's characteristic bonuses equal to the degrees of success on the Scrutiny Test. The Shaper may select which characteristic bonuses he discovers when using this ability. The Shaper may use this ability once per target per encounter.

### Shamanic Powers (Trait)

One of the many roles of a Shaper within Kroot society is to act as a focus for the practice of ancestor worship. Kroot Shapers have a great mastery of rituals that call upon the ancestor spirits of their Kindred. These rituals often have unusual effects that lend Shapers a reputation for supernatural powers. Each must be activated by the Shaper, usually involving a sonorous chant and access to the powders, rocks and bones kept within the Shaper's fetish pouch. Activating a Shamanic Power is a Full Action.

### Ancestral Blessing

The Shaper's rituals are attuned to asking the warrior spirits of his ancestors for aid in battle. The Kroot may affect himself and a number of Kroot equal to his Willpower Bonus with this ability. The Shaper may apply the benefits of this Talent to non-Kroot allies, but he must first pass a **Challenging (+0) Willpower Test**. Those who benefit from this ritual gain a +2 bonus to melee damage rolls for a number of rounds equal to the Shaper's Willpower Bonus. This ability may be used only once per day.

### Blood of the Stalker

The Shaper daubs the blood of a local predator upon his exposed skin and those of his allies, cawing a prayer to gain the favour of his ancestors in the coming hunt. The Shaper may apply this Talent to himself and a number of Kroot equal to his Willpower Bonus. The Shaper may apply the benefits of this Talent to non-Kroot allies, but he must first pass a **Challenging (+0) Willpower Test**. Those who benefit from this ritual gain an additional degree of success on any passed Concealment, Shadowing, or Silent Move Tests.

### Prophetic Dreams

Many Shapers seek guidance from their ancestors in visions and dreams. Often, these visions may grant the Shaper insight into the future, although such glimpses are quite difficult to interpret. The Kroot may enter a trance during his normal sleep cycle. During this trance, he may receive a vision that grants him some foreknowledge of the future. The Kroot may re-roll one failed Test during the next 24 hours. The Shaper experiences visions that are clues to significant events that may come to pass in the near future. These visions may relate to something in the next week or even years hence.

## ADVENTURE SEEDS

**Alliance:** A large alliance of Kroot Kindreds appears to be operating not as auxiliary troops under the Tau Fire Caste, but as an independent mercenary group operating far from Tau worlds and apparently independently. The Shaper leading the alliance has offered his force's services to several rebel-held worlds in the regions spinward of the Hadex Anomaly, and the Crusade High Command have taken notice. The Deathwatch is petitioned to help, and the Chamber of Vigilance agrees to send a Kill-team on a mission to neutralise the Shaper. The mission takes the player characters deep into the anarchic reaches beyond the anomaly, where rebels, pirates and the vanguard organisms of Hive Fleet Dagon rule the void. The Shaper and his alliance are encamped on a lawless world, and engrossed in negotiations to sell their services to a rebel leader the Crusade has been looking to dethrone for some time. The leader cannot be allowed to recruit the mercenary force, for if he does he will be able to overcome his rivals and present a far more serious threat to the Crusade's progress. Of course, there is always the possibility that the Shaper will accept a better offer, should the player characters wish to talk rather than fight…

### USING KROOT SHAPERS

Shapers are quite capable adversaries in battle, and able field commanders of their Kindreds. However, they are not just "bad guys" to be engaged in combat, they are the leaders of their Kindreds and can make interesting characters in themselves. They interpret the will of the Tau into strategies their Kindreds can enact, and some of them even broker their services to factions other than the Tau. This is most likely to happen without the Tau's knowledge and approval, but it could of course be a ploy, an effort by the Tau to sow discord amongst their enemies by surreptitiously aiding one against another.

## Addendum by Codicier Taelon

Our knowledge of how this species reproduces is still incomplete, and we have yet to fully decipher the complexities of their relationship with the Tau. Cross-referencing various sources, I have come to form a picture, albeit incomplete, of Kroot society.

The Kroot are in essence mercenaries, in that they fight for the Tau in return for material benefit. Yet, this appears a simplistic interpretation of the relationship and one that applies in greater or lesser degrees amongst different groups. Various sources suggest that the Tau delivered the Kroot home world from an Ork invasion, and this intervention triggered the Kroot's integration into the Tau Empire. It is my belief that on a species-wide level, the Kroot are fully invested into the Tau's collectivist creed, accepting their place in what the Tau call the 'Greater Good'. Yet, on an individual level the Kroot are somewhat materialistic, placing great value in practical items such as tools, food and weapons. This to me appears to be an analogue of their genetic traits — they embrace their fate but seek to acquire new advantages, both genetic and material.

This notion is borne out when considering those Kroot who, perhaps in contravention of the terms of their membership of the Tau Empire, ply their mercenary trade across the stars. They do so in order to acquire a greater degree of genetic variance, and at the same time, I believe, a wider range of tools and weapons.

I have further noted in various writings the attitudes of the Kroot towards technology. They are not great innovators, but despite this display an innate, instinctual affinity towards certain forms of technology, generally those with a military application. This must surely have been inherited from the Orks, perhaps by way of the Kroot eating a number of the Orkoid "Mek" class and acquiring something of the greenskins' almost genetic understanding of machinery. I have noted some Kroot warriors discarding acquired weapons that have become unserviceable through simple lack of maintenance, but never those of their own manufacture. It appears that their affinity with their own weapons is instinctual, and does not extend to items constructed by others. This much surely be of use in the ongoing war against the Tau Empire.

# KROOTOX

*"When facing Krootox I have three main weapons of choice. Autocannon, autocannon, or autocannon."*

–Gunnery Corporal Vatis Jan, 76th Gathalamor Heavy Grenadiers fire support company

A salutary example of Kroot dead-end evolution, the Krootox are massive brutes descended from those Kroot who consumed the flesh of especially muscular and barbaric beasts. These kindreds became locked into a downward spiral of evolution, losing their intelligence and with it their ability to forge their own genetic future. The result is a hugely muscled, oversized variant of Kroot physiology, its mind capable of little more than unreasoning brutality. Were it not for the fact that the Kroot have found a use for the Krootox, the line might have died out generations ago, but instead, they are a common sight in Carnivore Kindreds all over the Tau Empire and beyond.

The Kroot utilise Krootox as beasts of war. They saddle them and mount upon their backs an overlarge version of the Kroot rifle, which is crewed by a single Carnivore rider. The Krootox are large and solid enough to provide a stable and mobile firing platform for the weapon, while at the same time serving as powerful assault troops in close combat. While relatively placid under the control of a Carnivore, the Krootox become enraged by the presence of an enemy and their hugely powerful arms and fists are capable of staving in vehicle hulls and power armour with equal ease.

Krootox and their riders are usually encountered in only small numbers and it is not uncommon for individual beasts to be found within a larger group of Kroot Carnivores. This provides the Carnivores with a degree of fire support as well as substantially augmenting its close combat capabilities. Some have noted that this deployment is not one learned or copied from the Tau, as the Fire Caste do not make use of team-level heavy weapons but instead rely on close integration and cooperation with specialised fire support units. Ordo Xenos savants have postulated that the Kroot are either more intelligent than they might appear, or else they copied the tactic from Imperial forces.

On several occasions, larger groups of Krootox have been encountered. Such formations are a formidable obstacle for even the most skilled of Kill-teams. The massed heavy weapons are capable of unleashing a withering hail of fire, and the beasts present a solid wall of muscle and sinew to any who attempt to engage them in a melee. To

## USING KROOTOX

Krootox make great complications when a Kill-team is having things a little too easy. Adding them in to larger hordes of Kroot Carnivores is a great way of forcing the players to rethink their plans and approach the combat in a different manner. Krootox can also be used on their own, perhaps in groups and positioned to defend key points in the mission. The combination of heavy firepower and brutal strength makes the Krootox formidable enemies that have to be approached with great caution.

date, the most effective tactic when faced with one or more Krootox has been to direct sniper fire at the rider, in the hope that, bereft of direction, the Krootox itself will run amok or amble off harmlessly. In reality, this tactic is not easy to accomplish, for the rider is almost entirely protected by the muscular bulk of the beast, and the first missed shot will draw an enraged charge.

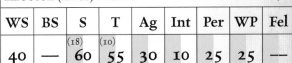

| Krootox (Elite) Profile | | | | | | | | |
|---|---|---|---|---|---|---|---|---|
| WS | BS | S | T | Ag | Int | Per | WP | Fel |
| 40 | — | (18) 60 | (10) 55 | 30 | 10 | 25 | 25 | — |

**Movement:** 3/6/9/18      **Wounds:** 80

**Skills:** Climb (S), Concealment (Ag) +10, Silent Move (Ag) +10.

**Talents:** Furious Assault, Leap Up, Resistance (Fear).

**Traits:** Auto-stabilised, Brutal Charge, Improved Natural Weapons, Natural Weapons (Beak, Fists), Quadruped, Size (Hulking), Sturdy, Unnatural Strength (x3), Unnatural Toughness (x2).

**Weapons:** Beak (1d10+18 R; Pen 0), fists (2d10+18 I; Pen 2; Concussive), kroot gun (150m; S/2/–; 3d10+8 I; Pen 6; Clip 10; Rld Full).

### Special Rules

**Kroot-served Weapon Platform:** Krootox are always accompanied by a rider (see page 20), a single Kroot who operates the Kroot Gun lashed to its back. The Krootox and the rider are treated as two separate targets. When fired at from the front, the rider may benefit from the cover afforded him by the sheer muscular bulk of the Krootox. Any shot fired at either target that misses by one Degree of Failure or less will strike the other instead.

## Addendum by Codicier Taelon

I have recently inloaded to the data-repository a number of pict-feeds showing the beasts known as Krootox in action. One was captured via the sensorium of Brother Skasith's Tactical Dreadnought armour, and shows in graphic detail an engagement fought at extremely close range between Skasith's team and a number of Krootox. Another was captured by the machine spirit of a Rhino belonging to the White Scars Chapter, during the assault on the Tau city of Gel'Bryn during the Damocles Gulf Crusade. Both show the creatures' incredible physiology, and serve to emphasise the damage they can inflict in both close combat and at range. The weapon carried on the Krootox's back is in essence a simple, large bore, breach-loaded cannon, but as is common amongst Kroot firearms, the ammunition has been modified by the Tau. Instead of the solid slug or explosive rounds the guns must once have utilised, they now consist of an impact-fused, high-yield plasma core that affords the round improved armour-piercing capabilities for its size and weight. One feed shows the weapon penetrating the side armour of a Rhino, and subsequent examination of the damage confirmed its properties. While the rounds should not be able to penetrate ceramite by chemical effect alone, their velocity and ballistic characteristics certainly make them a threat that all brethren should be made aware of.

In terms of the beasts' close combat potential, it has been observed that their muscle density and bone strength is extremely high in comparison to their size and mass, even compared to the already elevated characteristics of Kroot Carnivores. They are extremely tough and in addition have a high tolerance to tissue damage and the resulting pain. This is perhaps due to a regressed nervous system, a factor which in the wild might be a disadvantage but in service to the Kroot is a significant advantage, as it causes the Krootox to fight on when others might be incapacitated.

According to the footage captured by Brother Skasith's sensorium, the beasts are capable of causing significant damage using their fists alone. During that action, one crippled a Battle-Brother wearing Mark 7 armour, and significantly damaged Skasith's Terminator suit. Fortunately, Brother Skasith was equipped with a chainfist, a weapon against which even the toughest of creatures have little defence. While he was not able to recover an intact specimen, Skasith's Kill-team returned with many samples of Krootox blood.

## Further Addendum, added 767.M41:

It was on my ill-fated, third deployment to the cursed warzone of Baraban that I first encountered Kroot Knarlocs in the field. I was attached to Brother Djan's Kill-team, and my attentions were focused entirely upon holding at bay the aetheric manifestations that bedevil the forests of that world. I had been doing so for almost an entire day, and while my efforts had spared my Battle-Brothers from the worst of the effects, I myself was suffering considerable strain. It was as we approached a forest glade three hundred kilometres out from Bastion Delta-9 that the Kroot attacked. The air was split by the thunder of heavy calibre gunfire, and Brother Nahn went down straight away having sustained a direct hit to the head. We deployed as per standard contact drill, rallying around Brother Silsten who laid down a withering suppressive fire with his heavy bolter. I extended my senses into the treeline, and detected there the presence of at least half a dozen brutal, if simple minds – Knarloc. I shouted a warning, and seconds later the treeline exploded into motion as the beasts burst forth. Thanks to my warning, my brothers were able to direct their fire on the enemy and three were down before they could cross the glade and strike our line. We were ready and able to repulse them, but only just.

# KNARLOC

Knarlocs are voracious and highly successful predators from the Kroot home world of Pech. They live in small packs and hunt together through the forests of Pech, cooperating to bring down larger foes such as the Great Knarloc or coordinating complex pursuits of fleet Kroot Hound packs. The term Knarloc actually covers a wide variety of creatures, all exhibiting similar characteristics and habits. Some, for example, are broad and muscular and lack the clawed forearms that others display, while some are tall and lean. All of these varieties are highly prized by the Kroot, who capture entire packs and domesticate them, as far as is possible with such a wild creature. Kroot Kindreds utilise Knarlocs for a wide range of uses, most commonly as scouts and trackers. Because the beasts are native to the dense forests of Pech, they are well able to negotiate any type of rough terrain, from sweltering rain forests to urban warzones.

When Imperial forces first encountered Knarlocs and the Ordo Xenos set about analysing them, the beasts were taken as a form of raptor—agile, bird-like lizards. As more of the Kroot's unique evolution and physiology became understood however, the savants of the Ordo Xenos all but abandoned hope of understanding or cataloguing the boundless variety displayed by the species. They realised that the Knarloc was not a bird-like creature at all, but more resembled a Kroot Carnivore whose form has become stooped and distended by the rapid development that characterises the species. The genetic ties between Kroot and Knarloc are plain to see and the two groups share many common physical traits, including the razor-sharp beak that makes the mounts effective as assault troops as well as scouts.

Groups of Knarloc-mounted trackers are most often encountered ranging far ahead of their force. While not as fast in the open as a Pathfinder team mounted upon its modified Devilfish carrier, the Knarlocs are far better suited for moving through terrain that armoured vehicles would have problems traversing. When moving through forests, jungles and swamps, the Knarlocs are all but silent and make use of every possible scrap of cover to remain concealed. When launching an ambush it is common for the riders to dismount, sometimes using their mount's form as additional concealment or cover. Other Kindreds, generally those in possession of more vicious beasts, utilise them more like heavy cavalry, launching devastating charges from their ambush positions and overwhelming their target within seconds.

Knarloc riders equip themselves according to the character of their mount and the tactic they intend to employ against the enemy. Those riding the more aggressive mounts sometimes carry crude spears or lances, while those utilising the more stealthy beasts carry a longer version of the Kroot rifle. Others carry the more common version of the standard fire arm, which, thanks to its muzzle- and stock-mounted blades, makes an effective weapon close up as well at range.

I: THE ALIEN THREAT

## ADVENTURE SEEDS

**Kidnapping:** A Knarloc-mounted Kindred has kidnapped a senior Adept of the Departmento Tacticae, presumably on the orders of their Tau masters (this presumption is based on the fact that the Kroot don't normally take live prisoners, unless it's to keep the meat fresh on a long journey!). The Kill-team answers a plea for aid in tracking down the Knarloc riders and recovering the Adept, and a tense pursuit ensues across the wilderness. Matching their skills against the Kroot is a trial indeed, and if the Kroot detect their pursuers they make every effort to counter-attack and misdirect the Battle-Brothers. Eventually however, the Kindred reaches a Tau lander and hands over the prisoner. The Kill-team has one last chance to intervene before the Adept is shipped off to the Velk'Han Sept, along with whatever military secrets he holds in his head.

**Pursuit:** One way of using Knarloc-riding Kroot Kindreds is as an additional complication at the end of the mission, once the Kill-team's primary objective is completed and they are in the process of extricating themselves from the theatre of operations. The Knarlocs can be used to pursue the Battle-Brothers, harrying them all the way to their exfiltration point. Knarloc riders are capable of harassing their foe from a distance using their long rifles, and have the speed and stamina to keep the pursuit up for days on end, forcing the Kill-team to engage their pursuers before they can return to their vessel and leave.

### Knarloc (Elite) Profile

| WS | BS | S | T | Ag | Int | Per | WP | Fel |
|----|----|----|----|----|----|----|----|----|
| 40 | — | (10) 50 | 45 | 50 | 10 | 35 | 10 | — |

**Movement:** 8/16/24/48      **Wounds:** 50
**Skills:** Awareness (Per) +10.
**Traits:** Bestial (only applies if rider is killed), Fieldcraft, Improved Natural Weapons, Natural Weapon (Beak), Size (Hulking), Unnatural Strength (x2).
**Weapons:** Beak (1d10+10 R; Pen 2).

# GREAT KNARLOC

When Ordo Xenos savants and Adeptus Mechanicus biologists accompanying the Achilus Crusade first saw footage of the huge Great Knarloc, they took it for some kind of archaic precursor remnant of the Kroot species. They compared it to the saurian creatures that are found on many other planets across the galaxy, seeking to explain the creature's bizarre form. Of course, with such a narrow frame of reference, the Great Knarloc made no sense, and it was only when the unique genetic traits of the Kroot species was discovered that a deeper understanding dawned. The Great Knarloc was not, the savants realised, some primitive, pre-historical ancestor that somehow survived into the present day. It was instead a close relative of the Kroot, representing a branch of the same genus or family and as such shared many of its basic characteristics.

Great Knarlocs are large beasts, their powerful bodies powered by massive, muscular rear legs which while not especially fast are capable of bearing heavy weights and allow the Great Knarloc to trek huge distances without tiring. They have smaller frontal limbs, which they use to grasp food and to scavenge in undergrowth or soft earth. Their heads are visibly similar to the Kroot's, though the proportions are different. Great Knarlocs have small eyes and poor eyesight, and massive beaks that they use to disable prey and tear flesh and bone apart. Great Knarlocs are solitary creatures, dwelling in the deep forests of Pech. They rarely actively hunt, subsisting on a range of food sources, from carrion to creatures they happen to stumble upon in their environment. They remain relatively docile most of the time, but when angered they display savage bursts of violence. These characteristics make them ideal for use as domesticated beasts amongst the Kroot, who utilise them in a variety of roles.

Many Kroot Kindreds, especially the mercenary groupings that range far from their home world, utilise Great Knarlocs as baggage animals. The beasts are loaded with all the supplies the Kroot may require, acting as both mobile arsenals and pantries. Great Knarlocs utilised in this manner are attended by a small group of handlers and often muzzled in case they become enraged and attack their keepers. While it is not intended that these baggage beasts should be required to fight in battle, if a supply column should be ambushed they are quite capable of defending themselves. The handlers use their sharp goads to enrage the creature, driving it towards the enemy on which it vents its anger until little more than the crushed and broken bodies of the foe remains.

Other Great Knarlocs are used as living battering rams, driven into battle by highly experienced handlers. These beasts are selected for their speed and aggression, which is moderated by pheromone excretions produced by the handlers. In battle, they are driven straight at the enemy, scattering their formations and crushing any not fast enough to get out of the way. A fully-grown and suitably goaded Greater Knarloc is capable of tearing armour panels with its huge beak and smashing an armoured vehicle apart. It is a truly terrifying opponent to face.

More easily controlled Great Knarlocs are sometimes used as platforms for a variety of primitive heavy weapons. Huge crossbows and cannons are strapped to a crude saddle and crewed by two or more Kroot. These weapons are similar in nature to the Kroot rifle, in that they represent the simple technology of the Kroot upgraded by the Tau. Instead of iron bolts for example, the Kroot bolt thrower fires explosive-tipped rounds, utilising the same technology normally seen in Tau smart missile systems.

Imperial forces facing Great Knarlocs have found it necessary to treat them as enemy vehicle targets and bring anti-armour weaponry to bear in order to halt their charge before it hits home. The creatures' large mass makes them mostly invulnerable to small arms fire and they are tremendously resilient to wounds that would cripple most other beasts. Targeting the handlers is a risky tactic, for without them the beasts become even more enraged and often attack the nearest prey, friend or foe, with renewed savagery. It has been found that pinpoint sniping while the Great Knarloc is surrounded by other Kroot is the most effective tactic, for repeated shots can drive it to attack nearby troops out of sheer rage.

## Great Knarloc (Elite) Profile

| WS | BS | S | T | Ag | Int | Per | WP | Fel |
|----|----|----|----|----|-----|-----|-----|-----|
| 40 | — | (18) 65 | (10) 50 | 30 | 15 | 45 | 35 | –– |

**Movement:** 6/12/18/36 **Wounds:** 120

**Skills:** Awareness (Per).

**Traits:** Fieldcraft, Unnatural Strength x3, Unnatural Toughness (x2), Size (Enormous), Stampede.

**Weapons:** Beak (1d10+18 R; Pen 2). If equipped with a howdah, then a Kroot Bolt Thrower (60m; S/–/–; 2d10+10 X; Pen 2; Clip 20; Rld Full; Blast [3], Mounted) or a twin-linked Kroot Gun (150m; S/2/–; 3d10+8 I; Pen 6; Clip 10; Rld Full; Twin-linked) will be mounted.

### Special Rules

**Irascible:** Every time a Great Knarloc takes Damage it must take a **Challenging (+0) Willpower Test** as per the Stampede Trait rules. If the test is failed by one Degree of Failure or more it will charge the nearest target, friend or foe. Otherwise, a failed test results in the beast charging straight forward.

**Handlers:** Great Knarlocs are accompanied by one to five handlers. These either run alongside the beast on foot, or if it has a weapon mounted on its back, hang on for dear life to a crude saddle. At least half of the handlers are equipped with goads (see below) and the remainder with Kroot Rifles.

**Goad:** Kroot handlers use their goads to enrage the Great

## Adventure Seeds

Great Knarlocs are most likely to be encountered in one of two situations. The first is when the Kroot are launching a large scale, all-out assault upon a strong enemy, in which case they utilise the huge beasts as living engines of war and as battering rams. In all likelihood, it is the Imperial Guard regiments that have to endure these attacks rather than the smaller Kill-teams, but the Battle-Brothers might find themselves present during such an attack and be forced to take a hand to stave off the collapse of an entire defence line. The other situation is when the Kill-team is engaged upon a mission against a Kroot camp or settlement. In this case, Great Knarlocs might be present and as such can provide the Kill-team with a major obstacle if the Kroot are able to goad them into action. Should a Kill-team discover that their target includes one or more Great Knarlocs, they would be well advised to deal with the beasts from afar using heavy weapons or perhaps to use a sniper rifle to enrage the beast and sow confusion amongst the Kroot as the Battle-Brothers sneak in and complete their mission.

Knarlocs and cause them to stampede. A handler equipped with a goad, who is riding or within 2 metres of a Great Knarloc, may force the beast to take a Willpower Test as per the Stampede Trait rule and modified by the Irascible rule above.

---

**To Codicier Taelon, by the hand of Watch Captain Æthan, 406817.M41**

It is both my sad duty and my great honour to report to you the death of our brother Tariaq, and to commit to the archive the manner in which he gave his life. Tariaq was serving under me on a mission to Veren, a reconnaissance intended to penetrate the furthest reaches of the coral tunnels that run northwards beneath the Umbra Sea. Remote prognost rituals had raised the possibility that the Tau were using previously unknown technology to move troops around the contested world, a disturbing possibility that had to be investigated as matter of urgency. Three days out of Cavern Sub—223, we picked up the auspex spoor of a large enemy force, and followed it for another two days before coming upon its source. The spoor was that of a Kroot supply column consisting of a dozen of the beasts known as "Great Knarlocs" and around a hundred Kroot. We observed the column entering a massive cavern three kilometres beneath the sea bed, and followed. What we saw within was astounding. The mighty, naturally formed cavern was aglow with bioluminescence cast from hundreds of rearing fungal forms growing from the cavern's floor and walls. Furthermore, we soon saw that these flora were being used by the Kroot as the basis for a substantial settlement. Crude dwellings constructed of hide, wood and metal clung to the side of the huge fungi, connected by way of hundreds of precarious walkways.

Seeing an opportunity to disrupt the enemy's operations in this region of Veren, we set a series of demolition charges designed to bring down as much of the cavern as possible. The charges were set and Tariaq was the last of the team to return to our position, when our presence was betrayed. The Kroot exploded into action, unleashing the Greater Knarlocs and goading them towards us. Tariaq was cut off and faced with the charge of three of the beasts. To my utter amazement, he killed two of them and wounded the third before he was overrun, and in so doing afforded the remainder of the team the time we needed to withdraw and detonate the charges. The first beast he slew by hauling himself up onto its back, cleaving a deep wound in its side and planting a melta bomb within. The second he brought down by way of hamstringing its huge rear legs with his power sword, and beheading it once it was down. The third he blinded with pinpoint bolt pistol shots to its eyes, but not before it had him in its terrible grip. I did not see how Tariaq fared in the last seconds of his life, for I was forced to detonate the charges that brought a vast section of the cavern down upon him and the beast, and many more of our enemies.

I commit his memory to the archives that he shall live on forever in the annals of glory.

# KROOT HOUND

*"Recon Lead in position, Kroot encampment in sight. Recon Two, commence infiltration, over. Recon Two? Recon Two, report status, over…"*

–Scout Captain Khorvah, Volg 91st Light Infantry

As the name suggests, Kroot Hounds are dog-like creatures of the Kroot genus, evolved to a standstill as savage and agile attack beasts. Kroot Hounds are highly intelligent in a bestial sort of way, and well able to understand the instructions of their handlers. They are also highly temperamental, and prone to attacking their keepers should they get the opportunity. Those Kroot tasked with keeping the Kroot Hounds in line are often covered in scars, but they develop a close bond with their charges over time and act as one in the field.

The beasts are the size of a large dog, with a series of sensory ganglia running along their spine with which they are able to detect the presence of enemies and prey even within very dense terrain. They are wiry of frame, yet just like the Kroot themselves, possessed of a toughness that belies their apparent fragility. Facially, Kroot Hounds are ugly beasts, and they share the under-bite beak of the Carnivores.

Kroot Hounds serve many functions within Kroot society. They serve as watch-beasts in Kroot settlements, both the permanent ones on Pech and the other Kroot worlds, as well as the temporary encampments that spring up wherever the Kroot travel. In this role, they are able to detect the approach of even the stealthiest foe, through a combination of sensory input gathered by the ganglia along their backs. Should any creature other than one of the Kroot genus approach, the Kroot Hounds emit a fearful shrieking and snarling sufficient to deter most infiltrators from pressing on. When accompanied by a handler, the Kroot Hounds can be trained to emit low sounds that do not alert the intruder to discovery, allowing the Kroot to set up and spring an ambush on their foolhardy foe, who soon after is likely to become the Kroot's next meal.

Kroot Hounds are often used to patrol the area around a Kroot camp. If there are no Tau around, the Kroot sometimes set the hounds free in the knowledge that they will hunt as a pack as they do in the forests of Pech, ambushing any they encounter and bringing them down with ruthless efficiency. If there are Tau or other allies in the vicinity, the pack is accompanied by one or more Kroot handlers in order to avoid any unpleasant incidents.

The beasts are also employed on the field of battle, serving as guards for high-ranking Kroot such as Shapers and Master Shapers, and in packs controlled by handlers. The handlers must be fleet of foot indeed to keep up with their charges once their blood is up, for the Kroot Hounds are used to move swiftly around the flanks of the enemy and launch lightning-fast attacks upon exposed units. When attacked by large numbers of Kroot Hounds, even the largest of foes can be dragged down and gored to death by their beak-like maws, a fate many Imperial Guardsmen have been executed for running away from.

## ADVENTURE SEED

A great way to make use of Kroot Hounds is to have savage packs of them ranging the area in which the Kill-team is operating, hunting down intruders and launching vicious ambushes at the worst possible moment. The player characters will have to keep their eyes, ears and auspexes on high alert if there are Kroot Hounds in the area, for the beasts are well able to track even the most stealthy and cunning of enemies. They also have the intelligence to strike when their prey is most vulnerable, a fact that makes them ideal for use by the GM when he wants to add an additional layer of challenge to a mission.

### Kroot Hound (Troops) Profile

| WS | BS | S | T | Ag | Int | Per | WP | Fel |
|----|----|----|----|----|----|----|----|----|
| 40 | — | (8) 40 | 30 | 40 | 18 | 45 | 30 | — |

**Movement:** 8/16/24/48      **Wounds:** 18

**Skills:** Awareness (Per) +20, Concealment (Ag) +20, Silent Move (Ag), Tracking (Int) +20.

**Talents:** Heightened Senses (Hearing, Smell), Sprint, Takedown.

**Traits:** Bestial, Improved Natural Weapons, Natural Weapon (Kroot Beak), Quadruped.

**Weapons:** Beak (1d10+8 R; Pen 0).

**Horde:** Kroot Hounds can be used as a Horde (see page 359 of the **DEATHWATCH** Rulebook).

# TAU PATHFINDER

*"Recon gamma three reports contact with Tau Pathfinders, single squad. That means we can expect company. Operations? I want all companies deployed and ready within the hour or we're all dead!"*

–Lord Colonel Silvestri, 9th Scintillan Heavy Infantry prior to the Battle of Loath

Pathfinder teams provide Tau Hunter Cadres with long-range reconnaissance capabilities. Utilising specially adapted, anti-grav Devilfish troop carriers, Pathfinder teams range far ahead of the Cadre in search of enemy forces. They maintain a close watch on the foe while remaining expertly hidden, reporting details of the enemy's nature and disposition by way of highly encrypted, nigh undetectable communication systems. Pathfinder teams are also deployed in the role of aggressive patrol groups, maintaining dominance over a wide area around a stationary Hunter Cadre and detecting any enemy forces that attempt to approach. Occasionally, an entire Hunter Cadre of Pathfinders is tasked with a mission, such as exploring a newly discovered planet and ascertaining if it is suitable for colonisation.

Pathfinders are equipped with a range of specialised equipment to aid in their mission. Every member of the team carries a Markerlight, a laser designator device attached to his firearm that projects an all but invisible, highly focused beam of light at a potential target. The Markerlight is networked to a support weapon platform such as a Hammerhead gunship, and transmits precise targeting information in order to guide the fire of such units. When used to guide the armour-piercing seeker missiles carried as additional weapons on many Tau tanks, the Pathfinders are able to remain hidden as they call in devastatingly powerful and unerringly accurate fire right onto the target. Many Imperial troops have come to fear the small, red dot of light that appears on the body on those about to be slain, and some refer to it as the "Valkyrie's Mark."

The Devilfish troop carriers used by Pathfinder teams are fitted with a larger variant of Markerlight technology called a Marker Beacon. This is used to designate a position to which jump troops and orbital insertion craft can be guided, allowing units such as battlesuit-equipped Crisis teams to drop directly onto their target.

Each individual Pathfinder is equipped with a pulse carbine, which is fitted with an underslung photon grenade launcher. The blinding, disorienting effect of the grenades is utilised by the Pathfinders when reacting to sudden and unanticipated contact with their enemies, and they are adept at rapid deployment using their anti-grav carriers. Some Pathfinders replace their carbines with rail rifles, sniper weapons as accurate and deadly as any similar weapon the Imperium is capable of fielding.

## ADVENTURE SEEDS

**Infiltration:** The Deathwatch has discovered the presence of numerous Tau Pathfinder teams, apparently scouting an uncatalogued world near the Black Reef. This is a worrying development, and the Kill-team is dispatched to discover the Tau's intentions. Upon making planetfall, the player characters encounter numerous Pathfinder teams. The Kill-team must ascertain what it is that the Pathfinders are looking for and if their presence is a precursor to a Tau takeover of the world. There are many ways the Kill-team can approach the mission, from stealthy observation to capturing a Pathfinder and interrogating him. Whatever approach they take, a deadly game of cat and mouse ensues, as the Pathfinders are adept at discovering enemy movements. Ultimately, the Kill-team must decide how to deal with the Tau presence. Will they attempt to disrupt the Tau, engage them or exfiltrate to return later with a larger force?

### USING PATHFINDERS

Pathfinders are most likely to be encountered in the early stages of a mission, perhaps when the Kill-team is reconnoitring the lay of the land and planning an assault on their objective. They can also be present as a precursor to a Tau attack, when their presence, if detected, should be taken as a sign that a significant Tau force is not far behind.

The Deathwatch considers Pathfinder teams high priority targets. When encountered acting as perimeter sentries patrolling the region around a Tau facility they can compromise an entire mission without the Kill-team even knowing they have been detected. The first indication of imminent contact is the telltale red dot appearing upon a Battle-Brother's armour, followed an instant later by a barrage of seeker missiles. On several occasions, Pathfinder teams have held back while observing an infiltrating force, only calling in fire when their enemy was too far forward to extricate safely. When facing Tau forces likely to be accompanied by Pathfinder teams, the Deathwatch takes exceptional measures to ensure mission security, equipping Kill-teams with all manner of sensor and countermeasure devices.

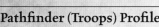

| Pathfinder (Troops) Profile | | | | | | | | |
|---|---|---|---|---|---|---|---|---|
| WS | BS | S | T | Ag | Int | Per | WP | Fel |
| 25 | 35 | 30 | 30 | 25 | 35 | 30 | 30 | 30 |

**Movement:** 3/6/9/18      **Wounds:** 12

**Skills:** Awareness +20 (Per), Common Lore (Tau Empire) (Int), Concealment (+10) (Ag), Dodge (Ag) +10, Shadowing (Ag), Speak Language (Tau) (Int), Tracking (Int).

**Talents:** Exotic Weapon Training (Tau Pulse Weapons).

**Armour:** Tau Pathfinder Armour (Head 7, Body 7).

**Weapons:** Pulse Carbine (60m; S/–/3; 2d10+2 E; Pen 4; Clip 24; Rld Full; Gyro-Stabilised) (with integral Markerlight and underslung photon grenade launcher) or Rail Rifle (150m; S/–/–; 2d10+10 I; Pen 9; Clip 16; Rld Full; Devastating [1], Overheats).

**Gear:** Micro-bead, photo-visor and magnoculars incorporated into helmet.

## PATHFINDERS AND HORDES

Pathfinders usually operate in smaller squads and will only very rarely be encountered as a Horde. When they form a Horde, Pathfinders gain the Fighting Withdrawal and Fire Drill Traits.

## Addendum by Codicier Taelon

I was serving under Watch Captain Kasman, the Emperor guard his soul, the first time I encountered Tau Pathfinders. My team was traversing the polar wastes of a nameless world spinward of Andronicus, tracing the mortis-cant echo of a long dead star-seer. Eighty-three point five hours into the mission, I detected a timid mind-trace belonging not to our target, but to some other group. I informed the Watch Captain, and we continued on our path as if nothing were awry, allowing whoever was trailing us to become lulled into false confidence. Eventually, we came upon a mountain range, and Brother Helskadt peeled off as we entered the pass, doubling back to identify our pursuers.

After a further nine hours, Helskadt reported in, having identified the others as a group of Tau Pathfinders. The Pathfinders themselves were of little concern to us, but their mission was. Why were they there? Was it coincidence that we should encounter one another, against all the odds, in such a barren and isolated place? Kasman had his orders from the Watch Commander himself—the spoor of the star-seer had to be traced, so he ordered the team split in half. The Watch Captain took Helskadt, Borsun and Ardikus and led them south with the intention of drawing the Pathfinders away from our objective. I myself led Usto, Alonnso and Llon eastwards, towards the source of the mortis-cant.

It appeared to us all that Kasman's ruse had worked, for we completed the mission successfully without interference from the Tau. Yet, as we extracted by Thunderhawk, I caught the slightest of mind-traces and looked south through the cockpit canopy. There, racing away from us across the cobalt sea was a grav-tank, a Tau Devilfish. The Pathfinders had not fallen for Kasman's plot at all, and must have observed us the whole time.

Upon investigating this matter further, I discovered how. The Tau appear to have a reduced mind-spoor. They are not blanks, let me be quite clear on that, but their presence in the Sea of Souls is somehow muted, as if only tenuously anchored in the material universe. I cannot explain any further at this time, but I intend to make the issue a subject for further study. We were fortunate in that our mission was not ultimately compromised and the Tau were only observing. The next mission may not be so lucky.

# VESPID STINGWING

*"Let me tell you son, when you hear that sound, you've got three seconds to grab your lasgun and then they're on you."*

–Corporal Hahnsen of the 45th Scintilla Guard

Vespid is a world within the Tau Empire, located approximately three light years from the Sept world of D'yanoi. The world is home to a single sentient species, known as the Vespid, or "mal'kor" in the Tau tongue. The term Stingwing was coined by the first Imperial units to survive contact with the species, and has become almost universal amongst the Imperial Guard.

The world of Vespid is a gas giant, its dark, violet-hued skies wracked by continuous and violent storms. This environment would appear an unlikely crucible for any form of life, yet alone a sentient species, but the Vespid are far from conventional in their biology. The upper layers of the planet's atmosphere are host to many thousands of floating islands of rock, kept aloft by lighter-than-air gas trapped within. The islands are flat-topped and become narrower towards the base, giving them the appearance of vast, floating stalactites. The Vespids make their homes within these structures, using their diamond-hard claws to hollow them out like termite mounds. Because the islands are so large, the air pressure varies significantly between topmost and bottommost levels. The lower levels are host to all manner of exotic and unique types of crystal, which only the larger female Vespids have the constitution to reach and harvest. These crystals are the basis of the species' technology, one type of which is used in the construction of the deadly neutron blaster utilised by the Stingwings in battle.

The Vespids themselves are a vaguely insectoid species, though this narrow term is an imperfect one that fails to account for many aspects of their unusual physiology. Their bodies are encased in a chitinous exoskeleton, and sports many lethally sharp barbs. They see by way of three pairs of eyes, one pair perceiving the ultraviolet range, one the normal visible spectrum, and the last the infrared. It is assumed that the Vespids see in all three ranges simultaneously, and therefore have a perception of their surroundings unique to their race. Vespids can fly by way of a pair of hard chitin wings, which also emit a continuous ultrasonic tone with which the species appears able to modulate and control the workings of their crystal technology. The functioning of the wings is a great mystery to the biologis of the Adeptus Mechanicus accompanying the Achilus Crusade, who flatly state that the Stingwings should not be able to fly according to any known laws of bio-aerodynamics.

When the Tau first encountered the Vespids, they saw a species of great potential value to the Greater Good and much coveted their crystal-based technologies. Although the species had developed a reasonably stable planetary government and was able to utilise its technology for a wide variety of uses, it had not yet achieved space flight. Tau Water Caste cadres established contact, yet were unable at first to communicate with the species. This was not a mundane matter of vocalisation or the understanding of language, for the Vespids have an utterly alien mindset. Initially, the Tau were not only unable to communicate, but incapable of getting the Vespids to even register that they were fellow sentients. The matter was eventually resolved at the command of the Ethereal Caste, who issued instructions for the construction of an interface device that forged a connection between the two species and facilitated communication. The moment the device was employed, the Vespid not only registered the Tau, they instantly understood the concept of the Greater Good and their place within it. By gifting senior Vespids with "communion helms" fitted with the interface device, the Tau are able to communicate with the species at large. Their will is disseminated to those under the command of these "strain leaders," and they become able to decipher their role as befits the Greater Good. Needless to say, certain factions within the Inquisition would very much like to learn more of the workings of this device.

## Vespid Stingwing (Troops) Profile

| WS | BS | S | T | Ag | Int | Per | WP | Fel |
|----|----|----|----|----|----|----|----|----|
| 35 | 45 | 30 | (8) 45 | 60 | 25 | 30 | 30 | 15 |

**Movement:** 4/8/12/28      **Wounds:** 15

**Skills:** Acrobatics (Ag), Awareness (Per), Dodge (Ag) +10, Speak Language (Tau, Vespid) (Int), Survival (Int).

**Talents:** Exotic Weapon Training (Vespid Neutron Blaster), Catfall, Chem Geld, Hard Target, Lightning Reflexes.

**Traits:** Dark Sight, Flyer (10), Natural Armour (Chitin), Improved Natural Weapons, Natural Weapons (Claws), Unnatural Senses (see in normal, infrared and ultraviolet bands), Unnatural Toughness (x2).

**Armour:** Chitin (All 3).

**Weapons:** Claws (1d10+3; Pen 4), neutron blaster (30m; S/–/–; 1d10+12 E; Pen 8; Toxic).

**Gear:** Strain Leader has Communion Helm.

**Horde:** Vespid Stingwings can be used as a Horde (see Hordes on page 359 of the DEATHWATCH Rulebook).

## Special Rules

**Strain Leader:** One member of the Horde must be designated a Strain Leader. This individual has the same profile as the rest of the Stingwings, but wears the Communion Helm.

## VESPID COMMUNION HELM

Communion Helms are Tau-manufactured masks or helmets worn by Vespid Strain Leaders. Even among the Tau, the technology utilised in the Communion Helm is largely a mystery, as the Earth Caste created the devices following the directives of the Ethereals. What is known is that the Vespids view the world around them in a very different way to most other sentient beings, and their frame of reference is so far removed they often fail to relate to other species as even sentient, yet alone a friend or enemy. The Communion Helm allows for communication between the two species, although some amongst the Ordo Xenos believe that the helm actually attunes its wearer to the worldview of the Tau.

As long as the Strain Leader is alive and conscious, the Stingwings act normally. The Communion Helm effectively grants the wearer the Speak Language (Tau) Skill, and counts as a micro-bead. If the Strain Leader is killed however, the remaining Stingwings must take a **Willpower Test** each turn. The first such test is **Trivial**, but every turn the Horde is without a Strain Leader it increases by one level of Difficulty until it eventually becomes **Hellish**. Each turn that the test is passed the Stingwings act normally. Each turn it is failed however the Vespid lose track of their surroundings and act increasingly erratically, in a manner of the GM's choosing. They may, for example, simply disengage and fly off, but they might equally attack former allies, start firing at harmless rocks, or attempt to burrow into the earth.

## ADVENTURE SEEDS

**Recovery:** An Ordo Xenos Inquisitor has petitioned the Chamber of Vigilance to allow him to lead a Deathwatch Kill-team on a mission to recover a Communion Helm from a Vespid Strain Leader. The Kill-team is ordered to accompany the Inquisitor to the Vespid-held world of Krrk'tikit. While not a great distance from the leading edge of the front, the Kill-team must negotiate the perils of the Black Reef in order to reach their target, and slip past numerous Air Caste patrols before making planetfall. Setting foot upon the world, the Kill-team is in entirely new territory, for no Imperial force has been there before them. They must scout out the Vespids' holdings so that the Deathwatch's records can be updated, and locate a suitable Strain Leader to target. Doing so is far from simple however, for Strain Leaders are invariably accompanied by their Strains! The best tactic might be to lure a single group away into the wilderness, but doing so might bring the Battle-Brothers into contact with the strange beings that exist deep beneath the surface. Couple these factors with the hazardous radiation bathing the tunnels in which the Vespid live, and the mission is a perilous one indeed.

### USING VESPID

Vespid Stingwings can be used by the GM to spring an unexpected trap on unwary player characters. They are often used by the Tau to launch rapid counter attacks against enemies seeking to outflank less manoeuvrable units such as Broadside battlesuit teams or static positions. The Vespid lurk nearby, out of sight, allowing the Kill-team to approach before leaping through the air to bring their short-ranged, but highly effective, weapons to bear.

### Addendum by Codicier Taelon

After-action reports relating to these so-called "Stingwings" are fragmentary and often contradictory. I have compiled multiple sources, from Imperial Guard battle tank gun-cam exloads to the sensorium feeds captured by our own Battle-Brothers. The most vivid of these was retrieved on Ravacene, from the sensorium core of the sergeant of a Tactical Squad of the Executioners Chapter, and it showed the Xenos and their weapons in action in graphic detail. The squad was engaging a substantial Kroot force at the eastern extent of the twelfth parallel when the Vespid attacked. The first our Brothers of the Executioners knew of the assault was the high-pitched whine of what later cogi-dissemination revealed to be the creatures' wings vibrating at incredibly high speed. The xenos burst through the treeline at speed, negotiating the close terrain with apparent ease. While the Executioners deployed faultlessly into a defensive stance, the Vespids were all around them, bringing their weapons to bear from every angle. The sensorium core feeds show the ash-chocked air aglow with arcs of weirdling energy, great cones of radiation pulsing through the jungle. The trees withered and died in seconds and the airborne ash motes flash-burned all around. The squad was slain, but not, I am glad to say, before the Battle-Brothers could exact a terrible cost upon the attackers, slaying several dozen of their number. Most of the sensorium cores were too damaged by the radiation of the Vespids' weapons to be of any use, but one survived to describe something of the effect the weapons inflicted. The Battle-Brothers' power armour was of scant use, for the radiation bypassed it, inflicting unutterable damage upon the body within. The armour we recovered was functionally intact, even if the contents of the sensorium core were severely corrupted. The bodies however were not. Perhaps worst of all, the radiation caused such damage that the Battle-Brothers' gene-seed could not be harvested, for risk of passing on corrupted material. For that, the Vespids shall surely pay dearly.

# TYRANIDS

*"There is nothing as mindless and terrible as a Tyranid swarm, like a starving beast it falls upon world after world, consuming and devouring everything it touches. All we can do is try to hold back the flood, hurling men and machines into its path in the hopes that if we cannot stop its advance perhaps we can slow it and buy ourselves a few more precious moments of existence."*

—Adept Ibin Glar, from *The Endless Tide of Night*

Remorseless, completely alien and without mercy, the Tyranid hive fleets threaten not just the Imperium but all life in the galaxy. Invaders from across the vast empty gulf of space between galaxies, the Tyranids are a relentless tide of bio-horrors, deadly killing machines with but a single purpose, to devour all living things in their path. The worst hit regions of the galaxy are those along the Eastern Fringe, where multiple hive fleets have crashed into the outlying systems and sectors, consuming whole races and empires in their advance and leaving only dead and lifeless worlds in their wake. The Jericho Reach is no exception to this assault, and has drawn the attention of Hive Fleet Dagon, which is in the process of rolling up the rimward edge of the sector and has pushed deep into the Orpheus Salient. Against this implacable advance, dozens of Imperial worlds are desperately holding out, while dozens more are threatened by splinter fleets and advanced Tyranid scouting forces that constantly range forward in search of more life to consume.

The Tyranids are a unique and deadly foe and a regular adversary of the Deathwatch. This chapter expands on the selection of Tyranid creatures for the **DEATHWATCH** game, adding new adversaries, new weapons and new powers for the GM to challenge his players with. For more details on the Tyranids, and profiles for other Tyranid creatures, refer to page 369 of the **DEATHWATCH** Rulebook.

## NEW TYRANID WEAPONS

This section covers a number of new Tyranid Weapons. These weapons follow all the standard rules for Tyranid weapons found on page 372 of **DEATHWATCH** and as such have no Clip or Reload values because Tyranid weapons are living bio-constructs and use neither. It is also important to note that Tyranid Heavy Weapons, unless otherwise noted, do not require Bracing (see page 140 in the **DEATHWATCH** Rulebook).

### Spike Rifle

Essentially a long tube of muscle, the spike rifle fires a short harpoon-like bone into its targets over a considerable distance. Razor sharp and fired with great force, the spike is able to punch through light armour and even right through unarmoured targets. Once embedded in flesh it becomes very difficult to remove as it has tiny barbs which dig into the victim, holding it in place.

Spike Rifles are usually carried by Termagants (see **DEATHWATCH** page 371) and these creatures may replace their Fleshborer with a Spike Rifle should the GM choose.

### Spine Fists

Carried in pairs, these weapon beasts attach to a Tyranid creature's arms and can fire a sustained volley of razor sharp darts. The speed at which the Spine Fist can fire, and thus its rate of fire and its deadliness, is related directly to the creature using it. It has tubes attached to the creatures airways allowing a stronger creature to expel more force into the weapon and fire more darts. Thus a Tyranid creature can fire only single shots from its Spine Fists unless it has the Swift Attack or Lightning Attack Talents. Creatures with the Swift Attack Talent can fire them with a semi-auto rate of fire of 2, and a creature with the Lightning Attack Talent can fire them with a full-auto rate of fire of 4. Creatures may of course choose to fire them at a lower rate of fire. Finally, a Spine Fist draws directly from the strength of its user and adds their Strength Bonus to the damage it deals.

## TABLE 1-2: TYRANID WEAPONS

| Name | Class | Range | ROF | Dam | Pen | Clip | Rld | Special |
|---|---|---|---|---|---|---|---|---|
| Spike Rifle | Basic | 80m | S/–/– | 1d10+4 R | 0 | — | — | — |
| Spine Fist | Pistol | 25m | Special† | 1d10 R | 4 | — | — | Twin-linked |
| Strangleweb | Basic | 30m | S/–/– | 1d10 I | — | — | — | Deadly Snare, Devastating (1) |

† *A Tyranid creature can fire only single shots from its Spine Fists unless it has the Swift Attack or Lightning Attack talents. Creatures with the Swift Attack Talent can fire them with a semi-auto rate of fire of 2, and a creature with the Lightning Attack Talent can fire them with a full-auto rate of fire of 4.*

### Strangle Web

A composite creature, like all Tyranid weapons, the Strangle Web fires a spray of sticky mucus at its target, enveloping them in strands of glistening web. Almost immediately the web begins to harden and those covered become enmeshed in a cocoon of constricting fibers which begins to crush them. Those that survive the crushing are the left to the mercy of the swarm.

Strangle Webs are usually carried by Termagants (see page 371 in the DEATHWATCH Rulebook) and these creatures may replace their Fleshborer with a Strangle Web should the GM choose. This weapon uses the Flame Quality rules (see page 142 in the DEATHWATCH Rulebook) but does not set anyone on fire.

# TYRANID PSYCHIC POWERS

Many Tyranid bio-forms possess potent psychic powers, manifested not from drawing the power of the warp but by tapping into the vast gestalt will of the Hive Mind itself. Such is the potency of the Hive Mind that a fully fledged Tyranid fleet can blanket entire regions of space with its presence, casting a shadow in the warp and projecting its ancient and terrifying consciousness across the barrier between Materium and Immaterium. When a Tyranid creature with a particularly strong connection to the Hive Mind, or the ability to channel its power, taps into this vast store of will, it can create deadly psychic effects, subverting minds, incinerating flesh or even bending reality to aid the Tyranids' all consuming hunger.

Tyranid creatures with a Psy Rating, such as a Hive Tyrant or Zoanthrope, follow all the normal rules for psykers as detailed in Chapter VI: Psychic Powers of DEATHWATCH with the exceptions that if a Tyranid psychic creature suffers a Psychic Phenomena or Perils of the Warp, it does not roll on either table. Instead it suffers 1d10 Energy Damage, not reduced by armour or Toughness, as it loses control of the power and the immense strength of the Hive Mind backlashes upon it; otherwise, the power has no effect.

Tyranid psykers may possess the powers listed on pages 34-35.

### Catalyst
**Action:** Half
**Opposed:** No
**Range:** 75 metres
**Sustained:** No
**Description:** This power functions as described under the Hive Tyrant's special rules in DEATHWATCH page 370.

### Dominion
**Action:** Half
**Opposed:** No
**Range:** Special
**Sustained:** Yes
**Description:** The Tyranid creature reaches into the depths of the Hive Mind and strengthens its links to the indomitable alien will, projecting a blanket of control and purpose through its synapse to all Tyranid bio-forms nearby. While this power is in effect, the Tyranid creature's Synapse range (see DEATHWATCH page 135) is doubled. In addition, the hardened resolve of the Hive Mind gives both the creature and all other creatures with the Tyranid Trait affected by the power +10 to all Willpower test for its duration.

### Hypnotic Gaze
**Action:** Half
**Opposed:** Yes
**Range:** 10 metres
**Sustained:** Yes
**Description:** The Broodlord can use its powerful gaze to snare the mind of a nearby warrior, holding it immobile and helpless as long as its stare remains unbroken. The Broodlord can affect a single enemy with this power, provided it can make eye contact with its intended target. If the target succumbs to the power, it is then held immobile (counts as being Helpless) until it can break free by winning an Opposed Willpower Test at the start of any of its turns, or the Broodlord's gaze is somehow broken.

## HIVE TYRANT PSYCHIC RULES

Note that the rules for dealing with Tyranid psychic powers presented here replace the Hive Tyrant's Monstrous Tyranid Psyker special rule (DEATHWATCH page 370) and it must test as normal to manifest its powers using the normal psychic rules.

## Leech Essence

**Action:** Half
**Opposed:** Yes
**Range:** 10 metres x PR
**Sustained:** No
**Description:** Using the raw power of the Hive Mind, the Tyranid creature tears the life-force from a nearby foe, devouring its essence and healing its own wounds. The target (which may be a Horde) suffers 1d5 damage (or Magnitude), plus an additional 1d5 damage for each degree it fails the Opposed Test, not reduced for either armour or Toughness. The Tyranid creature is then immediately healed by an amount equal to the damage inflicted, up to its total number of starting wounds. When working out the effects of Leech Essence, the GM should calculate each 1d5 damage roll separately, because if the target dies (or burns a Fate Point) before all the damage is applied, no further wounds can be drained from their desiccated corpse.

## Onslaught

**Action:** Half
**Opposed:** No
**Range:** 25 metres x PR
**Sustained:** Yes
**Description:** The Tyranid creature infuses a nearby brood with burning energy and the pitiless drive of the Hive Mind to devour all in its path. The creature chooses a single Master, Elite or Troop Horde within range, allowing it to either make a Full Move, Standard Attack (Ranged or Melee), or Charge Action as a Free Action once per Round. The warrior or brood continues to benefit from the effects of this power as long as the creature sustains it and they remain in range.

## Paroxysm

**Action:** Half
**Opposed:** Yes
**Range:** 25 metres x PR
**Sustained:** Yes
**Description:** Summoning the power of the Hive Mind, the creature assails its foes with crippling pain, tearing at their nerve endings and filling their minds with agony that makes it difficult for them to stand let alone fight. The Tyranid creature chooses a number of foes within range equal to its Psy Rating (or a single Horde of any Magnitude). Those that fail their Opposed Test reduce both their Weapon Skill and Ballistic Skill to 10 while they remain affected by the power. The pain is also quite distracting when trying to concentrate and therefore targets under the effects of Paroxysm suffer a –10 to all Intelligence, Perception, Willpower and Fellowship Characteristic and Skill Tests.

## Psychic Scream

**Action:** Half
**Opposed:** No
**Range:** 20 metre Radius
**Sustained:** No
**Description:** This power functions as described under the Hive Tyrant's special rules on page 370 of the DEATHWATCH Rulebook.

## The Horror

**Action:** Half
**Opposed:** No
**Range:** 75 metres
**Sustained:** No
**Description:** This power functions as described under the Hive Tyrant's special rules on DEATHWATCH page 370.

## Warp Blast

**Action:** Half
**Opposed:** No
**Range:** 50m x PR
**Sustained:** No
**Description:** By sending out a burning bolt of warp energy, the Zoanthrope blasts an area with power. The Zoanthrope must choose a single creature within range as the target, through others nearby may be affected. The Zoanthrope does not need to hit with the Warp Blast, though its Focus Power Test is modified as if it were making a ranged attack at the target, taking into account such things as range and concealment. Warp Blast inflicts 1d10 Energy Damage x PR, with a Penetration of 2 x PR. Creatures within 1m x PR of the target are also affected and suffer damage as well.

## Warp Lance

**Action:** Half
**Opposed:** No
**Range:** 30m x PR
**Sustained:** No
**Description:** More focused than a Warp Blast, the Warp Lance is primarily used against heavily armoured targets and vehicles. Taking the form of a single concentrated beam of energy, it can strike a single target within range. The Zoanthrope does not need to hit with the Warp Lance, though its Focus Power Test is modified as if it were making a ranged attack at the target, taking into account such things as range and concealment. Warp Lance inflicts 2d10 Energy Damage x PR, with a Penetration of 5 x PR.

# CARNIFEX

Carnifexes are giant creatures that can be found at the forefront of Tyranid assaults. These multi-ton monsters act like living battering rams that can smash through almost any obstacle whether it be a platoon of men, enemy tanks or a fortified position. They are specially evolved for use in shock assaults, spaceship boarding actions and massed battles where they can put their overwhelming strength and preternatural toughness to best effect. A Carnifex is a living engine of destruction and the attack of just one of these creatures is a terrifying thing to behold, a primeval force of nature unleashed in a killing frenzy.

Carnifexes have been encountered in every major encounter with Tyranids since the arrival of Hive Fleet Behemoth, most notably at the Battle of Macragge where large numbers of them were killed during the siege of the polar fortresses. These, the first Carnifexes to be seen by Imperial forces, became known as Screamer Killers because of the high-pitched scream they made as they charged into combat.

The Screamer Killer had four great sickle-shaped claws of diamond-hard chitin, bone and cartilage. The combined assault of these mighty scythes driven by the creature's huge muscle mass was powerful enough to rip through even armourplas and ceramite with ease. The source of their high-pitched screaming was found to be rasping plates in their esophagus that were used to energize a form of bio-plasma in their gut. This bio-plasma 'vomit' made a dangerous short range flamer-like weapon. In some instances Screamer Killers were reported using an electrical field around their claws to build up an incandescent bio-plasma ball before launching it at a target over longer ranges. The Screamer Killer had a massive body that was found to be extremely tough. It was also covered with a thick, chitinous hide that protected it from damage.

The Screamer Killer is now believed to be just one extreme mutation of the Tyranid warrior genus Tyranicus Tyranicii with a massively enlarged exoskeleton and musculature. It is accounted as a stable enough mutation to be given its own classification of Carnifex Primus. An ever-widening variety of sub-classifications of Carnifexes developed over the first Tyrannic war and subsequent attacks by Hive Fleet Kraken and Hive Fleet Leviathan. Over time it has been discovered that each Hive Fleet, perhaps even each hive ship, has its own variants on the basic Carnifex.

As with so many of the more extreme warrior mutations, Carnifexes lose much of the synaptic reception of the Hive Mind native to Tyranid Warriors and revert to a more animalistic intelligence level. It should be noted, however, that when this is mated to their ferocious capacity for violence, even a solitary Carnifex should not be underestimated. Many reports exist of lone Carnifexes that turn the tables on their would-be hunters and terrorize outlying colonies.

All Carnifex species seem well able to adapt to extremes of environment from arctic cold to desert heat. Their tremendous strength allows them to plough through swamps and jungles without hindrance and their endurance seems, to all intents and purposes, inexhaustible. If Carnifexes demonstrate one vulnerability, it is possibly that their bipedal nature and great weight give them a high ground pressure footprint that can exceed the load bearing strength of bridges and gantries or break through ice unexpectedly. Knocking one down is best achieved

with an armoured vehicle but getting one into close proximity with any Carnifex is a dangerous proposition.

Most Carnifex kills registered come from high energy attacks—lascannon, plasma and melta weapon strikes to critical locations. Carnifexes can shrug off other small arms fire and even bolt gun hits with minimal loss of function. Some great heroes have successfully pitted their speed and agility against a Carnifex to overcome it in close combat, but many more have died trying.

## Carnifex (Elite) Profile

| WS | BS | S | T | Ag | Int | Per | WP | Fel |
|----|----|----|----|----|----|----|----|----|
| 35 | 25 | (21) 70 | (18) 65 | 22 | 20 | 35 | 45 | –– |

**Move:** 5/10/15/30 **Wounds:** 100

**Skills:** Awareness (Per), Climb (S), Swim (S), Tracking (Int).

**Talents:** Ambidextrous, Berserk Charge, Combat Master, Fearless, Furious Assault, Heightened Senses (Sound, Smell), Iron Jaw, Swift Attack, True Grit, Two-weapon wielder (Melee).

**Traits:** Brutal Charge, Dark Sight, Fear 3 (Horrifying), Improved Natural Weapons (Scything Talons), Multiple Arms, Natural Armour (Bonded Exoskeleton), Regeneration (5), Size (Massive), Sturdy, Unnatural Strength (x3), Unnatural Toughness (x2). Tyranid.

**Armour:** Bonded Exoskeleton (All 10).

**Weapons:** Scything Talons (1d10+23 R; Pen 3), Bio-Plasma (30m; S/–/–; 3d10+10 E; Pen 9; Clip —; Rld —; Blast (5)).

## Special Rules

**Living Battering Ram:** During a Turn in which it charged, the Carnifex's melee attacks gain the Concussive Quality.

**Biomorphs:** At the GM's discretion, a Carnifex may be given the following changes to represent a different Carnifex variant.

**Thornback:** +10 BS, +5 Per. Replace the Talents Two-weapon wielder (melee) and Swift Attack with Two-weapon wielder (ballistic). Add the Trait Toxic (1d10). Replace Scything Talons and Bio-Plasma with Devourer (Basic; 30m; –/–/6; 1d10+6 R; Pen 0; Clip —; Rld —; Twin-linked, Living Ammunition, Storm, Tearing) and Stranglethorn Cannon (Heavy; 80m; S/–/–; 2d10+10 I; Pen 3; Clip —; Rld —; Blast (10), Deadly Snare, Devastating [2], Living Ammunition, Tearing).

**Venomspitter:** +15BS, +10Per. Replace the Talents Two-weapon wielder (melee) and Swift Attack with Two-weapon wielder (ballistic). Add the Talent Heightened Senses (Sight). Add the Trait Spore Cysts[††]. Replace Scything Talons and Bio-Plasma with two Heavy Venom Cannon (Heavy; 100m; S/–/–; 4d10+10 I; Pen 6; Clip —; Rld —; Blast (6), Living Ammunition, Toxic 1d10).

**Bile-Beast:** Remove the Talent Two-weapon wielder (melee). Add the Traits Spore Cysts[††] and Dorsal Chimneys[†††]. Replace Scything Talons and Bio-Plasma with Deathspitters (Basic; 40m; S/3/–; 1d10+6 E; Pen 4; Clip —; Rld —; Living Ammunition, Twin-linked, Tearing), Rending claws (1d10+ 18 R; Pen 3; Razor Sharp) and Prehensile tongue (count as Lash Whip (1d10+21 R; Pen 3; Flexible, Snare).

**Other Options:** At the GM's Discretion, the Carnifex can lose the Swift Attack Talent and gain one ranged weapon from the Tyranid Weapons list in this chapter or from page 373 in the **Deathwatch** Rulebook.

[††]**Spore Cysts:** Fat spores bloated with vile pathogens develop in the creature's carapace before breaking free and floating away. On any turn the Carnifex can take a **Challenging (+0) Toughness** Test as a Free Action to create a Virus grenade (3D10 I; Pen 0; Blast (2), Toxic) that drifts 1d5 metres per turn towards the loudest noise in the vicinity (randomly if indeterminate). If the Toughness Test is failed, the Carnifex suffers 1d10 damage per degree of failure with no reduction for Toughness Bonus or armour.

[†††]**Dorsal Chimneys:** Non-Tyranid creatures within 60 metres of a Bile-Beast must pass a **Challenging (+0) Toughness Test** each turn or suffer one level of fatigue even if in fully sealed armour. Characters and NPC's in unsealed armour take a **Hard (–20) Toughness Test** instead. The belching dorsal chimneys also generate a smoke cloud that covers everything within 15 metres of the Bile-Beast.

### Adventure Seeds

**Hunt the Alien:** Reports from a Watch Station monitoring a feudal world indicate that peasants have accidentally released a Carnifex that was trapped in ice during an attempted Tyranid invasion centuries ago. The locals have sent out several 'heroes' to slay the beast but none have returned and now they're terrified. The Kill-team must hunt down and destroy the Carnifex before the people turn to human sacrifice as a way to appease the monster.

**Venom:** A Bile-Beast has broken through the lines and is heading for the water supply of an important city. If the creature survives long enough to reach the reservoir, or even dies in close enough proximity, the death toll will be catastrophic.

**Gatecrasher:** Tyranid forces besieging a vital installation have brought up a Carnifex to batter down the front gate. Unless the Kill-team can find a way to stop the Carnifex the defences will be fatally compromised.

### Addendum by Codicier Taelon

Through extensive examination of the data crypts I have identified three core sub-variants of the Carnifex genus in Hive Fleet Dagon that appear to be stable enough to warrant examination.

Carnifex Vorantii: Commonly called the "Thornback," these creatures are living batteries of symbiote weaponry equipped with short to medium range ballistic parasites and living bomb projectors. Several of the intimidating-looking thorns on this subspecies are in fact sensory organs for sniffing out prey. They are murderous infantry hunters that seem to take pleasure in rooting out hiding men. Despite its lack of specialized melee limbs the Thornback is extremely dangerous at close quarters, where its speed and bulk allow it to easily impale incautious enemies.

Carnifex Arbylis: A sub-classification of extreme Carnifex variants that meld both pairs of upper limbs into complex ranged weapon symbiotes. Most common of these is the "Venomspitter" Carnifex, a beast capable of launching hyper-velocity crystalline shards of pure poison that can knock out a tank or easily kill a warrior in power armour. Carnifex Arbylis generally have improved ocular acuity and excellent depth perception from multiple eyes, although specimens employing a kind of stereoscopic echo-location have also been found on night worlds.

Carnifex Bilius: Commonly called "Bile-beasts," these creatures have been converted into walking biological weapons factories. Their carapaces are pitted with bubbling spore cysts and their guts writhe with lethal pathogens and molecular acids that gout from dorsal vents. The combined attack of necrotizing spores and acids used by these beasts will fatally overwhelm most bio-chem defences in moments; more resistant enemies are crushed by the creatures' crab-like claws and digested by its drooling, acidic maw.

# DAGON OVERLORD

*"It is the very embodiment of a predator; a soulless, remorseless beast which carries with it the weight of uncounted alien minds all hungry for our flesh."*

–Brother Talsharn, Dark Angels 5th Company

From the edge of the galactic rim, the first tendrils of Hive Fleet Dagon have coiled around the edge of the Jericho Reach, choking the life from worlds and feeding on the Imperium itself. Among this new hive fleet, ancient and now all too familiar horrors have arisen, creatures spawned and unleashed in dozens of other sectors and across countless other battlefields. Alongside the familiar, however, come new and disturbing Tyranid variations, proving once again that as soon as the Imperium believes it understands the Tyranid, the Tyranid changes and adapts once more. For the Jericho Reach, the force of the Tyranid assault was like a mighty hammer blow, catching the Achilus Crusade off balance and forcing Imperial Commanders to scramble to face this new and encroaching threat before too much ground was lost and too many worlds had fallen. Meeting the swarms head-on, millions died in those first desperate years of Dagon's arrival, and many planets could not be saved, disappearing forever under a tide of chitin and claws.

It was also during this dark time that Hive Fleet Dagon took on its own identity among the dozens of other major hive fleet incursions from the Eastern Fringe. Commanders and soldiers alike came to know the signs and character of the swarm, the nature of its beasts and the unique hunger it seemed to possess for the Jericho Reach, as if it had a taste for that sector specifically and the worlds that lay within it. They also noted how it adapted and changed with each world it consumed, each battle it won (or lost) and with each light year it came closer to the Iron Collar and the Warp Gate. This kind of rapid adaption had been observed in other fleets of course, however in Hive Fleet Dagon it seemed to take on an even more sinister slant, as if the fleet were aware of the pain and suffering it was inflicting and the terror in the hearts of the soldiers trying to stop it. In the space of a few short years, this evolution and mutation within Dagon led to a number of unique bio-constructs and weapons never seen before by Imperial scholars; the most terrible of them all being the Overlord.

The rise of the Dagon Overlord, or simply the Overlord as it became known, seemed to occur in conjunction with those first victories scored by the hive fleet, as if the Hive Mind had taken the measure of the foes it has faced and chose to evolve a specific tool for their eradication. Other theories speculate that the Overlord was a genus specific to the hive fleet that existed long before its arrival in the Imperium, and that it was simply a superior warrior construct, brought out of storage to face a more stubborn than excepted adversary. Whatever the case, the Overlord first appeared during the opening days of the battle for Castobel, leading a mighty swarm against the amethyst spires of the Trimalov Hive, rending through its walls and dispatching its defenders in a month-long orgy of carnage and slaughter. Those fortunate enough to escape the fall of the hive city with their lives took with them tales of terror and the memory of a beast which stood apart from even the worst horrors the swarm has to offer.

The Dagon Overlord is in appearance similar to a Hive Tyrant, a creature of terrible and horrific majesty all on its own, but is different enough to stand apart from its lesser brethren and be remembered by those that see it looming across the battlefield. Covered in slimy plates of chitin which constantly drip and leak fluid, the Overlord projects an aura of horror and menace like nothing else within the swarm. Its importance and power are also readily apparent when it strides alongside other Tyranid creatures, its powerful presence emboldening and maddening the lesser creatures more so than would be expected by any link to the Hive Mind. It is almost as if the Overlord is the embodiment of Hive Fleet Dagon's ire toward the Jericho Reach and its alien hatred infects creatures with a personal desire to murder, maim, and kill all those in their path. It has been suggested that this notion of the beast's personal vendetta is just the fanciful imagining of terrified Imperial Guardsmen, though only by those who have not seen the Overlord beast in the flesh themselves.

Since its first appearance, the Dagon Overlord has been sighted in almost all of the major combat zones of the Orpheus Salient, leading swarm after swarm into the ranks of Imperial defenders. This has led many to believe that the Overlord is just one of many, and not a unique creature at all. However such notions of individuality are hard to determine when dealing with the Hive Mind, as it is constantly recycling its troops and adding to them by consuming worlds. This means the Overlord may well be a veteran of many wars, and may have even fallen countless times to the foe, only to be re-spawned by the Hive Mind with a fresh body and a will for vengeance. Both the Ordo Xenos and the Deathwatch have made attempts to find the truth behind the Overlord, if for no other reason than to catalogue a new and deadly variation of the Tyranid race. Neither has met with much success, and both agents and Battle-Brothers have been lost during the process. Even when the Dagon Overlord seems defeated, it invariably rises again in another place or another time.

## Dagon Overlord (Master) Profile

| WS | BS | S | T | Ag | Int | Per | WP | Fel |
|----|----|----|----|----|-----|-----|----|-----|
| 81 | 35 | 65 (18) | 63 (18) | 45 | 45 | 49 | 70 (14) | —— |

**Movement:** 7/14/21/42  **Wounds:** 180

**Skills:** Awareness (Per), Climb (S), Swim (S).

**Talents:** Ambidextrous, Combat Master, Crushing Blow, Fearless, Heightened Senses (All), Psy Rating (8), Two-Weapon wielder (Melee), Swift Attack, Lightning Attack.

**Traits:** Brutal Charge, Dark Sight, Fear 4 (Terrifying), Natural Armour (Bonded Exoskeleton), Multiple Arms, Unnatural Strength (x3), Unnatural Toughness (x3), Unnatural Willpower (x2), Improved Natural Weapons (Scything Talons), Shadow in the Warp, Size (Massive), Synapse Creature, Tyranid.

**Armour:** Bonded Exoskeleton (All 10).

**Weapons:** Scything Talons (1d10+22 R; Pen 3), two Boneswords (1d10+20 R; Pen 6, Drain Life), Twin-linked Devourer (30m, –/–/6; 1d10+6 R; Pen 0; Clip —; Rld —; Living Ammunition, Storm, Tearing, Twin-linked).

**Gear:** None.

### Special Rules

**Biomorphs:** At the GM's discretion, the Dagon Overlord may have Acid Blood (when wounded in melee combat all non-Tyranid creatures in melee with it must make a **Challenging (+0) Agility Test** or suffer 2d10 Damage with a Pen of 5), Adrenal Glands (gaining the Furious Assault Talent), Toxin Sacs (gaining the Toxic (1d10) Trait on all melee and ranged attacks, which stacks with the Miasma of the Depths Trait), or Regeneration (5) (gaining the Regeneration Trait).

**Tyranid Psyker:** The Dagon Overlord is a Tyranid Psyker and follow the rules for Tyranid Psychic Powers on page 34. It has access to all the standard Tyranid psychic powers.

**Death Shock:** When the Dagon Overlord is slain, its death sends a shockwave through the Hive Mind. All Tyranid creatures that do not have the Fearless Talent or Synapse creature Trait will automatically break and flee as quickly as they can (this effect overrides the effects of Instinctive Behaviour in this instance). Any Tyranid creature with the Fearless or Synapse Creature Trait must pass a **Challenging (+0) Willpower Test** or be stunned for one round.

**Old Adversary:** The Overlord is an ancient Hive Tyrant and a veteran of countless battles within the Jericho Reach. Even when it is slain, the Hive Mind resurrects it anew with memories of its past deeds and a hatred for its foes. The Dagon Overlord gains the Hatred (Deathwatch) Talent when facing members of the Deathwatch.

**Blood of Dagon:** When the Overlord leads a swarm of Tyranid creatures it can spur them on to greater acts of fury and force them to fight on even when grievously wounded.

Any Horde of Tyranid creatures which fights alongside the Dagon Overlord benefits from its presence and regenerates 1d5 points of Magnitude at the start of each of its turns.

**Miasma of the Depths:** The Dagon Overlord has a cloud of toxins constantly oozing from its joints and creates a virulent haze of haemotoxins, neurotoxins, and deadly phage organisms all around it much in the same way as a Venomthrope. It counts as having the Toxic Trait, but the damage is 2d10, ignoring Toughness and Armour. The Toughness Test to resist the poison is Very Hard (–30).

**Body Collector:** The Overlord is selective about those it chooses to devour, and picks only the strongest and most powerful of its adversaries to consume. Often it will task lesser Tyranid creatures with gathering together these bodies after, or even during a battle, and piling them at its feet so it may feast on them and grow stronger. A Dagon Overlord which devours the body of a creature with 15 or more wounds and a Toughness of 40 or more, heals 1d10 points of damage. At the GM's discretion, the Overlord may also over time take on traits of those it devours as it assimilates their flesh.

### Adventure Seeds

**Rogue Psyker:** Whispers from the Ordo Xenos have indicated that a psyker named Aralon managed to escape the fall of Trimalov Hive on Castobel. It is said that Aralon witnessed the horror of the Dagon Overlord first hand. In addition, the agents and spies of the Ordo believe that Aralon touched minds with the Overlord and has formed some kind of unholy bond with the beast. If this is true, Aralon would be a valuable asset indeed, as he could be used both to track the creature and also grant vital insight into its actions and motives. Unfortunately, Aralon, driven near to complete insanity by his experience, has been running ever since and has fled most of the way across the Jericho Reach. Tracking him down will be no easy task, as Aralon is also a talented telepath and has been using his abilities to cover his trail and wipe away memories of his passing. Worse still, he has been heading for Tau-held space.

**A Foe Reborn:** The Deathwatch have faced the Dagon Overlord numerous times since the arrival of the hive fleet in the Jericho Reach. It has vanquished more than one Kill-team, devouring Battle-Brothers and stoking the flames of its hatred for the Deathwatch. Now a new hunt is being organised to destroy the creature and recover a measure of honour for the Deathwatch. The Dagon Overlord has been traced to the Cadron system, a dismal feral world covered in untamed jungles and jagged mountains of volcanic glass. It is believed that the hive fleet will imminently launch an assault on the world, giving the Kill-teams a chance to bring it down. Such a prize, however, has led to rivalry among the Kill-teams, which could hinder the mission should chance of glory cloud the tactical sense of some of the Battle-Brothers.

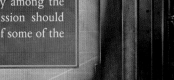

# The Shadow of Dagon

+++For the Attention of Codicier Taelon, White Scars Chapter+++
Confirmed Sightings Xenomorph Designation X65a "Dagon Overlord"
+++Time Frame Codes Fleet Standard Epsilon+++

**0.865:** The Overlord is first identified as a unique Tyranid Genus on Castobel during the battle for the Trimalov Hive. Though few live to tell the tale of the beast, a handful escape with their lives and news of a monstrous beast leading the swarm to victory.

**0.877:** As the battle for Castobel rages on and the remaining hive cities fortify themselves, the Dagon Overlord appears again at the Battle of the Nine Bridges, crushing an entire Planetary Defence Force regiment and sweeping the defenders from the field. Hazy pict images gathered after the battle from a servo-skull show what seems to be a mountain of corpses gathered at the feet of the Overlord.

**1.101:** During an engagement around the world of Jove's Descent, the Imperial Gothic-class Cruiser *Spirit of Defiance* is boarded and gutted by an assault led by the Dagon Overlord. Vox transmissions from the dying ship identify the beast as it smashes its way through deck after deck until reaching the ship's bridge and dismembering her captain.

**1.132:** The first agents of the Ordo Xenos attempt to gather information on the Overlord and hard evidence of its existence, following a trail of destruction from the ruins of Freya to the shores of Vanir. Some agents vanish without a trace while others fall in Tyranid incursions and battles, none return with so much as a sighting of the creature or any evidence as to its whereabouts.

**1.288:** During the Battle of Xin-Cyn, pict images and vox echoes gathered from combat servitors seem to indicate the presence of the Dagon Overlord, though the Death Spectres presence report no sighting of the beast, leading to speculation that it may be sizing up the threat of the Adeptus Astartes in the Jericho Reach and gaining the measure of this new foe.

**1.563:** Two Deathwatch Kill-teams dispatched to clear the space hulk *Eye of Desolation* as it drifts close to the edge of the Vanir system confirm contact with the Dagon Overlord. After opening a vault deep inside the space hulk, they unleash a tide of Genestealers, apparently held in some kind of stasis. During their extraction, Tyranid vanguard organisms appear from nowhere and they must fight their way back to their craft, narrowly escaping the arrival of the Overlord.

**1.671:** The psychic council of Ynai, long preparing for the arrival of the hive fleets to their world, are found dead within their inner chambers. No sign of their killers can be found, nor is the exact method of their demise clear, however, painted in their blood are crude images that appear to match the appearance of the Dagon Overlord, resplendent atop a pile of corpses.

**2.001:** The Dagon Overlord appears again during the invasion of Whispers Crossing on the edge of the Orpheus Salient. The primitive natives of the world liken the Overlord to their ancient god of destruction and bringer of the end days, throwing themselves at the feet of the swarm to be killed and devoured in their millions.

**2.015:** Brother Heroitus, a Deathwatch Space Marine of the Storm Wardens Chapter, faces down the Dagon Overlord in the tunnels of Arsati and slays the beast with the aid of his Kill-team. Reliable evidence of the creature's demise, however, is not forthcoming, as Heroitus is forced to retreat when the swarm caves in the tunnels and seals the underhives of Arsati from the outside world.

**2.344:** The Ordo Xenos uncover some disturbing patterns in the appearance of the Dagon Overlord. Mapping its appearances during Tyranid attacks across the sector, they discover it seems to be reacting to the intervention of the Deathwatch—as if it is actively hunting Kill-teams...

# GARGOYLE

Flying at the head of the swarm, Gargoyles are often the first sign of the onrushing wave of Tyranids, as they blot out the sun and choke the sky with their leathery wings and infernal screeching. Not dissimilar in appearance to a Termagant, albeit with the addition of wings, a Gargoyle is individually weak, and relies as much on its speed and ranged weapons as it does tooth and claw. However, in great numbers (as Gargoyles are almost always encountered) they can make as fearsome a foe as any Tyranid. The primary goal of Gargoyles, in their role as part of the Tyranid vanguard, is, it seems, to sow confusion. They achieve this by peppering foes with their fleshborers and then darting away before retaliatory fire can find them, always staying out of arm's reach and using their speed to move from target to target before they can be outmatched.

This command of the air and their agility makes Gargoyles a particularly fearsome foe to fight, especially as they often descend on enemies from hundreds of metres, swooping down to strike lethal blows. This forces foes to constantly scan the skies and be alert for any shadow or flicking form that could be the first sign of a descending Gargoyle brood. Gargoyles are also a menace for aircraft and can make air travel across a Tyranid-contested world extremely dangerous, as they hunt ceaselessly for prey, often supported by other, more massive Tyranid bio-forms such as Harpies and Harridans. Fast and manoeuvrable, it is not unheard of for Gargoyles to ambush craft many times their own size, latching onto the hulls in large numbers and chewing through power cables, couplings and other vital components to bring them down in flames.

Dangerous when beyond the range of Tyranid synapse creatures, they become even more so when driven forward by the implacable will of the Hive Mind, pouring down from the sky upon their foes like clawed rain, forcing their way through small openings and blanketing sensors and observation towers with their bat-like wings. Under the direction of the Hive Mind, Gargoyles will even throw themselves into vents, exhausts and exposed gears, fouling machinery and weapons with their bodies. In this way Gargoyles are very difficult to defend against or trap in a bottleneck, as their ability to fly allows them to come at their foes from all angles and exploit any opening they can find. A Gargoyle which becomes trapped in an enclosed space (as sometime happens when they force their way through openings) is deadly indeed as it goes into a frenzy to escape, fighting as only a cornered beast can.

**Armour:** Chitinous Carapace (All 3).
**Weapons:** Fleshborer (20m; S/–/–; 1d10+5 R; Pen 3, Clip —, Rld —; Living Ammunition, Tearing), Teeth and Claws (1d10+3 R; Pen 3, Primitive).
**Gear:** None.

## Special Rules

**Biomorphs:** At the GM's discretion a Gargoyle may have Adrenal Glands (gaining the Furious Assault Talent) and/or Toxin Sacs (gaining the Toxic (1d10) Trait on all melee and ranged attacks).

**Blinding Venom:** Attacks in melee from a Gargoyle have a chance of blinding its foes. If a blow from a Gargoyle with its Teeth and Claws strikes an opponent's head, they must make an **Easy (+20) Toughness Test** or become Blinded for 1d5 turns. Enclosed helmets (such as those on a suit of power armour, negate this ability).

**Enclosed Spaces:** Gargoyles are feral creatures and sometime become trapped in places where they cannot fly, and go crazy in an effort to escape. A Gargoyle which becomes trapped in an enclosed space (i.e., where it cannot spread its wings or use its Flyer movement) gains the Frenzy and Furious Assault Talents until it escapes or dies.

**Gargoyle Hordes:** Gargoyles make ideal horde creatures and can use the Horde rules (see **DEATHWATCH** page 359).

| Gargoyle (Troops) Profile | | | | | | | | |
|---|---|---|---|---|---|---|---|---|
| WS | BS | S | T | Ag | Int | Per | WP | Fel |
| 30 | 33 | 32 | 30 | 40 | 10 | 40 | 30 | — |

**Movement:** 4/8/12/24      **Wounds:** 9
**Skills:** Acrobatics (Ag), Awareness (Per), Climb (S), Contortionist (Ag), Dodge (Ag).
**Talents:** Death from Above, Leap Up.
**Traits:** Dark Sight, Flyer (20), Natural Armour (Chitinous Carapace), Natural Weapons (Teeth and Claws), Instinctive Behaviour (Lurk), Tyranid.

# LICTOR

*"It was like the shadows just came alive and took him, right from under our noses. One moment he was there, the next he was gone... and none of us saw an Emperor-damned thing."*

—Sergeant Morvik, 351st Castobel Rifle Brigade

Lictors are the lone hunters of the Tyranid swarm, roving ahead of the hive fleet, seeking out prey and leading the Hive Mind to concentrations of enemies. As tall as a Tyranid Warrior, Lictors are distinct in appearance from other Tyranid creatures in a number of ways, such as a pair of long mantis-like claws extending over the creature's shoulders which it can use for climbing and impaling its prey; long, drooping feeder tendrils that hang from its maw and greatly increase its senses, and shimmering chameleonic scales which allow it to hide with ease. A natural predator, the Lictor is patient and stealthy and can move past even the most alert foes, or spend days hiding immobile, waiting for a chance to strike once its prey's guard is down. This behaviour has given the Lictor an almost mythical reputation amongst its foes, as a ghost-like horror which can strike at any time and place, before vanishing into thin air just as easily.

A Lictor's primary purpose is to lead the Tyranid swarm to fresh prey and seek out large groups of foes that might be hiding or fleeing before the swarm. In this role, they move silently and almost completely invisibly across all kind of terrain, using their enhanced senses to find their foes. When they locate prey, they will move in and begin to stalk it, avoiding open conflict or situations where it might be outnumbered or outmatched and instead choosing to pick off its targets one by one. During the course of these attacks, the Lictor will be exuding a pheromone trail which other Tyranid creatures can then follow to the location of this fresh prey.

The Lictor also gathers information for the Hive Mind. Part of the creature's unique genus means that it is capable of literally devouring a victim's memories by eating their brain, learning more from them in a single bloody meal than hours of brutal interrogation might yield.

Fighting Lictors is very difficult, as first a solider needs to find one. Even then, bringing one to battle can be difficult as they strike and kill a handful of men before vanishing, sometimes right before the eyes of their enemies, and leave no trail to follow. Lictors are usually only brought down by quick thinking heavy weapons teams or powerful Imperial heroes, such as well-armed Space Marines, which have the strength and nerve to slay the beast before it can melt away into the terrain. Another less reliable method of destroying Lictors, and one favoured by many Imperial Guard commanders, is the recon by fire method. Once even the slightest evidence of a Lictor is detected, they will isolate the area they believe it to be lurking in (sometime kilometres across) and carpet bomb it into ash and dust. While this only rarely works (Lictors being cunning enough to either slip away or hide where you least expect them) it does raise morale among the local soldiers, at least until the Lictor strikes again...

## Lictor (Elite) Profile

| WS | BS | S | T | Ag | Int | Per | WP | Fel |
|----|----|----|----|----|----|----|----|----|
| 65 | — | 65 (12) | 40 (8) | 40 (8) | 25 | 45 (8) | 45 | —— |

**Movement:** 6/12/18/36  **Wounds:** 40

**Skills:** Acrobatics (Ag), Awareness (Per) +20, Climb (S) +20, Concealment (Ag) +20, Contortionist (Ag) +10, Dodge (Ag) +10, Shadowing (Ag) +20, Silent Move (Ag) +20, Survival (Int) +20, Swim (S), Tracking (Int) +20.

**Talents:** Ambidextrous, Assassin Strike, Berserk Charge, Blind Fighting, Catfall, Combat Master, Crushing Blow, Fearless, Furious Assault, Hard Target, Heightened Sense (Hearing, Sight, Smell, Taste, Touch), Leap Up, Lightning Attack, Sprint, Step Aside, Swift Attack.

**Traits:** Dark Sight, Fear 3 (Horrifying), Instinctive Behaviour (Lurk), Natural Armour (Reinforced Chitin), Multiple Arms, Size (Hulking), Unnatural Agility (x2), Unnatural Strength (x2), Unnatural Perception (x2), Unnatural Toughness (x2), Improved Natural Weapons (Scything Talons), Size (Enormous), Tyranid.

**Armour:** Reinforced Chitin (All 6).

**Weapons:** Scything Talons (1d10+14 R; Pen 3; Toxic), Rending Claws (1d10+12 R; Pen 5; Razor Sharp, Toxic).

**Gear:** None.

## Special Rules

**Flesh Hooks:** Lictors have dozens of tiny hooks which they can fire from their chests to snare prey and drag their victims toward them. These allow a Lictor to initiate a Grapple (see page 240 in the **DEATHWATCH** Rulebook) with a target up to 10m away. With every successful Opposed Strength Test the Lictor makes as part of the Grapple action, the target is pulled closer by 1m plus 1m for each degree of success.

**Chameleonic Scales:** A Lictor is covered in chameleonic scales which shimmer and shift to match its surroundings and can

## ADVENTURE SEEDS

**Countermeasure:** Deathwatch Apothecary Brother Galus has been tasked by the Watch Fortress Erioch command to hunt down and kill Lictors from at least a dozen warzones across the Orpheus Salient. With the aid of a Kill-team he is to hunt down the alien hunters and harvest their pheromone sacs, so that a counter might be found to negate them. Finding even a single Lictor should prove a momentous task, as Brother Galus and his team must follow rumours, unconfirmed sightings and ghost stories to probable locales and then try to track one of the swarm's most elusive creatures. As arduous a task as this may be, it is made even more so by the presence of countless other Tyranid creatures and predators, which will also be drawn to the location of the Lictor sooner or later...

**Devoured Data:** On the world of Eleusis, a brutal murder has been laid at the feet of a Lictor. In the shadow of the immediate Tyranid invasion, a high ranking Imperial Guard commander has been slain in his quarters and his brain devoured, a killing that bears all the hallmarks of an advanced Lictor scout. The Imperial Guard now fears that if the Lictor has assimilated the commander's memories, it will be able to pass on dangerous military secrets about the world's defence. What is unclear however is whether or not the encroaching hive fleet, and its Hive Mind, is close enough to make contact with the Tyranid creatures already on Eleusis. If there is even a chance that the Lictor has not yet been in contact with the Hive Mind, there may still be time for an elite formation, such as a Deathwatch Kill-team, to find the beast and slay it, keeping the commander's secrets safe.

make it practically invisible to the naked eye, plus most other methods of visual detection such as infrared and ultraviolet scopes. Whenever a Lictor uses its Concealment Skill to hide, all tests to detect it visually suffer a −30 penalty. In addition, the scales allow the Lictor to make Concealment Tests as a Half Action rather than a Full Action and it can even do so even when being observed or when there is no nearby cover.

**Memory Devourer:** When a Lictor devours the brain of its prey, it can learn some of its memories. Once the Lictor has eaten a brain, it gains access to all of the victim's recent, most distinct memories (usually the location of friendly troops or defences). If the Lictor wishes to learn something very specific from the victim, such as an old memory or one the victim does not remember well, it must make an **Easy (+20) Intelligence Test**.

## Tyranid Psychological Warfare and the Methodology of Fear

*During my studies of Hive Fleet Dagon and its splinter fleets I have made numerous observations as to the exact nature of the Tyranid understanding of fear and its uses as a battlefield weapon. All of the data thus gathered by the Imperium seems to suggest quite clearly that the Tyranid does not feel fear, or at least not in any way which we would understand—it operates only within the emotional parameters of the Hive Mind, and the Hive Mind's will to conquer and devour. What is less clear is if the Tyranid understands fear in its prey, beyond the normal responses of predator to prey, in which the former gives chase to the later and expects it to run, hide and generally try to get away.*

*I have been exploring these concepts largely in response to the behaviour of the bio-forms known as Lictors, which seem to be some kind of scout genus, but, like all Tyranids, is a highly evolved predator. More than any other kind of Tyranid creature, the Lictor seems to be an object of utter terror for many Imperial troops, given its tactics of hit and run and its superior stealth abilities, which allow it to strike without warning and then disappear without a trace. The questions that then arise from this are: does the Lictor behave as it does deliberately to sow terror, or is it simply following its basic biological programming to avoid open confrontation and pick off the weak? Does the Hive Mind understand the tactics of terror and did it create the Lictor to exploit them? Does the Lictor understand the benefits of leaving some of its foes alive to spread terror when it could easily finish them off?*

*As with most questions about the Tyranids, I imagine the answers will remain a mystery, as even if we were to find a way to communicate with the Hive Mind, I doubt it would have much to say to us.*

 *-Codicier Jaelon*

# PURESTRAIN GENESTEALER

*"I can think of few greater xenos threats to the Imperium than that of the Genestealer. An apex predator possessed of intelligence and cunning that rival our own, they exist for the sole purpose of reproducing in vast numbers and sowing utter chaos in their wake."*

—Inquisitor Kalistradi from the *The Nature of the Beast*

Genestealers are terrifying close combat horrors with the individual strength and speed to tear apart even an armoured Space Marine if they can get close enough to land a telling blow. They stand almost six feet in height, even hunched over as they are on hind legs, their four arms ending in claws, talons or other bio-weapons capable of cutting through ceramite and plasteel with equal ease. Cunning and independent, Genestealers are also one of the few Tyranid creatures which can exist away from the nurturing and controlling influence of the Hive Mind, using their own innate intelligence and brood telepathy to form tight-knit groups. These groups can survive for decades or even centuries on worlds, hiding their presence and infecting more and more of the population until the time to strike arrives, usually coinciding with the arrival of the hive fleet and the wholesale invasion and consumption of the world itself.

Few Tyranid creatures have earned such a terrible reputation or caused as much damage to the Imperium as the Genestealer. Detected long before the first tendrils of the hive fleets reached the galaxy, they were thought to be little more than another unusual and deadly alien xeno-form. It was only after the horrors of Behemoth and Leviathan that the Imperium came to realise their true purpose as advanced scouts for the Hive Mind and infiltrators of the most insidious kind. Hiding away on void ships and in the depths of space hulks, the Genestealer menace has travelled across the length and breadth of the Imperium of Man, seeding themselves onto worlds and subverting their populations. This perhaps is the greatest horror the Genestealers bring, as they can infect almost any life form with a "kiss," implanting some of their own genetic material into the host and taking complete control of it. When the host gives birth to offspring, these carry with them the Genestealer's genes and over a few generations a new Genestealer is born, albeit with some genetic traits taken from its host—such as the human-like hands many Genestealers encountered in the Imperium possess.

Purestrain Genestealers are Genestealers which have been spawned not through the process of infecting hosts but rather by the hive ships themselves in great bio-factories and birthing vats. Not polluted or altered by "inferior" genetic material, they are markedly stronger and faster than a normal Genestealer and possess a wider variety of adaptive bio-morphs. This is intentional, as Purestrain Genestealers are the creatures from which all other Genestealers are born, and even a single Purestrain Genestealer can create a vast brood from a local population given time and enough raw material.

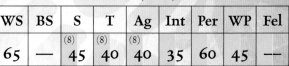

| Purestrain Genestealer (Elite) Profile | | | | | | | | |
|------|------|------|------|------|------|------|------|------|
| WS | BS | S | T | Ag | Int | Per | WP | Fel |
| 65 | — | (8) 45 | (8) 40 | (8) 40 | 35 | 60 | 45 | —— |

**Movement:** 8/16/24/48 **Wounds:** 20

**Skills:** Awareness (Per) +10, Climb (S) +10, Dodge (Ag) +10, Swim (S) +10.

**Talents:** Ambidextrous, Fearless, Hard Target, Leap Up, Lightning Attack, Lightning Reflexes, Step Aside, Swift Attack.

**Traits:** Dark Sight, Fear 2 (Frightening), Improved Natural Weapons (Rending Claws), Multiple Arms, Natural Armour (Reinforced Chitin), Unnatural Agility (x2), Unnatural Speed, Unnatural Strength (x2), Unnatural Toughness (x2), Tyranid.

**Armour:** Reinforced Chitin (All 4).

**Weapons:** Rending Claws (1d10+12 R; Pen 5, Razor Sharp).

## Special Rules

**Biomorphs:** At the GM's discretion, a Purestrain Genstealer may have Adrenal Glands (gaining the Furious Assault Talent) and/or Toxin Sacs (gaining the Toxic [1d10] Trait).

**Brood Telepathy:** Purestrain Genestealers have a constant telepathic link with each other which can function clearly and without restriction (such as from intervening objects or other forms of shielding) up to one kilometre. This allows them to communicate with each other and pass information to nearby Genestealers quickly and quietly.

## ADVENTURE SEEDS

**Surgical Strike:** The Ordo Xenos is tireless in its investigation and eradication of Genestealer infection, as if even a single Genestealer survives, the threat can spring up again in the space of a few short generations. Kalano Secondus is one such world, a brutal penal world nestled on the edge of Jericho Reach at the far extent of Imperial control. A subterranean rock, the world is home to countless connected prisons and work camps where military prisoners, deserters and dissidents are dumped from across the Reach. Over the past few decades there have been no less than three Genestealer infestations found and purged by the Ordo Xenos, prompting them to consider destroying the entire world so that it does not happen again. However, Kalano Secondus is too useful to the Imperial authorities and so an accord has been struck where by a Kill-team will be deployed to the world to seek out and find the cause of the recurring infestation (doubtless a powerful and cunning Broodlord) and end it for good.

**Infection:** The Halaran noble family of Eleusis has been the target of a Genestealer infestation, one of their mercantile members bringing the creatures back from a void-faring mission. While the infestation has been dealt with (though Eleusis still faces imminent Tyranid attack) and the Halaran family largely decimated, those that remain are burning for revenge against the brood which enslaved them, some of which they claim have escaped to other nearby worlds. The Ordo Xenos also takes this threat seriously and have graciously allowed the Halarans to fund their investigations into the location of the brood. It is likely that the Ordo will eventually call in a Kill-team to track this specific brood across the Orpheus Salient and run it to ground.

**Genestealer's Kiss:** A Genestealer possesses an ovipositor within its maw that implants the alien's genetic code into its victims. This seeds the host's body with a parasite that will grow into a monstrous hybrid creature, mixing the genes of the Genestealer and the host. Over a number of generations, these hybrid will give birth to more hybrids until eventually a new Genestealer is born. A host can resist such an implantation, but only if they pass a **Challenging (+0) Toughness Test** as soon as it occurs. Once infected, the host become beholden to the Genestealer which infected it and loves the hybrid offspring it carries as if it was its own progeny. Special Deathwatch treatments and a Space Marine's own physiology ensure that Deathwatch Space Marines are immune to this effect.

## BROODLORD (MASTER)

Genestealer broods are often led by ancient and powerful Genestealers know as Broodlords. The GM can create a Broodlord by making the following additions and changes to a Purestrain Genestealer profile:

- +10 Weapon Skill
- +10 Agility
- +10 Intelligence
- +10 Willpower
- +30 Wounds
- Increase Unnatural Strength and Toughness to (x3)
- Replace Natural Armour (Reinforced Chitin) with Natural Armour (Hardened Carapace) giving it 6 armour points on all locations.

Broodlords are also psykers with a Psy Rating of 5 and access to the Tyranid Psychic Powers (select two). In addition, they have their own unique psychic power: Hypnotic Gaze (see page 34).

## Signs and Portents of Infestation
### by Codicier Taelon

*During the course of my studies of the Genestealer, I have come across numerous accounts from Inquisitors, planetary lords and even Deathwatch Kill-teams as to the signs and portents of a suspected Genestealer infestation. Some of the more common ones include:*

*The rise of variant and divergent cults of the Imperial Creed, often restricted to certain social classes or locals.*

*Elevated instances of citizen disappearances, missing or mutilated livestock, and seemingly senseless local vandalism.*

*Breakdowns in command of local enforcers or planetary defence forces, as key officers go missing for a number of days or become mysteriously ill, only to return to their posts oddly different.*

*Rise in rumours and sightings of "monsters," also numerous local legends coming to life involving cursed woods, haunted vaults or "evil" locales.*

*An increase in citizen lethargy or restlessness in a given area, often at odds with surrounding areas or locales.*

*The presence of large numbers of strangers or travellers in an area, all with a similar look or a 'too familiar' manner with each other.*

*Strange markings, tracks or symbols appearing in and around settlements or well travelled areas, as well as a reduction in local traffic as citizens become wary of being outside.*

# RAVENER

*"The thing I learnt was to trust nothing; not the air, not the water, not the ground beneath your feet. Make no assumptions, and you might live to tell someone else."*

–Advice to fresh troops on fighting the Tyranids, given by Sergeant Gorth of the Volg 3rd "Mercy Bringers"

Raveners are horrific predators that burrow through the earth with frightening speed and precision. They are twisted, serpentine creatures whose armoured bodies are several times the size of a grown man's, and yet they move with a lightning-like speed that can see their victims slashed apart into bloody chunks, having never seen their assailant. Vulnerable only to massed firepower and heavy weapons, the Ravener's prey stands little chance if caught alone or off guard, as they often exploit their ability to burrow through almost any substance to surprise their victims, sensing their way by vibrations as faint as a beating heart, through many metres of intervening material. Often Raveners strike deep behind a battle line or in strongholds thought impregnable to outside assault, and worse yet for those that must face them; Raveners rarely hunt alone, but are instead often encountered in broods of half a dozen or more creatures. In several recorded cases, when such a brood breaks in to a shelter or underground bunker, they have inflicted utter carnage in minutes, ending the lives of hundreds in a few scant moments of screaming, blood-soaked fury.

While Raveners do appear similar in size and basic design to Tyranid Warriors, with the major exception being their serpentine tail rather than legs, they are in fact very different beasts and bred for a very different purpose. Possessed of little more than animal intelligence, unless directed by the Hive Mind they will wilfully chase fleeing prey or become distracted by fast moving targets disregarding all other concerns. The role of a hunting beast however is one they excel at, and they possess extraordinary senses for tracking foes, able to feel the slightest tremor made by passing footfalls even kilometres away and see into dozens of light spectrums, even following the pulsing waves of a vox transmission to its source. This makes it very hard to hide from a Ravener, and it is especially dangerous if being directed by the Hive Mind and its senses used to guide the bulk of the swarm toward the location of its prey.

Perhaps the most disconcerting aspect of the serpentine Raveners is their ability to appear in almost any location and usually where their foes least expect them. By burrowing through even some of the hardest substances, they can worm their way into heavily fortified structures, squeezing through opening much smaller than themselves and slinking off to hide in dark places to await the time to strike. This known tactic of the Ravener often prompts Imperial commanders to send their men on patrol looking for Ravener "nid holes" which might be hidden in subterranean tunnels or deep cellars. Needless to say, should an Imperial Guard patrol find such a "nid hole," more often than not it is their dying screams which alert their comrades.

| **Ravener (Elite) Profile** | | | | | | | | |
|---|---|---|---|---|---|---|---|---|
| WS | BS | S | T | Ag | Int | Per | WP | Fel |
| 60 | — | (8) 45 | (8) 40 | 50 | 17 | 50 | 35 | — |

**Movement:** 7/14/21/42 **Wounds:** 40

**Skills:** Awareness (Per) +20, Climb (S) +20, Concealment (Ag), Silent Move (Ag), Swim (S) +10, Tracking (Int) +20.

**Talents:** Fearless, Heightened Sense (Hearing, Sight, Smell), Sprint, Swift Attack, Lightning Attack.

**Traits:** Dark Sight, Fear 3 (Horrifying), Burrower, Instinctive Behaviour (Feed), Natural Armour (Reinforced Chitin), Multiple Arms, Unnatural Strength (x2), Unnatural Toughness (x2), Improved Natural Weapons (Scything Talons), Size (Enormous), Tyranid, Unnatural Senses (30m).

**Armour:** Reinforced Chitin (All 6).

**Weapons:** Scything Talons (1d10+14 R; Pen 3) or Rending Claws (1d10+12 R; Pen 5; Razor Sharp), or Devourer (30m, –/–/6; 1d10+6 R; Pen 0; Clip —; Rld —; Living Ammunition, Storm, Tearing) or Death Spitter (40m, S/3/–; 1d10+6 E; Pen 4; Clip —; Rld —; Living Ammunition, Tearing), or Spine Fists (20m, S/2/4; 1d10+12 R; Pen 2; Clip —; Rld —).

**Gear:** None.

## Special Rules

**Extraordinary Senses:** Raveners can see in many spectrums of light and also sense changes in the air around them or slight tremors in the ground. Raveners may therefore make Awareness Tests to detect enemies even if they would not normally be able to do so due to intervening terrain or other conditions. In addition, Raveners' senses are so good that they never suffer more than –30 to Perception Test regardless of modifiers.

**Surprise Strike:** Raveners can appear from almost anywhere without warning, usually from under the feet of their prey, bursting up and taking entire squads by surprise. If a Ravener attacks by emerging from the ground or wall, it automatically gains Surprise (see page 235 in the **DEATHWATCH** Rulebook) over its enemies.

# Adventure Seeds

**To Slay Fear:** The world of Garynar's Run sits just within the spinward edge of the Orpheus Salient, close to the Castobel system and the worst conflicts with Hive Fleet Dagon. For months now, the Imperial Guard garrisons in the great plains of ash and salt have been waiting for attack to fall from the sky and have built an intricate network of forts connected by hundreds of kilometres of underground tunnels. Commanders fear however that these tunnels have already been compromised as reports of disappearances and "nid holes" have been discovered. With morale dipping and invasion imminent, the planetary governor has laid a formal request at the feet of the Ordo Xenos for a Deathwatch Kill-team to find the problem and eradicate it before the real invasion begins, suggesting the morale of his men is equal to his world's chances of survival.

**Convoy:** Raveners constantly strike behind enemy lines, bursting from the ground in ambushes and killing all in their path. On the world of Castobel, locked in battle with swarms of Tyranid bio-creatures, links between the remaining hive cities are slowly disappearing as the planet's surface becomes a hunting ground for beasts like Raveners. In an act of desperation, the citizens have resorted to moving goods and men in massive, heavily armoured road trains, though even these have only a slim chance of making it through. With the arrival of Inquisitor Dolan on Castobel, and his mission to assess sedition within the hives, he has requested a Kill-team to guard him as he travels by road train from hive to hive (the skies being choked with Tyranid creatures). Such a series of journeys are likely to become running battles as the Battle-Brothers try to hold out and keep the road train moving from one ambush to another.

## Horror on Hyperion Station

During my investigations into the various forms and natures of the Tyranid bio-form known as the Ravener, I have come across a wealth of information (most of it regrettably second- or third-hand), mostly relating to their abilities as hunters and infiltrators. A good example of the extraordinary abilities of these beasts and the tactics they use is well illustrated by some transcripts and after-action reports I came across concerning their role in the fall of Hyperion Station, a geo-sync waypoint on the edge of the Kalvarsh system.

**—Codicier Taelon**

+++Vox Records 25B1—Hyperion Station Charter Command and Control—0.8873.35+++

+Transcript Begins+

Hyperion C&C: Squad Echo Nine please advise status. Squad Echo Nine please advise status. Squad Echo Nine please advise...

Echo Nine: We copy command; status is green across the board, though we seem to have found... something. I'll try and get the pict recorder on it.

Hyperion C&C: Your pict images are coming though fuzzy, move in for a better look.

Echo Nine: Affirmative command; it appears to be a hole of some kind in the station superstructure, though from the looks of this edge I'd say it was chewed. It looks like it leads down into the secondary waste reclamation tunnels. What are your orders command?

Hyperion C&C: Our internal sensors aren't picking anything up down there... hold on... we seem to be getting some kind of thermal disturbance below your chamber. Do you detect anything?

Echo Nine: Negative command, all is quiet here... wait, I think I hear something... its coming from the hole... moving in to take a closer look... command do you see this, there's something down there... it looks like...

Hyperion C&C: I can't quite see that Echo Nine, move in and...

***sounds of weapons fire and screams***

Hyperion C&C: Echo Nine your pict recorder is down, report. Report!

Echo Nine: The walls! They're coming out of the walls! Check your angle 12, back to the shaft...

Hyperion C&C: Echo Nine I'm not getting you, report!

***a few sporadic shots then silence and static***

Hyperion C&C: Echo Nine report, Echo Nine report... we are getting movement all over the place... what are these things? Echo Three, Echo Six, come in. Is anyone on station? Echoes report! We are sensing movement in the main transit shafts... the vault door should keep them out... what's that noise... it's coming through the Emperor-damned wall! Emperor save us all...

+Transcript Ends+

# RIPPER SWARM

One of the most terrifying aspects of a Tyranid hive fleet is the speed and scale of its operations in stripping a planet. Even while the Tyranids are overrunning a world's defences, they are in the process of rapidly assimilating the genetic imprint and biomass of every living thing on the planet. Eventually, once all resistance has been eliminated and everything consumed, the world will be stripped down to its bedrock, as all of its moisture, atmosphere and nutrients are absorbed by the hive ships. By the time the hive fleet moves on, nothing but a lifeless ball of rock will be left in their wake.

In the initial phases, billions of voracious Tyranid organisms are released all over the planet. Vast waves of these creatures move across the surface of the world, constantly multiplying and consuming everything in their path. The empty deserts left behind are devoid of even the bones of their former inhabitants, thanks to the relentless efforts of the ravenous hordes.

Eventually these organisms will be reabsorbed by the Hive Mind and in some cases evolved to perform higher functions depending on the genetic material they have absorbed. The majority become biomass to be rendered down to their base cells and reshaped by the Norn Queens to fulfill the hive fleet's needs. Tyranid-held worlds have been reported to feature "digestion pools" at the base of impossibly tall capillary towers that project beyond the atmosphere. Endless streams of Tyranid creatures have been seen sacrificing themselves in the searing acids of the pools so that their biomass can be sucked up in to the hive ships orbiting high above.

These small harvesting organisms are extremely varied but the most numerous are those known to Adepts as the Tyranicus Omniphagea, more commonly known to Imperial forces as Rippers. Rippers have serpentine bodies, around half a metre long, that terminate in a broad head above a set of vestigial gripping claws. The head is split by a wide maw filled with rows of exceedingly sharp ripping hooks and razor-edged boney ridges. The Ripper's powerful jaws can bite through flesh and bone with alarming ease, and they have been known to gnaw their way through plasteel to reach food.

Rippers are energetic and fearless organisms, quite capable of pulling down creatures many times their own size, from a rampaging Grox to an armed man. Huge swarms of Rippers are often seen on the battlefield, advancing behind Tyranid assault forces. These gorge themselves on the fallen, tearing apart the wounded and cannibalising the dead. It might appear that an armoured Space Marine would be safe from the attacks of individual Rippers, but en masse they can immobilise and drag down even the strongest Battle-Brother.

In certain instances, hive ships have been driven away from a world, leaving Tyranid ground forces isolated. Rippers appear to respond to such circumstances by burrowing below ground and metamorphosing into higher life forms. This has led many among the Magos Biologis to believe that Rippers are an immature form of the prime Tyrancii genus. This would mean they are theoretically capable of gestating into any kind of Tyranid creature with the right impetus from the Hive Mind, from Hive Tyrants to Hormagaunts. The wonder that Tyranids routinely produce and sacrifice their young so prodigiously serves only to reinforce how inhuman they truly are.

| Ripper Swarm (Troops) Profile | | | | | | | | |
|---|---|---|---|---|---|---|---|---|
| WS | BS | S | T | Ag | Int | Per | WP | Fel |
| 35 | — | 25 | 30 | 40 | 10 | 30 | 30 | — |

**Move:** 2/4/6/12      **Wounds:** 10
**Skills:** Awareness (Per), Climb (S), Dodge (Ag), Silent Move (Ag), Swim (S), Tracking (Int) +10.
**Talents:** Fearless, Heightened Senses (Smell).
**Traits:** Burrower (1), Crawler, Dark Sight, Improved Natural Weapons (Mandibles), Instinctive Behaviour (Feed), Natural Armour (Exoskeleton), Size (Puny), Tyranid.
**Armour:** Exoskeleton (All 2, Horde 2).
**Weapons:** Mandibles (1d5+3 R; Pen 3).

## Special Rules

**Horde:** Rippers can be used as a Horde (see the Horde rules on page 359 of the **DEATHWATCH** Rulebook). While in a Horde, Rippers gain the Rampage, Relentless, and Overwhelming Traits, the Swift Attack Talent, and their attacks gain the Tearing quality. A Horde of Rippers has the Fear 1 (Disturbing) Trait. Alter the Size Trait as appropriate for Horde magnitude.

**Biomorphs:** At the GM's discretion, Rippers may be given any of the following **Traits:**

- Toxic (1d10)
- Flyer (3)
- Unnatural Toughness (x2)

**Spinespitter:** +30 BS and gain ranged weapon (Pistol; 20m; –/3/–; 1d10+1 I; Pen 0; Clip —; Rld —; Living Ammunition).

**Tenacious Grappler:** Rippers drag down their prey by grappling with it so that others can latch on more easily. When attempting to grapple an opponent armed with a melee weapon, Rippers suffer a –10 to their WS instead of the normal –20.

## ADVENTURE SEEDS

**Lurking Death:** After a failed Tyranid attack, tens of thousands of Rippers have gone to ground on a planet by digging themselves into the surface over hundreds of square kilometres of forbidding wilderness. The Kill-team must locate and eliminate the Ripper concentrations before they have a chance to metamorphose into higher Tyranid organisms and renew the attack all over again.

**Collection:** Rippers are so close to the core Tyranid genome that fresh samples of them can give key indicators about a hive fleet's composition and status. If the Kill-team can visit a succession of different battlefields and collect Rippers from each one, the Tech-adepts can index the hive fleet's most recent mutations. Such invaluable information will allow the Deathwatch to devise new defences and stratagems against the alien menace.

---

### From the annals of Codicier Taelon

This after-action report from Kill-team Lucien graphically illustrates the perils of underestimating these Tyranid vermin.

Investigation of communications blackout: Watch Station Straven.

Report begins.

Three (3) member Kill-team Lucien arrived at Watch Station Straven twenty-one (21) days subjective time from receipt of orders. Watch Station presented heavy damage from apparent xenos assault. Inspection revealed eighty-seven (87) corpses of Tyranid organisms killed by automated defences and tracks of same. Battle-Brother Vertigus volunteered to patrol the perimeter while pict logs and sensor data were recovered from station archives. Battle-Brother Maed entered the data crypt alone while Squad Leader Lucien re-activated external defences.

Squad Leader Lucien received a call for assistance from Battle-Brother Maed approximately ten (10) minutes after entering the data crypt. Call indicated a surprise attack by multiple assailants. Squad Leader Lucien and Battle-Brother Vertigus arrived in the data crypt approximately two (2) minutes later. Battle-Brother Maed found prone, covered by small Tyranid organisms approximately fifty (50) centimetres long, with large jaws fastened onto his limbs and armour. Battle-Brother Maed eventually freed by a combination of unarmed attack (pulling organisms from him bodily) and application of Promethium (due to limited success of unarmed attack). Battle-Brother Maed found to be moderately injured and armour breached in five (5) locations. Battle-Brother Maed later testified that without assistance he would have been unable to free himself and felt he would have been consumed within his armour.

Watch Station Straven declared terminally compromised by Squad Leader Lucien and set to auto-destruct. Destruction of Watch Station witnessed by Kill-team Lucien during egress.

Report ends.

# TRYGON

*"Hey! Did you feel the ground shake just now?"*

–Guardsman Prall at the Battle of Table Mountain

The largest Tyranid creatures can become hard to accurately categorise as they increasingly appear as strange aggregations of symbiotes and parasites on a colossal scale. This is not the case with the Tyranid Trygon however, a distinct genus of vast serpentine creatures that tower above even the mighty Carnifex. Adepts have postulated a link between the Trygon and the smaller but equally ophidian Ravener, but it remains unclear whether Trygons are massively mutated Raveners or Raveners are underdeveloped, perhaps even immature, Trygons. Certainly adult Trygons can reach truly monstrous proportions, with examples of up to thirty metres in length on record, although twelve to fifteen metres is more common.

Trygons are extremely heavily armoured by a coat of overlapping scales that covers them from jaws to tail. In addition to offering excellent protection, these specialised scales form an essential part of the Trygon's natural weaponry. The thick armour plates include high concentrations of silicates and as the Trygon moves they become agitated, generating a powerful bio-static charge that is captured by subdermal platelet stacks. The Trygon directs this energy by exhaling an ionised spray from its gills, to prompt a deadly, high-voltage discharge.

Trygons have two sets of diamond-hard scything talons folded beneath their hood-like carapace that they use with lethal effect in close combat. Driven by a Trygon's size and strength, these wicked blades can easily impale an armoured vehicle or cut an armoured man in two. However, the primary purpose of the Trygon's claws is to allow it to burrow though practically any material at a terrifying rate. These creatures have shown themselves capable of detecting an enemy from below and seem to have a singular fondness for bursting out of the ground beneath them with shocking suddenness. Tanks and troops surprised in this way seldom have a chance to reply to the barrage of sweeping claw strikes and bio-static lightning unleashed upon them.

Seismic detectors have been used with some success to provide early warning of a Trygon's approach. Unfortunately, on many worlds, natural seismic activity can mask a Trygon's motion and in some instances Tyranid swarm activity seems to have been deliberately coordinated to cover the approach of burrowing Trygons. Trygons have forced tunnels through just about every material known to man, although they are considerably slowed by adamantium plating.

It appears that Trygons use their bio-static charge to assist with tunnelling, as their tunnels have been found coated with a fused, glass-like silicate layer on the inside. This effect stabilises the tunnel walls and prevents them from collapsing behind a burrowing Trygon. Other Tyranid organisms will take advantage of these tunnels to move around unseen and follow up on Trygon attacks. The emergence of a burrowing Trygon is often just the harbinger of a tidal wave of nightmarish horrors.

Commanders have found static defences become virtually useless once Trygons are operating in the area, unless tunnel torpedoes or mole mortars can be brought to bear to keep them at bay. Over an extended period, Tyrgons are capable of excavating a network of underground tunnels covering a huge

area, which makes it difficult to wipe out Tyranid forces even with saturation bombardment. Clearing out Trygon sub-surface tunnel networks is dangerous work even for a Deathwatch Kill-team and is a duty given only to the most experienced and well-equipped Battle-Brothers.

Trygons have also been known to dig deadfall traps by leaving a thin crust over a deep conical hole. Sufficient weight in troops and armour will collapse the roof of the sinkhole and deposit the victims into the Trygon's waiting claws. A Trygon's greatest weakness is probably that it can be baited or misdirected while burrowing by the first tasty morsel to cross its path. Under the direction of the Hive Mind, a Trygon becomes even more dangerous, as it will tunnel deep into the heart of the defences before bursting forth.

Unfortunately, a mutation now dubbed the Trygon Prime has been confirmed, that appears to have the relevant synapse development to make it a conduit for the influence of the Hive Mind. A Trygon Prime can be easily spotted by their elongated jaws and the containment spines running the length of their bodies. These are extended platelet stacks that enable the Trygon Prime to store up even greater charges of bio-electricity. A Trygon Prime is swathed in sheets of lightning whenever it moves, and when it opens its jaws, searing arcs of energy leap forth that leave only charred corpses in their wake. The strong synaptic link a Trygon Prime shares with the Hive Mind allows it to dominate lesser Tyranid creatures, including other Trygons, and it will rarely be found without an attendant horde of Termagants and Hormagaunts.

## Trygon (Master) Profile

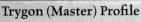

| WS | BS | S | T | Ag | Int | Per | WP | Fel |
|----|----|------|------|----|----|----|----|-----|
| 50 | 30 | (18) 60 | (12) 60 | 40 | 15 | 25 | 45 | –– |

**Move:** 4/8/16/32      **Wounds:** 160

**Skills:** Awareness (Per), Swim (S), Tracking (Int).

**Talents:** Ambidextrous, Combat Master, Fearless, Furious Assault, Heightened Senses (Touch), Swift Attack, Two-weapon Wielder (Melee).

**Traits:** Burrower (3), Crawler, Dark Sight, Fear 4 (Terrifying), Improved Natural Weapons (Scything Talons), Instinctive Behaviour (Feed), Multiple Arms, Natural Armour (Thickened scales), Size (Massive), Unnatural Strength (x3), Unnatural Toughness (x2). Unnatural Senses (Ground sense)[†], Tyranid.

**Armour:** Thickened Scales (All 10).

**Weapons:** Scything Talons (1d10+20 R; Pen 3), Bio-Electric pulse (Basic; 30m; –/–/12; 2d10+2 E; Pen 4; Clip —; Rld —; Storm, Living Ammunition).

### Special Rules

**Biomorphs:** At the GM's discretion, a Trygon may be given the following changes to represent a Trygon Prime.

**Trygon Prime:** +10 Int, +15 Per, +5 WP. Replace the Trait Instinctive Behaviour (Feed) with Synapse Creature and Shadow in the Warp. Upgrade Bio-Electric pulse to (Basic; 60m; –/–/12; 2d10+6 E; Pen 4; Clip —; Rld —; Storm, Living Ammunition).

## ADVENTURE SEEDS

**Tunnel Hunt:** The Kill-team must enter a network of Trygon tunnels and carry seismic charges down to its deepest points to collapse them. As well as the Trygons themselves, the Kill-team will also have to deal with broods of Tyranid Hormagaunts and Rippers that make their lair within the twisting underground passages.

**Capture:** A Trygon Prime is spotted alone and apparently injured in the aftermath of a battle. A live sample of a Trygon Prime would be of incomparable value for study and this represents the best opportunity to date to procure one. The Kill-team must find a way to capture the gigantic creature, relatively unharmed, and transport it back to their Watch Fortress. Of course the "injured" Trygon Prime might also be setting itself as bait to lure the Kill-team into a trap.

**Caravan:** A convoy of ground crawlers carrying vital supplies has to get through an area known to be frequented by Trygons. The Kill-team must take point to draw out any Trygons and locate their deadfall traps before the ground crawlers blunder into them.

[†]**Ground Sense:** A Trygon can detect enemies while burrowed, through the vibrations they make. It can easily detect anything in contact with the ground within 15 metres and receives a +10 bonus to tracking prey in constant motion. Large vehicles and similar give greater bonuses.

## From the annals of Codicier Taelon

*This excerpt from the witness report of an Imperial Guardsman of 632nd Ganf Magna Regiment details an unconventional Trygon assault on a prepared position at Table Mountain on Phonos.*

*+++++ Excerpt Begins +++++*

*…The next morning we found ourselves cut off, with swarms of Tyranids covering the valley as far as the eye could see. They'd clearly come for the defence laser installation on the flat top of the mountain, wanting to put it out of action before it took more of a toll on the hive ships and spores still in orbit. They tried rushing our defences with a direct assault first, but we'd used our time well and dug in deep. The slopes of the mountain turned purple with the ichor of their crushed bodies.*

*They tried winged creatures next and the sky was soon black with flocks of Gargoyles. The defence laser made short work of those flapping clouds though, burning them to cinders that fluttered helplessly downwards into the mass below. We were feeling pretty good about our chances right about then, but they cut loose with some of their big guys and another swarm attack next. Those giant, roaring monsters clambered right up the side of mountain like a man would scramble up a hill. They hit the forward redoubts hard but Captain Heskund stood right by the heavy weapons crews and directed their fire. We put enough holes into the monsters to stop them in their tracks and then mopped up the little ones when they were milling around confused. Afterwards we brought up a Leman Russ tank with a dozer blade and shovelled the corpses back down the mountain.*

*It got quieter then. The Tyranids pulled back out of range but we weren't fooled—they'd be back for a night attack or trying to tunnel their way in next. We had screamers and tremor sensors up around the perimeter so we felt pretty secure but nothing came all night. The Tyranids were still out there, thundering around like great herds of animals, shrieking and calling in their horrid alien voices, but we stood watch after watch and they never came.*

*Next morning there looked to be less Tyranids than before and we cheered. That was when the ground cracked open and we found out where they'd all gone. I don't know how we survived what came after; the first thing out of the hole was like a giant snake with claws, easily the length of three Chimeras, hissing and spitting lightning. Right after it came such a swarm of little ones that we were knee deep in them in seconds. We brought up flamers and burned the hole, the little ones and everyone near it. The big snake got away, I think—none of them like fire much. We figured out afterwards that the Tyranids had been thundering around outside all night to cover up the sound the snake made digging its way in. Those sneaky little b—*

*+++++++++++++ Excerpt ends +++++++++++++*

# TYRANID WARRIOR PRIME

*"Don't be fooled by its appearance, this is no simple soldier of the Hive Mind. Note the way it moves, the colours on its chitin and the subtle deference those around it exhibit, like an alpha male leading a pack of wolves."*

–Scout Sergeant Veraz, Storm Wardens

The leadership cast of the Tyranids is often difficult for Imperial commanders to identify, and there is often the mistaken assumption that larger Tyranid creatures are more important; a mistake that has cost more than one officer his rank and countless men their lives. This is especially true of Tyranid Warrior Primes, an evolution of the Tyranid Warrior genus with elevated intelligence and a stronger link to the Hive Mind. It has in fact only been in recent times that the Primes have been identified and reported among the ranks of the hive fleets, though as many scholars and magos are quick to point out, this is less likely to be because they are a recent evolution and more likely because they blend in with the rest of a Tyranid Warrior brood. Primes are also being encountered in greater and greater numbers within Hive Fleet Dagon, perhaps as a direct response to the constantly evolving tactics of Imperial forces and the hive fleet's need to deal with the elevated Deathwatch presence in the Orpheus Salient after several costly encounters.

In function, Tyranid Warrior Primes take on the role of commanders and captains within the swarm. Much in the same way as a Hive Tyrant might lead a host of Tyranids, a Prime will oversee a smaller section of the battlefield or direct a smaller strike force of warriors. When close to a more powerful synapse creature they will defer their control, acting as lieutenants and sergeants, often personally leading broods. However, should they find themselves alone, they can easily bind together those Tyranid creatures nearby into an effective fighting force and carry on with little trouble. In this way, a Tyranid Warrior Prime is just as capable of directing a swarm as a Hive Tyrant and many an Imperial officer has suffered as a result of underestimating their ability to project the Hive Mind and lead lesser Tyranid creatures.

Tyranid Warriors Primes have also earned a fearsome reputation as resourceful and cunning tacticians, directing nearby Tyranid creatures through the Hive Mind to take advantage of terrain, enemy movements and other prevailing battlefield conditions. It is often the failing of the Imperium (and even some xenos races such as the Tau and the Eldar) that the Tyranids are seen as mindless animals, driven forward by the will of the Hive Mind with no thought to tactics or strategy. The truth is of course that creatures like the Tyranid Warrior Prime and the Hive Tyrant are just as capable as any other commander, perhaps more so as they have unshakable faith in their troops and are fearless in battle, making them almost the perfect battlefield leaders.

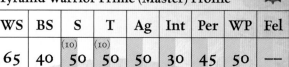

## Tyranid Warrior Prime (Master) Profile

| WS | BS | S | T | Ag | Int | Per | WP | Fel |
|----|----|----|----|----|-----|-----|----|-----|
| 65 | 40 | (10) 50 | (10) 50 | 50 | 30 | 45 | 50 | –– |

**Movement:** 7/14/21/42      **Wounds:** 80

**Skills:** Awareness (Per), Climb (S), Swim (S) +10.

**Talents:** Fearless, Lightning Attack, Swift Attack.

**Traits:** Dark Sight, Fear 3 (Horrifying), Natural Armour (Bonded Exoskeleton), Multiple Arms, Unnatural Strength (x2), Unnatural Toughness (x2), Improved Natural Weapons (Scything Talons or Rending Claws), Shadow in the Warp, Size (Enormous), Synapse Creature, Tyranid.

**Armour:** Bonded Exoskeleton (All 10).

**Weapons:** Scything Talons (1d10+14 R; Pen 3), or Rending Claws (1d10+12 R; Pen 5; Razor Sharp), or two Boneswords (1d10+12 R; Pen 6; Drain Life), or Bonesword (1d10+12 R; Pen 6; Drain Life) and Lashwhip (1d10+15 R; Pen 3; Flexible, Snare), Devourer (30m, –/–/6; 1d10+6 R; Pen 0; Clip —; Rld —; Living Ammunition, Storm, Tearing) or Death Spitter (40m, S/3/–; 1d10+6 E; Pen 4; Clip —; Rld —; Living Ammunition, Tearing), or Spine Fists (20m, S/2/–; 1d10+12 R; Pen 2; Clip —; Rld —).

**Gear:** None.

### Special Rules

**Biomorphs:** At the GMs discretion a Tyranid Warrior Prime may have Adrenal Glands (gaining the Furious Assault Talent), Toxin Sacs (gaining the Toxic (1d10) Trait on all melee and ranged attacks), or Regeneration (2) (gaining the Regeneration Trait).

**Alpha Warrior:** When in the presence of other Tyranid Warriors, a Tyranid Warrior Prime may enhance their coordination in battle and make them even more efficient killers, granting them a +10 on all melee attack rolls and an extra Reaction each turn. This ability works automatically and affects all Tyranid Warriors within synapse range of the Tyranid Warrior Prime.

**Tyranid Psyker:** Tyranid Warrior Primes sometimes exhibit psychic powers, if their link to the Hive Mind is strong enough. If the GM chooses, he can give a Tyranid Warrior Prime a Psy Rating of 3 and access to the Tyranid Psychic Powers on page 34 (select up to three).

## ADVENTURE SEEDS

**Glory:** Tyranid Warriors are seen as worthy opponents for a Space Marine, and many tales of glory have been sung about Battle-Brothers which have tackled these beasts singled handed. It can be imagined then the renown a Space Marine would earn if he could best a Tyranid Warrior Prime, among the most deadly of the Tyranid bio-forms a Battle-Brother might conceivably defeat alone. During a chance meeting in the Chapter House the Battle-Brothers have been challenged by Battle-Brother Yurgan (a member of the Space Wolves seconded to the Deathwatch) to find and best such a creature bringing back proof of its demise. While there is nothing stopping the Battle-Brothers from declining such a challenge, especially from such a loud and boorish Brother there would be much glory in doing so, and prove their ability against some of the worst the Tyranid hive fleet has to offer.

**Field Test:** Inquisitor Zathras of the Ordo Xenos has been travelling across the warzones of the Orpheus Salient, gathering information on the nature of Hive Fleet Dagon, as part of a decade-long "conclave subjecture" into the relation of the fleet to other fleets also encroaching from the Eastern Fringe. As part of his investigations, he has identified several distinct variations of Tyranid Warriors and believes some of them may in fact be Tyranid Warrior Primes, though without a live specimen or being able to observe one in the "wild," he cannot be sure. He is therefore requesting the support of a Deathwatch Kill-team to help him infiltrate the systems outlining the closest points of the hive fleet's advance and try to discover conclusive methods of identifying Tyranid Warrior Primes. Such a mission would be extremely hard, as it involves not only getting close enough to a Tyranid Warrior brood to study their markings and behaviour (possibly on a world already fallen to the Tyranids or one engaged in total war against them) but also getting out alive.

## Notes on the Nature and Hierarchy of Tyranid Leadership

*Concerning the rise of the leadership caste and the presence of the Hive Mind consciousness within Tyranid bio-forms: Many scholars have speculated on the nature of the Hive Mind, its limitations and the exact length and breadth of its reach across the stars. While proof exists to support the theory that separate hive fleets can communicate across entire sectors, no concrete evidence has yet arisen as to how its presence is disseminated or distributed among vessels and creature. This of course ties directly into the notion of Tyranid commanders and other leadership figures as such they are. It has been postulated on more than one occasion that the Hive Mind exists in no one place or one single creature (such as some vast and unseen intergalactic queen or system spanning hive ship) but exists in varying strengths in all Tyranid creatures, and in essence exists as long as even a single Tyranid remains alive.*

*The Tyranid Warrior Prime is a good example of this concept, and proves that a creature developed from one of the more common Tyranid bio-templates can become very strong in the Hive Mind and rise up to a leadership position, just as a talented human or gifted soldier might in more traditional armies. Of course, such analogies are poor at best and do not fully capture the unique nature of the Tyranid Warrior Primes, which have in effect been bred for the specific role in which they are employed. Rather it would be more accurate to say that they have been selected, even before birth, to be a special receptacle of the Hive Mind and boost its presence on the battlefield while aiding in the direction and control of lesser Tyranid creatures.*

*This final sentiment leads us full circle however, for if a Tyranid Warrior Prime contains and embodies the Hive Mind, in effect representing its presence in the material universe, then what chooses it to be so? Much in the same way as the ancient debate over what came first, the chicken or the egg, we are left to wonder whether or not the Hive Mind existed before the creation of the first Tyranid bio-form or whether it was spawned from the bio-forms themselves.*

*-Codicier Jaelon*

# TYRANT GUARD

*"Emperor's blood...it's still alive! Hit it with another round from the battle cannon before... it's coming right for us! Hit it again! HIT IT AGAIN!"*

–Last words of Captain Fulher, 12th Ascandian Armoured

Tyrant Guard exist for a single purpose and a single purpose alone, the defence of the Hive Tyrant they are charged with protecting. In this capacity they excel like no other kind of bodyguard in the galaxy. Their armoured hides and thick muscles are almost impervious to small arms and highly resistant to even the heaviest weapons which means they can soak up an appalling amount of damage before they are destroyed. Though similar in size to a Tyranid Warrior, a Tyrant Guard has more of the appearance of a hound or boar, loping alongside the Hive Tyrant on four limbs, their massively armoured heads close to the ground and alert for danger to their master. When they detect a threat to the Hive Tyrant, they immediately move to block lines of sight and throw themselves in front of bolts, blasts and missiles. When in close combat, they swarm around their Hive Tyrant, keeping the bulk of its foes away so it may deal with them more easily.

Never encountered without the presence of a Hive Tyrant, and never straying far from its side in battle, Tyrant Guard are nevertheless vicious opponents in their own right, tearing at their foes with large, bladed talons and gnashing teeth, with an animalistic fury notable even in the midst of a Tyranid swarm. They do however always remain close to their Hive Tyrant, like loyal dogs running at their master's feet and unlike more independent Tyranid creatures, they cannot be tempted or lured into pursuit, remaining steadfastly in the Hive Tyrant's shadow regardless of the presence of nearby foes. Some scholars speculate that the Tyrant Guard, not encountered in the early stages of the hive fleets, were an evolution to combat the tactics of Imperial forces which quickly found that destroying Hive Tyrants with heavy weapons fire was a good way to break up a swarm. Like so many Tyranid creatures, however, this is merely speculation, as Tyrant Guard have only been observed on the battlefield, and most specimens recovered are extensively damaged by the efforts of destroying them.

What has been established by Imperial scholars and tacticians is that the Tyrant Guard are among the dimmest of the Tyranid creatures, on a par with many of the smaller gaunt genus creatures in their intellect. This seems to be a deliberate evolution of the Hive Mind in creating a lumbering, heavily defended and utterly loyal bodyguard with no sense of personal safety, only the continued survival of its master. To this end, Tyrant Guard are blind, their heads encased entirely in rock-hard chitin, save for a razor-lined maw with which to bite and savage their prey. This is doubtless a further protection against damage, as the presence of eyes would only create a weak spot which their foes could exploit. Despite this seeming disability, Tyrant Guard seem to have little trouble detecting enemies, and appear to have a kind of sense link with their Hive Tyrant, seeing what it sees and reacting to danger instinctively as it becomes aware of its foes.

## Tyrant Guard (Elite) Profile

| WS | BS | S | T | Ag | Int | Per | WP | Fel |
|----|----|-----|-----|----|-----|-----|----|-----|
| 55 | 30 | (10) 50 | (18) 60 | 30 | 10 | 35 | 40 | — |

**Movement:** 6/12/18/36      **Wounds:** 45

**Skills:** Awareness (Per), Climb (S), Swim (S) +10.

**Talents:** Fearless, Swift Attack.

**Traits:** Blind, Fear 3 (Horrifying), Natural Armour (Bonded Exoskeleton), Unnatural Strength (x2), Unnatural Toughness (x3), Improved Natural Weapons (Scything Talons), Instinctive Behaviour (Feed), Size (Enormous), Sturdy, Tyranid.

**Armour:** Bonded Exoskeleton (All 10).

**Weapons:** Scything Talons (1d10+14 R; Pen 3) and Rending Claws (1d10+12 R; Pen 5; Razor Sharp), or may replace their Scything Talons with either a Lash Whip (1d10+15 R; Pen 3; Flexible, Snare) or a Bonesword (1d10+12; Pen 6; Drain Life).

**Gear:** None.

## Special Rules

**Bodyguard:** Tyrant Guard only ever appear when acting as the bodyguard for a Hive Tyrant and usually only in groups of 1–3, though at the GM's discretion larger groups may be encountered. Tyrant Guard will never stray more than a few metres from their master, and if for any reason separated from it, will endeavour to return to its side as soon as possible. While within 20 metres of their Hive Tyrant, a Tyrant Guard may use its Reaction to move (up to its normal movement allowance) into combat with a foe, before that foe enters melee with the Hive Tyrant, effectively interrupting the enemy's charge or move. Tyrant Guard may alternatively use their Reaction to interpose themselves between the Hive Tyrant and a ranged attack, effectively becoming the new target of the attack.

**Master's Eyes:** Though Tyrant Guard are blind, while within 20 metres of their Hive Tyrant, they can use his Perception and senses as their own, including any Traits or Talents which improve them.

**Rampage:** If a Tyrant Guard's Hive Tyrant is killed, it will go berserk, attacking any non-Tyranid creatures it can reach. While in this state, it gains the Frenzy and Furious Assault talents. Once begun, Rampage lasts until the Tyrant Guard is destroyed.

# ADVENTURE SEEDS

**Subdual:** As the forces of Hive Fleet Dagon press in upon the Orpheus Salient, and more and more larger Tyranid creatures are encountered, the Imperium seeks every advantage it can in defeating them. To this end the Magos Biologos has devised a plan to capture a Tyrant Guard alive, so that it might be studied and its weaknesses uncovered. They want a Kill-team to travel deep into the warzones of Castobel, where Tyranids are slowly devouring the world. Such a task is no mean feat. It will require the Kill-team to infiltrate into the midst of one of the great ongoing battles for Castobel's hives and tackle a Hive Tyrant head-on while trying to subdue one of its rampaging bodyguards. For the Battle-Brothers which could recover such a specimen, the glory would be great indeed.

**Return to Avalos:** In the wake of the Tyranid invasion of Avalos and subsequent defeat of the bulk of those invasion forces, countless Tyranid bio-forms have been left scattered across the world. As the citizens of Avalos pick up the pieces of their broken world, they must also contend with these hidden horrors lurking on the edges of their farms and in the wild regions of the planet. Once such horror has been dubbed the Beast of Barrowdown (for the region which it terrorises) and sketchy reports seem to indicate that it might be a lone Tyrant Guard, wounded and abandoned after the destruction of its swarm. Needless to say, both the Ordo Xenos and the Magos Biologos would have an interest in such a beast, dead or alive, and it falls to the Kill-team to travel to this blighted world and hunt it down.

```
After-Action Report: Defence of Xin-Cyn

ATT: Codicier Taelon; ++Priority
Vermillion++

As requested, I have assembled the
fragmented pict files taken from our
Battle-Brothers' stand at the luna city
of Xin-Cyn against a tendril of Hive
Fleet Dagon (hereafter referred to as
Fleet X18a). As you know, X18a was
tracked for some time as it intercepted
the Orpheus Salient from the galactic
south, not far from the doomed world
of Freya. Our scouts were to determine
X18a's relation to the main hive fleet
when it suddenly changed course and
engulfed the outpost world of Xin-Cyn.
In a peerless act of bravery, two squads
of Death Spectres Space Marines landed
on the moon world to ensure the escape
of the Magos stationed there. Of course,
while the engagement was nothing we
have not seen before, our Brothers did
managed to recover detailed recordings
of the so-called "Tyrant Guard" before
being forced to withdraw. If you examine
the picts provided (see attachments
5xi through 61xi), recovered from some
of the Xin-Cyn heavy combat servitors,
you will note the extreme resistance
of these beasts and the savagery with
which they defend the Hive Tyrant. Pict
43xi especially demonstrates the damage
these things can sustain, as you will
note the combat servitor's power weapon
has clearly penetrated deep into the
creature's cranial cavity, yet it shows
no signs of slowing. In fact, following
the sequence from 44xi though 49xi, we
can see it easily dispatches the combat
servitor and continues to function at an
almost undiminished capacity.


It is my assessment from this data,
along with that drawn from various other
sources within the Orpheus Salient where
engagements with Hive Fleet Dagon have
occurred, that further study and data
on these creatures should be gathered
as soon as possible, so that we might
devise new tactics or weaponry to
combat them. I have already presented
a recommendation to the Ordo Xenos for
the use of a Deathwatch Kill-team in the
tracking down and recovery of one of
these beasts, and have every confidence
in their ability to complete this task.
Emperor willing, it should help us to
move one step closer to taking back
the initiative from the Tyranids in the
Jericho Reach.

—Scout Sergeant Syrbel, 10th Company
Death Spectres
```

# VENOMTHROPE

*"More than a minute in that cloud and you'll be bleeding out of your eyes, ears and mouth, praying for the pain to stop."*

—Captain Ascote, pointing out a Venomthrope to his men at the Battle of Twelve Bridges

Many Tyranid creatures carry toxins on their claws and fangs, but none more so that the Venomthrope; a veritable factory of poisons, its tendrils drip with vile substances and it is constantly surrounded by a cloud of lethal vapours. Held aloft by numerous gas-filled bladders (also the source of the toxic cloud that fills the air around it) it moves along by using its tentacle-like hooked tendrils to drag itself across any surface. These same tendrils are also used to snare enemies and drag them into its poison cloud, where it holds them fast until their feeble struggles cease and it can devour them at its leisure. Not as powerful a combatant as a Tyranid Warrior or Ravener, the Venomthrope relies mostly on its poisons to do its work, expecting only mild resistant from its prey once it gets close enough to envelope them with its cloud or touch them with its deadly tendrils.

Venomthropes are not just toxic to non-Tyranid life forms, but also to any environment they enter. Over time their miasma of toxic spores infects the very ground and air of a world, rendering it hostile to even its own indigenous species. The Hive Mind uses this aspect of the Venomthrope by gathering them together in large numbers and unleashing them on a region to gradually poison it, making it harder for non-Tyranid life forms to continue the fight. Venomthropes can be especially deadly in enclosed areas or underground, where their toxins can fill ventilation systems and foul air-scrubbers, making the corridors and chambers of a fortress or void ship deadly to its garrison or crew. In efforts to combat these tactics, the Adeptus Mechanicus has tried repeatedly to study the Venonthrope and develop either more sure methods of protecting troops against its venoms or to discover an antidote to them. So far no successes have had any large or lasting effects on the Imperium's efforts against the Tyranid swarms, and as soon as a new method or antidote is found to counter the Venomthrope, it seems the creature quickly adapts and overcomes it.

A Venomthrope's feeding instincts means that it can operate quite effectively even while beyond the range of the Hive Mind, drifting into formations of troops and spreading its deadly toxins or lashing out at exposed warriors. In battle, Venomthropes are therefore often found on the flanks of the swarm, or exploiting gaps to get at rear-echelon troops where their toxic presence can cause as much havoc as possible and they can force troops to abandon defensive positions lest they become caught up in its slowly spreading mist of death. As a general rule, the only sure way to deal with such an attack is a quick response from heavy weapons and a sustained blast of fire to tear the creature apart before it can get to close, even then it still leaves a toxic corpse which can be almost as deadly as the creature was in life.

## Venomthrope (Elite) Profile

| WS | BS | S | T | Ag | Int | Per | WP | Fel |
|----|----|----|----|----|-----|-----|----|-----|
| 48 | — | 55 (10) | 55 (10) | 40 | 20 | 35 | 40 | — |

**Movement:** 6/12/18/36      **Wounds:** 40
**Skills:** Awareness (Per), Climb (S), Dodge (Ag) +10.
**Talents:** Ambidextrous, Swift Attack.
**Traits:** Dark Sight, Fear 3 (Horrifying), Hoverer (6), Instinctive Behaviour (Feed), Multiple Arms, Natural Armour (Reinforced Chitin), Size (Enormous), Spore Cloud, Unnatural Strength (x2), Unnatural Toughness (x2), Toxic Miasma, Tyranid.
**Armour:** Reinforced Chitin (All 4).
**Weapons:** Lash Whips (1d10+13 R; Pen 3, Flexible, Snare).

## Special Rules

**Toxic Miasma:** The Venomthrope is an exceedingly toxic creature, its flesh and flailing tendrils dripping with the most virulent haemotoxins, neurotoxins, and deadly phage organisms. It counts as having the Toxic Trait, but the damage is 2d10, ignoring Toughness and Armour. The Toughness Test to resist the poison is **Very Hard (–30)**.

**Spore Cloud:** Additionally, the Venomthrope emits a thick and choking spore cloud from gas bladders and vents in its carapace that causes all non-Tyranid beings within 10m of the creature to suffer from the Toxic Miasma as well. This cloying vapour partially obscures the Venomthrope, imposing a –30 penalty to all shooting attacks made against it.

## ADVENTURE SEEDS

**Harvest:** The Magos Biologis of the Adeptus Mechanicus are always seeking new Tyranid samples and toxins in their research into defences and antidotes against them. To find the right materials means tracking down specific species of creatures in specific locations and at specific times. To this end, the Magos have identified a pure strain of Venomthrope, tracked from the edges of the Orpheus Salient and part of the core of Hive Fleet Dagon. If the creature can be harvested before it spends more than a few hours on a world (and starts to adapt its poisons for life specific to that planet) it could prove invaluable in creating a universal antidote, one that the Venomthrope would find hard to overcome given its pure nature. Of course this means the Kill-team must either find the creature in space before it is deployed (boarding and scouring a Tyranid vessel) or catch it during the chaos of the first hours of the Tyranid landing as it emerges from its mycetic spore.

**Clear the Decks:** While in transit aboard the Imperial Luna Class Cruiser *Imperial Wrath,* the Kill-team aids the ship's captain in fighting off a chance encounter with a cluster of vanguard ships, seeing off several brutal boarding actions. Unfortunately, during the fray a Venomthrope has somehow boarded the cruiser and is hiding down in the lower decks. Hour by hour, the creature's poisons are slowly turning the cruiser's atmosphere into a deadly fog, and the captain has not yet been able to find or destroy it. Now only the Kill-team, with their power armour and enhanced physiology, stand a chance of killing it in time. Of course there will be a 'nid hunt below decks, wading through a thick mist of poison vapour and almost certainly encounters with other Tyranid creatures left over from the raids.

## Tyranid Neurotoxins and Biological Toxin Production

*Brother Codicier Taelon,*

*As you requested, I have secured samples of corpses from a platoon of Imperial Guard that came into contact with Venomthropes during the Avalos incursion. Due to the extremely toxic nature of the samples (and the bodies themselves) I have for transport placed them in stasis caskets, the only means it seems of completely stopping the spread of the pathogens. I have also considered your questions on the nature of Tyranid toxins and their propensity for biological toxin production. Much in the same way as some specific organisms found on ancient Terra, it seems an innate trait of the Tyranids that they are toxic to all other forms of life not sprung from the same biological foundation as themselves. Their flesh cannot be eaten or used for sustenance by non-Tyranids, and even those that survive wounds from Tyranids often succumb to the toxins inherent in their touch. This of course is found to the greatest extent in the Venomthrope, and in my years serving the Deathwatch I have come across few creatures with such an array of toxins and toxin creating abilities as the this beast. Even the most advanced labs of the Adeptus Biologis would be hard pressed to create or replicate such virulent poisons in anything like the potency or quantities of the Venomthrope. I can only imagine that this ability of the Venomthrope, and the Tyranids in general, comes from their opposition to all life but their own, and their natural imperative of biological domination. If we imagine our galaxy as a living thing, then surely the Tyranid is a poison that runs through its veins.*

## –Brother Apothecary Dynis

# ZOANTHROPE

*"Can't you feel it? It's like a claw crushing my mind in its grasp, squeezing my brain between its talons. I can feel it scratching behind my eyes, tearing at my sanity... Emperor save us!"*

–Sanctioned Psyker Euos Dax, Castobel Regional Command

Zoanthropes are amongst the strangest and most bizarre of all Tyranid creatures. Their feeble atrophied bodies hang limp and seemingly lifeless beneath their massive craniums, far too large for their weak limbs to support. Only their immense psychic power allows them to move at all, drifting across the battlefield on a cushion of psychic energy. This vast store of energy and their ability to focus it is also what makes them such terrible foes, for a Zoanthrope is capable of conjuring up earth-shattering bolts of warp energy with the strength to smash apart even the most heavily armoured troops or vehicles. In this role, the swarm uses Zoanthropes as psychic cannons, blasting apart strong points and tanks with equal ease or raining warp fire down upon the heads of massed foes, slaying dozens of warriors in a single, blinding flash of power.

There is an unknown and alien intelligence which lurks within the chitin cranium of the Zoanthrope, its actions seemingly governed by both the Hive Mind and some inner psychic instincts to seek out particular enemies and use its powers in certain ways. Despite their power, however, Zoanthropes sometimes seem to be victims of their own massive energy reserves and there have been numerous after-action reports of Zoanthropes "burning out" in battle. After hurling numerous bolts or sustaining their shield for an extended period, their craniums have been observed to burst and bleed out, sending them crashing limply to the ground. Psykers who have witnessed these events liken it to the perils of the warp which normal psykers can suffer when psychic energy overloads their minds.

In addition to their ability to hurl terrible bolts of warp energy at their foes, Zoanthropes are also very difficult to destroy, especially considering how weak and feeble their bodies appear. This resilience stems from their ability to create a powerful warp bubble around themselves, shielding them from all kind of weapons and even turning aside blows in close combat. Like their ability to drift above the ground, the shield seems a constant part of the Zoanthrope and is always present as long as the creature lives. It has been noted that the shield seems to strengthen or coalesce around particularly powerful attacks, flashing bright for an instant to turn aside the blow before fading back to a uniform shimmer.

## Zoanthrope (Elite) Profile

| WS | BS | S | T | Ag | Int | Per | WP | Fel |
|----|----|----|----|----|----|----|----|----|
| 30 | 45 | (8) 45 | (8) 45 | 10 | 35 | 45 | 60 | — |

**Movement:** 3/6/9/24  **Wounds:** 32
**Skills:** Awareness (Per), Psyniscience (Per) +10.
**Talents:** Fearless, Improved Natural Weapons, Improved Warp Sense, Psy Rating (6), Warp Sense.

**Traits:** Dark Sight, Fear 3 (Horrifying), Hoverer (6), Natural Armour (Reinforced Chitin), Shadow in the Warp, Size (Enormous), Synapse Creature, Tyranid, Unnatural Strength (x2), Unnatural Toughness (x2).
**Armour:** Reinforced Chitin (All 6).
**Weapons:** Teeth and Claws (1d10+4 R; Pen 3).
**Gear:** None.

## Special Rules

**Warp Field:** Zoanthropes are protected from harm by a powerful psychic warp bubble. This functions as a Force Field (see page 166 in the **DEATHWATCH** Rulebook) and counts as having a protection rating of 65 and overloads on a roll of 01–05. If a Zoanthrope's Warp Field overloads, the creature can spend a Full Action to restore it, the effects coming back into effect at the start of its next turn.

**Tyranid Psyker:** Zoanthropes are Tyranid Psykers and follow the rules for Tyranid Psychic Powers on page 34. They have access to all the standard Tyranid psychic powers plus Warp Blast and Warp Lance.

## ADVENTURE SEEDS

**The Hive Mind:** Ordo Xenos Inquisitor Heltor Zyr has long speculated on the powerful connection a Zoanthrope shares with the Hive Mind, and a way in which it might be exploited to better combat the Tyranid menace. Zyr believes that if a sufficiently powerful psyker could "tap into" the link a Zoanthrope shares with the Hive Mind, he might be able to sense communications to the swarm before they occur. Perhaps, if he was powerful enough, he could even use the Zoanthrope as a conduit to nearby Tyranid creatures, sowing confusion and conflicting commands via its powerful synaptic link. Of course this is all mere speculation unless Zyr can get close enough to one of the beasts to test his theories, and is also dependent on keeping this psyker alive long enough to make a serious attempt at breaking down the Zoanthrope's mental shields.

**Take Captive:** Unlike many other kinds of Tyranid creature, a Zoanthrope seems to undergo a significant change when it dies, something within it expiring and melting away as its psychic energy ebbs away. Recorded instances of Zoanthropes taken alive and contained for any length of time are next to nil, though it has not stopped the Magos Biologis from making repeated attempts. The Deathwatch also have an interest in taking such a creature alive (mostly so they can learn how to better kill it) and have considered allowing a team of Tech-Priests and Magos the protection of a Kill-team to make the attempt. Such an undertaking would take a great deal of planning, and the only sure way to transport such a creature would likely be in a stasis chamber, requiring either some heavy lifting or a cunningly laid trap.

# Psychic Manifestations of the Tyranid Hive Mind

*There can be no doubt that the Hive Mind is a potent psychic entity. Simply by observing its effect on the warp, the creatures with its countless broods and the senses of our own psykers, we can determine that it does in some way exist in both the Materium and Immaterium simultaneously. What is less clear is how and from where Tyranids draw their psychic power. Creatures like the Zoanthrope exhibit particularly massive amounts of psychic energy, dealing out bolts of power and blasts of fire as strong as any lascannon or artillery strike. Is the power of a Zoanthrope drawn from the warp itself like that of a normal psyker, perhaps channelled through the great consciousness of the Hive Mind, or is it the Hive Mind itself that provides the power for its psychic manifestations?*

*While to the solider on the ground, such speculation may seem one of pure semantics (a warp blast that cuts your men in half is just as deadly no matter how it came to be), it is of interest to the Codiciers like myself. If we could somehow know for sure where such a beast drew its power, we would be far better equipped to deal with it, and could over time create more effective counters. Perhaps, with enough research and skill, we might learn of a way to cut it off from the Hive Mind completely, permanently robbing it of its power. After all, as with all my studies on the Tyranids, the old maxim "To kill the Beast, you must first know the Beast" rings truer than ever.*

*—Codicier Jaelon*

# ORKS

*"Dey'z comin' for us like we some kind a humie gitz. But we ain't. We'ze da orks and dis here is gonna be one great fight! So get your choppas and shootas ready boyz , cos dere's some killin' to do!"*

—Warboss Gorgutz 'Ead 'Unter

A particularly barbaric and warlike race of aliens, Orks infest large portions of the known galaxy. In many sectors of space, Ork empires are constantly being built and torn down, waging war amongst themselves or against races unheard of by the Imperium. Orks are incredibly violent and numerous, so much so that if they were ever to combine forces under one ruler, they could potentially sweep away nearly all other races in the galaxy.

It is fortunate for the rest of the galaxy that the Ork's propensity for violence precludes such a fate, for Orks enjoy fighting amongst themselves as much as against other races. Most would-be Ork empires fall apart into petty squabbles and skirmishes before they can become more than a minor threat. However, there are some occasions where a powerful Ork warlord rises amongst his kind, possessing sufficient brutish strength and cunning to bully other greenskins into line and concentrate their efforts into a significant force. When this occurs, a Waaagh! is raised—a great invasion of Orks that can decimate entire sectors of the galaxy, if given the time to grow in momentum and size.

The Ork presence in the Jericho Reach is small and scattered, rarely touched by the presence of the greenskin menace (although few locations in the Galaxy are truly completely safe from Orks). Many worlds harbour an Ork presence, even those that are declared safe by Imperial authorities. Typically such greenskins are stamped out with overwhelming force whenever they are discovered, for the Imperium has learnt from considerable experience that there is a price to pay for leaving such seemingly harmless infestations unchecked—Orks multiply extremely quickly.

On some other worlds, Orks thrive in far greater numbers. Often, these are feral Orks who wage war against each other and ride into battle atop great wild boars or massive, reptilian creatures known as Squiggoths. These Orks are not to be discounted, for Orks evolve quickly and develop from possessing relatively primitive technology to mastering the basics of spaceflight (albeit in crude, ramshackle spaceships that carry Orks to invade other worlds) in the space of a few generations.

Cleansing a world of an Ork infestation is not a simple task. Ork spores may lie dormant beneath the soil for years before sprouting into a new generation of greenskins. Despite the best efforts of the local population, some worlds can have outbreaks of Orks rising up every few years.

Orks have two main methods of interstellar travel; space hulks and roks. A space hulk is an enormous floating mass of debris, normally comprised of wrecked spacecraft and other cosmic detritus that drifts in and out of warp space. As a space

hulk drifts near an Ork infested world, crude tractor beams and teleporters are used to seize it long enough for as many Orks as possible to embark. Once aboard, Ork Meks (Orks that have an inborn natural knack for technology) and Weirdboyz—Ork psykers—guide it back into the warp, navigating it into neighbouring systems ripe for plunder and war. Space hulks are often accompanied by great swarms of orbiting roks—hollowed out asteroids hurled across space, acting as makeshift drop pods and assault shuttles. Also, sometimes such creations enter the sector on their own, propelled by some great mass catapult deep in a neighbouring area of space. Orks have little control over where the roks go, but so long as they smash into an inhabited world (and some Orks survive the impact long enough to fight), they are happy enough.

Fortunately, roks and space hulks are a rare occurrence in the Jericho Reach, and the Achilus Crusade would need to muster significant resources to oppose such a force.

## ORK PHYSIOLOGY

An Ork's body contains the genetic traits of both animal and fungal life forms. This plant-like nature is responsible for the Ork's incredible physique and toughness. Algae flows through an Ork's blood, breaking down and repairing damaged tissue at an advanced rate. This algae is the reason for the Ork's greenish coloration and freakish durability.

Ork reproduction occurs by dispersing spores that settle and mature over time. When an Ork dies, this triggers a mass release of spores that can develop into dozens of subterranean cocoons. These cocoons then may hatch Gretchin, Squigs, or just simple fungi depending on the surrounding conditions. A good number of these cocoons will mature into fully-grown Orks after a gestation period.

## ORK SOCIETY AND KLANS

For Orks, size equals respect and might makes right. These two elements are rooted in the Ork's physiology: natural leaders among their breed grow larger and stronger, enforcing their authority with physical abuse and the volume of his shouting in preference to cunning plans or charisma. These creatures thrive on conflict, and often gather into groups intent on finding the biggest and most violent battle to join in and escalate. These groups centre around a leader, known as a Nob, who forms a mob of his closest and most reliable Ork allies (including many Gretchin hangers-on and sycophants). The biggest and most powerful Nob becomes a Warboss and leads all the mobs in what is known as a Warband. Warbands are sometimes absorbed into larger tribes, and many tribes together often form the massive invasion hosts known as Waaaghs! In addition to this, Orks also have Klans, which embody a philosophy (for want of a better term) among Orks, each Clan emphasising particular elements of Ork culture above others. Orks belong to one or another Klan no matter what Tribe they are in.

## TEETH

The basis of Ork economics is teeth (known in the parlance of the alien as "teef"). Not any teeth will do—they must be the sharp tusks grown by Orks and periodically shed by the creatures as they grow. Teeth can be exchanged for almost anything in a crude form of market economics, from a choppa or a shoota to a buggy or bike. And, of course, because Ork money is grown by Orks, a good spot of fighting is great for shaking loose a few teeth and earning a bit more wealth for the victor.

## FREEBOOTERS

Not every Ork belongs to a warband or tribe. Some are misfits from Ork society, Orks who take more of an interest in looting and pillaging than in fighting. Outcasts amongst their own kind, these Flash Gitz and Freebooters are pirates, bandits, and mercenaries of ill-repute, selling their services to the highest bidder whether Ork or human ('umie, to use the Ork's parlance). Violence is always a major part of an Ork's life, no matter how much he may yearn after booty and adventure, and a Freebooter's agreement is fickle, lasting until the money runs out or he gets a fancy for bashing.

# ORK TRAITS

The following is a selection of Ork Traits that most Orks possess.

## MIGHT MAKES RIGHT

Amongst Orks, Intimidate can be substituted for Command Tests.

## MAKE IT WORK

Unreliable Ork weapons are not Unreliable in an Ork's hands.

## MOB RULE

All Orks are latently psychic, an ability that increases in strength the more of them there are in one place. This bolsters their confidence and courage to near-fearless levels when they gather en masse. For every additional Ork within 10m, the Ork's Willpower gains a +10 bonus to resist the effects of Fear and Pinning. In a Horde, Orks are immune to Fear and Pinning.

## WAAAGH!

When the Ork charges, he may make any additional attacks granted from other Talents (such as Swift Attack or Lightning Attack), rather than one. In addition, whenever this Ork charges into combat, all other Orks (or Ork Hordes) within 20 metres who charge that Turn may make one additional attack.

# ORK BOY

The majority of Orks encountered throughout the galaxy are Ork Boyz, the common, foot-slogging warriors that make up the bulk of the greenskin horde. They are neither rulers nor leaders, for that role belongs to the Nobz, but nor are they servants or slaves, for the Gretchin fulfil that role. They exist for one purpose, and one purpose alone—to wage war. Orks care not where war is waged or against whom, and in the absence of a worthy foe, they happily fight amongst themselves.

Ork Boyz are tough, hulking brutes with thick, gnarly green hides. Fully erect they stand somewhere between six and seven feet tall, but most stand hunched over. Their bestial, almost porcine faces have beady little red eyes and a jutting jaw brimming with long tusks. Their skulls are thick, their arms long and ape-like, and their torsos extremely well-muscled. They typically wear battered and worn clothing and armour, cobbled together from whatever scraps they can find, take, or steal, and wield crude weaponry ranging from loud slug-firing pistols to even louder rifles.

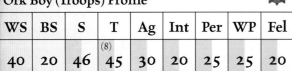

## Ork Boy (Troops) Profile

| WS | BS | S | T | Ag | Int | Per | WP | Fel |
|----|----|----|----|----|----|----|----|----|
| 40 | 20 | 46 | 45 (8) | 30 | 20 | 25 | 25 | 20 |

Speed: 3/6/9/18 　　　　　　　　　　Wounds: 15

**Skills:** Awareness (Per), Dodge (Ag), Intimidate (S)
**Talents:** Basic Weapon Training (Primitive, SP), Bulging Biceps, Crushing Blow, Furious Assault, Hardy, Iron Jaw, Melee Weapon Training (Chain, Primitive), Pistol Weapon Training (Primitive, SP), Street Fighting, True Grit.
**Traits:** Brutal Charge, Make it Work, Mob Rule, Sturdy, Unnatural Toughness (x2)
**Armour:** Flak armour (Body 2)
**Weapons:** Slugga (20m; S/3/–; 1d10+9 I; Pen 2; Clip 18; Reload Full; Inaccurate, Unreliable) or Shoota (60m; S/3/10; 1d10+8 I; Pen 2; Reload Full; Inaccurate, Unreliable), choppa (1d10+7 R; Pen 2; Tearing, Unbalanced).
**Gear:** Shiny bitz, really small Squig.
**Horde:** Ork Boyz can form a Horde, in which case they gain the Overwhelming Trait.

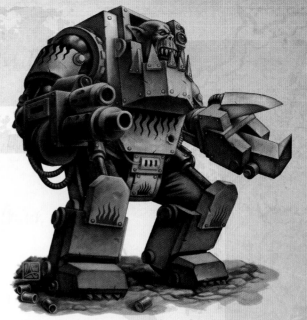

# ORK MEGANOB

Ork culture is a seething morass of violence where the strong constantly assert their position over upstart, ambitious young orks. Only the largest, toughest, and most aggressive Orks rise to leadership amongst the greenskins. This makeshift "nobility" results in a class of ork known as "Nobz" in their guttural language. Nobz lead by example, fighting where the fighting is thickest and "encouraging" any recalcitrant Orks or Grots with cuffs and blows to get them into the battle.

In many warbands, Nobz gain a favoured status for collecting loot or special wargear from the Meks, such as mega-armour. Such mega-armoured Nobz (known as Meganobz) often form an elite bodyguard for an Ork Warboss and accompany him into the heart of any fight with savage enthusiasm.

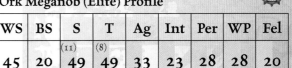

## Ork Meganob (Elite) Profile

| WS | BS | S | T | Ag | Int | Per | WP | Fel |
|----|----|----|----|----|----|----|----|----|
| 45 | 20 | 49 (11) | 49 (8) | 33 | 23 | 28 | 28 | 20 |

Speed: 3/6/9/18 　　　　　　　　　　Wounds: 35

**Skills:** Awareness (Per), Command (Fel) +10, Dodge (Ag), Intimidate (S) +20
**Talents:** Basic Weapon Training (Primitive, SP), Bulging Biceps, Crushing Blow, Exotic Weapon Proficiency (Any Ork Weapon), Furious Assault, Hardy, Iron Jaw, Melee Weapon Training (Chain, Primitive), Pistol Weapon Training (Primitive, SP), Swift Attack, Talented (Intimidate), Street Fighting, True Grit.
**Traits:** Auto-stabilised, Brutal Charge, Fear (1), Make It Work, Might Makes Right, Mob Rule, Size (Hulking), Sturdy, Unnatural Strength (x2) Unnatural Toughness (x2)
**Armour:** Mega-armour (Body 14, Arms and Legs 10, Head 6)
**Weapons:** Twin-linked Shoota (60m; S/3/10; 1d10+8 I; Pen 2; Reload Full; Inaccurate, Twin-Linked, Unreliable), power claw (1d10+20 R; Pen 8; Unbalanced).
**Gear:** 5d10 Ork Teeth ("teef"), lots of shiny bitz, small pet hair Squig.

# ORK WARBOSS

A large and aggressive Ork Chieftain, a Warboss has proven himself as a leader of a warband. As such, the Warboss gets the pick of any wargear and loot the warband accumulates, and gathers the best Ork fighters from the warband as his bodyguard. Warbosses often have their own entourage of Squigs, Gretchin, or other slave creatures. A Warboss is often decorated with huge horns on his helmet, a crude banner affixed to his back or carried by a Grot, or a massive iron jaw bolted onto his skull. He keeps the other Orks in line with the force of his domineering personality and a brutal beating from time to time.

At times a Warboss' authority may be challenged by his rivals. The outcome of such struggles for power can be resolved in a number of ways. Some Orks prefer low kunnin' (such as assassination or ambush), whilst others will engage in some ritual duel. Among the Orks in the Jericho Reach, the second option is much preferred, and every Ork settlement in the reach possesses a fighting pit for such challenges to be fought. In fact, many of these pit fights are used as a crude form of judicial system, with the outcome of the fight resolving any kind of dispute over loot or position.

## Ork Warboss (Master) Profile

| WS | BS | S | T | Ag | Int | Per | WP | Fel |
|----|----|----|----|----|----|----|----|----|
| 55 | 20 | (10) 55 | (10) 55 | 43 | 33 | 35 | 40 | 25 |

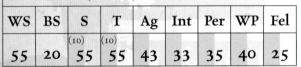

**Speed:** 4/8/12/24  **Wounds:** 55

**Skills:** Awareness (Per) +10, Command (Fel) +10, Dodge (Ag), Intimidate (S) +20

**Talents:** Basic Weapon Training (Primitive, SP), Bulging Biceps, Crushing Blow, Exotic Weapon Proficiency (Any Ork Weapon), Furious Assault, Hardy, Into the Jaws of Hell, Iron Discipline, Iron Jaw, Lightning Attack, Melee Weapon Training (Chain, Primitive), Pistol Weapon Training (Primitive, SP), Swift Attack, Talented (Intimidate), Street Fighting, True Grit.

**Traits:** Brutal Charge, Fear (2), Make It Work, Might Makes Right, Mob Rule, Size (Hulking), Sturdy, Unnatural Strength (x2) Unnatural Toughness (x2), Waaagh!

**Armour:** 'Eavy armour (Body 6, Arms and Legs 4, Head 6)

**Weapons:** Shoota (60m; S/3/10; 1d10+8 I; Pen 2; Reload Full; Inaccurate, Unreliable), power claw (1d10+20 R; Pen 8; Unbalanced).

**Gear:** 1d5 Space Marine Helmet trophies, 1d5 other trophies, crude banner, 1d5x10 Ork Teeth ("teef"), lots of shiny bitz. Some warbosses also own pet attack squigs.

## MORE ORK INFORMATION

Additional Ork profiles, rules, and equipment can be found in CREATURES ANATHEMA, a supplement for DARK HERESY, and INTO THE STORM, a ROGUE TRADER supplement. These additional sources for information can be very valuable for a GM who wants to involve Orks more heavily in his DEATHWATCH campaign.

## ADVENTURE SEEDS

**Lightning Strike:** Warboss Gobklaw has begun lightning strikes against both sides of an Imperial / Tau conflict. Initial attacks greatly weakened the Imperial Guard who are desperately holding a line against the advancing armies of the Tau. There is a brief respite, for now, as the Warboss lashes out against the enemy. Can the Kill-Team assassinate the Warboss while his forces are still deep within Tau territory so that his forces continue to attack the Tau blindly?

**Ominous Silence:** Astropathic communication with Watch Station Cosel has fallen silent. The Kill-team arrives to find the station infested with Orks as the remaining Adeptus Astartes forces are trapped defending the lower decks. In a desperate maneuver the Kill-team's Strike Cruiser disables the Ork Kroozer and they board the Watch Station to defeat the Warboss and reclaim what is rightfully theirs.

# BIG MEK WURRZOG

Some Orks possess a natural gift for engineering and tinkering with technology. These Orks are known as Meks or Mekaniaks, and it is they who build, modify, and maintain the machines and weapons of the greenskin race. Meks are often obsessed with creating ever more elaborate and powerful machines of war to unleash upon the enemy.

Some particularly visionary Meks gather a number of acolytes, followers, and other Meks under their authority. These Orks become known as Big Meks, and they are true masters of Orky technology. Big Mek Wurrzog is one such Ork, and he has gathered a small warband around him and his workshop, located somewhere in the Slinnar Drift region of the Jericho Reach.

Wurrzog has a fascination with the technology of the Tau Empire, and his band of Orks has made a number of raids against the Velk'han Sept. The Big Mek has, in fact, crafted a special "kustom" force field by looting one of the Tau Shield Drones and modifying it (often by applying various whacks with his wrench). He keeps the drone on a chained tether to keep its protection for himself. Wurrzog has somehow discovered the presence of a number of Deathwatch Watch Stations, and he is currently planning a particularly "kunning" raid to try and capture some of the Deathwatch's esoteric wargear for his own purposes.

## ADVENTURE SEED

Wurrzog is keenly interested in looting some more Tau technology. He has gathered a warband of Boyz and Meganobz for a most cunning plan: Wurrzog intends to find an ongoing battle between the Achilus Crusade forces in the Canis Salient against the Tau Empire, then lead his warband in a furious assault that is actually a raid. The Kill-team is present during this battle (perhaps assigned a mission to assassinate the Tau leader) when Wurrzog's warband add a third front to the raging battle. The Kill-team must now deal with the Orks as well as the Tau. For an additional complication, the Kill-team's target is captured by the Orks along with the technology that Wurrzog craves, making the mission much less straightforward than it initially appeared!

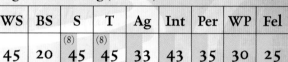

### Big Mek Wurrzog (Master) Profile

| WS | BS | S | T | Ag | Int | Per | WP | Fel |
|----|----|-----|-----|----|-----|-----|----|-----|
| 45 | 20 | (8) 45 | (8) 45 | 33 | 43 | 35 | 30 | 25 |

Speed: 3/6/9/18      **Wounds:** 45

**Skills:** Awareness, Command (Fel) +10, Demolitions (Int) +20, Intimidate (S) +20, Security (Int) +10, Tech-Use (Int) +20.

**Talents:** Basic Weapon Training (Primitive, SP), Bulging Biceps, Crushing Blow, Exotic Weapon Proficiency (Any Ork Weapon), Furious Assault, Hardy, Iron Jaw, Lightning Attack, Melee Weapon Training (Chain, Primitive), Pistol Weapon Training (Primitive, SP), Swift Attack, Street Fighting, True Grit.

**Traits:** Brutal Charge, Fear (2), Make It Work, Might Makes Right, Mob Rule, Size (Hulking), Sturdy, Unnatural Strength (x2) Unnatural Toughness (x2)

**Armour:** 'Eavy armour (Body 6, Arms and Legs 4, Head 6)

**Weapons:** Kustom mega-blasta (40m; S/–/–; 1d10+18 E; Pen 9; Reload Full; Overheat, Inaccurate, Recharge, Unreliable), Slugga (20m; S/3/–; 1d10+9 I; Pen 2; Clip 18; Reload Full; Inaccurate, Unreliable), 'uge orky wrench (1d10+15 R; Pen 2; Concussive, Unbalanced).

**Gear:** Speshul Force Field (see sidebar below), set of brutishly effective tools, 30 Ork Teeth ("teef"), lots of shiny bitz, six oil cans.

## WURRZOG'S SPESHUL FORCE FIELD

Wurrzog built this device from a looted Tau Shield Drone he keeps attached to a thick chain. The Drone wobbles a lot more since being "looted," but its power output has been modified by Wurrzog's tinkering. This device follows the rules for Force Fields (see page 166 in the **DEATHWATCH** Rulebook) with a strength of 35, but also provides the same benefit to other Orks or Ork vehicles within 15 metres. The Speshul Force Field does not work against melee attacks, and overloads on a roll of 01–05.

# OTHER XENOS

*"This blighted region of space teems with foul aliens, all of them inimical to man."*

–Deathwatch Chaplain Calderin of the Death Spectres

The Jericho Reach contains numerous alien foes, from the survivors of ancient civilisations to mindless beasts who have been brought into the Reach from unknown regions of space. This chapter focuses on those unusual aliens that are of particular interest to the Deathwatch.

## BRUUL PARASITE

*"The most horrific foes are not those that devour our bodies, break our minds with terror or tear us to pieces with their claws; they are those that take from us what we are, stealing away our very identity and turning us into living puppets to their foul alien will."*

–Magos Biologis Hypon Glass

As the Achilus Crusade spreads across the Jericho Reach it has encountered numerous new alien horrors and dangerous indigenous species. Among the strangest and most insidious of these are perhaps the Bruul Parasites—vile parasitic creatures which nest in sentient creatures, drawing energy from their prey's consciousness and controlling its body. First encountered among the blighted worlds of the Cellebos Warzone they were thought to be some vile new weapon of the Dark Gods; in time, however, they were discovered in other places and the Inquisition was forced to investigate, learning a great many disturbing facts about this new menace to the Crusade in the process. Unlike many kinds of parasites, the Bruul Parasite does not simply leech vitality from its host, hiding unseen in their flesh to devour them slowly from within over time; instead it wholly takes control of the subject, feeding as much on its memories and personality as its actual body. The Bruul Parasite also travels great distances to find its prey, seeking out centres of civilisation and centres of sentient population, often hitchhiking on lesser creatures until it can find a true host to latch onto. It then spreads slowly and carefully, using the hosts own memories to blend into its surroundings and create for its self a tight knit family or social grouping where it can breed and multiply.

Hosts infected with Bruul Parasites are easy to detect, their eyes sunken into their sockets and their lips pulled back as the worm wraps itself tightly around their brains. The hosts' movements are jerky and uncoordinated, though they can put on bursts of speed when threatened. Hosts also tend to become emaciated over time, as the Bruul Parasite does not really understand the concept of eating unless it comes across a memory or instinct that prompts it to feed. Bruul Parasites do act with cunning however, and seem well aware of the effect they have on the appearance of their hosts. They make every effort to disguise these effects where and when they can, at least until they have created a secure environment for themselves in which to hide from uninfected members of their host species.

It is difficult to determine whether or not the Bruul Parasite is a creature of intentional or accidental malevolence. Outside the host it is even difficult to determine if the Bruul Parasite has any intelligence at all, except the knowledge and memories it gleans from its hosts. What is clear is that when threatened, Bruul Parasites go to great lengths to protect themselves and their host, at least until the leap to a new host. This is especially true if the Bruul Parasite feels its social or family unit has been threatened, or that its supply of hosts is about to be cut off or destroyed. Even when discovered and brought to battle, Bruul Parasites are very difficult to kill, and there is only a short time to do so when they transfer from one host to another. This usually occurs from the eyes, mouth or ears and the worm can leap several metres to reach a new host. Those wishing to dispatch it have only the time before it can work its way into its host to squash it or hack it apart before it nests and once again must be driven out by destroying its new host body.

### CREATING A BRUUL PARASITE HOST

Bruul Parasites do not have their own profiles, instead taking on the profile of their hosts. These hosts can be anything that has a brain, though it is usually a sentient creature. To create a Bruul Parasite Host, make the following changes to its host's profile:

- +5 Strength
- +5 Toughness
- –10 Agility
- -5 Intelligence
- -5 Willpower
- –10 Fellowship

In all other respects (with the exception of psychic powers) the host functions as a normal member of its species.

#### Special Rules

**Mind Worms:** Bruul Parasites only exist within the body of their host and have no profile of their own. When they choose a host, they try to enter through the eyes, mouth or nose. The host must make a **Challenging (+0) Agility Test** (unless it is helpless, in which case it fails automatically) to resist becoming infected. Once within the host, the Bruul Parasite nests in 1d5 turns, after which it has complete control of the host. Removing a Bruul Parasite is extremely hard once it has nested and requires a full operating theatre, at least 6 hours and a **Hard (–20) Medicae Test**. Failure kills the subject, while even success reduces their Intelligence Characteristic by 1d5 points. A successful hit against a Bruul Parasite while it is outside a host, regardless of the weapon used, will kill it.

**Mixed Memories:** When inhabiting a host, a Bruul Parasite can draw upon its memories to a certain extent, though this level of recall is far from perfect and they can forget things. Whenever a Bruul Parasite wishes to call upon a memory of its host or use a skill based on Intelligence, Perception, Willpower or Fellowship, roll 1d10. On a result of 9 or 10 the Bruul Parasite cannot use the skill or recall the memory for the rest of the encounter. Bruul Parasites cannot use Psychic Powers even if their host possesses them, as they are far too difficult to command.

## ADVENTURE SEEDS

**Overdue Acolytes:** Strange whispers and odd rumours have been leaking out of the Kynis Mining Station. Traders and ship captains have reported unusual dealing with the miners, who seem bewildered or distracted, or don't seem to remember a trader they have met many times before. Worse yet, some of those visiting the mining station have failed to return, or decided abruptly to stay, even abandoning vessels and loved ones to do so. The Ordo Xenos has already sent in a team of Acolytes to investigate, but these have failed to report in and are feared lost. The Deathwatch is now poised to intervene and find out what kind of alien force or cult has taken over the station. Unfortunately the station is of considerable importance to the Crusade and supplies several nearby army groups with raw materials. This means the Kill-team must tread lightly, try to preserve as much of the infrastructure as possible and try to save as many of the miners that they can, while rooting out the truth behind the unusual goings on.

**Space Hulk:** Brother Tablin Kyn was a veteran member of the Deathwatch hailing from the Ultramarines Chapter. A champion of many battles, he was lost along with his Kill-team almost ten years ago while purging the space hulk *Ghosts of Jericho*. His body was never recovered and the Space Hulk was ultimately destroyed by vessels of the Imperial Navy, leaving little doubt in the minds of the Deathwatch that he had been killed. Now, years later, a Battle-Brother wearing Tablin's armour has been sighted during a pirate attack off the Shoals of Midnight, near the edge of the Iron Collar. Under interrogation, survivors have confirmed that the dead Space Marine, or something much like him was involved. This has led to much debate among the Ordo and the Chapter, and the launch of an investigation into the strange sighting. If it is indeed the lost Battle-Brother, then he must be found and captured, as he is either a traitor, the subject of foul sorcery or vile xenos control, and the truth must be uncovered.

**Hordes:** Bruul Parasites can inhabit a wide range of foes of all sizes and strengths, though usually they choose weaker social creatures as they are easier to control and feed off. If using creatures from the Troops category as hosts, then they will usually be encountered in Hordes and can use the Horde rules (see page 359 in the **DEATHWATCH** Rulebook).

## *Xenos Parasites*

### *On the Presence of the Unseen Enemy*

*During my time studying alien creatures and the enemies of the Imperium I have encountered a myriad of horrors both foul and fearsome. From the vile and animalistic Tyranid to the enigmatic and deluded Tau, there are countless alien empires and alien threats to the dominion of man. Of course, what is more worrying is those aliens we cannot see, those xenos which lurk in the invisible places of the world and infect us without our knowing. Against a Genestealer or Ork, a bolter serves as a reliable and trusty method of protection. However, against these unseen enemies, such as the Ghost Phage or the Bruul Parasite, we must be on constant guard and even then they seem to slip though our defences. This is especially true of the Bruul Parasite, a brain worm that feeds on sentient life and controls its host in a mockery of their normal function. Where these vile creatures come from is unknown, as is how they manage to take their first host, however once they take root in a society they seem to multiply with alarming speed and I have seen firsthand entire communities dominated by the tiny parasites. Though they do not destroy worlds as does the Tyranid or the Ork, they are no less deadly to the dominion of man, and prove time and again that even the smallest of things could bring about the fall of Mankind.*

*—Codicier Jaelon*

SEALED

DATA

# CROTALID

Crotalids are large, semi-aquatic carnivores that prefer to live in and around tropical and sub-tropical rivers. They are dangerous reptilian beasts with long scaly bodies carried on stubby, powerful legs capable of driving them forward with surprising bursts of speed over short distances. A long, finned tail drags behind the creature on land, leaving distinctive tracks, but in the water a Crotalid propels its whole body with powerful flicks of its tail.

The Crotalid's head is dominated by its ferocious jaws filled with serrated rows of triangular teeth. These teeth never stop growing throughout a Crotalid's life and Crotalid feeding grounds can be easily identified by the gnawed rocks and tree trunks found in the vicinity. Despite this, instances have been reported of dead Crotalids that were killed by their teeth growing so long that they finally pierced the creatures' own tiny brains. Aside from such examples of autophagia, Crotalids are protected by thick scales and a rudimentary nervous system that makes them extremely difficult to kill outright. Once injured or exposed to the scent of blood, Crotalids enter a kind of feeding frenzy which overrides any kind of pain or fear response, sending them into a berserk attack of thrashing limbs and snapping jaws.

Crotalids are primarily ambush predators, feeding on fish, other aquatic animals and wildlife drinking at the water's edge. Crotalids favour attacking from a submerged location and clamping their formidable jaws onto a victim before they have a chance to react, but they will also pursue prey a short distance out of the water, dragging it back to their aquatic home at the first opportunity. Crotalids are opportunists too and will quickly investigate any disturbances in the water, especially kills by other Crotalids, in hopes of snatching a mouthful or two for themselves in the resulting frenzy.

A full-grown Crotalid can easily overwhelm a man, and give a Space Marine a difficult fight. Unfortunately Crotalids often appear in large numbers, quickly making their way to the top of the food chain and completely dominating the area they inhabit. As such, any encounter with one Crotalid means that several more will soon arrive, and in a heavily infested area, dozens can appear in moments.

Crotalids in captivity have lived over seventy years, but Magos Biologis Xenologists have been unable to determine the life span of Crotalids in the wild with any precision. This is due to their curious migratory habits which are, as best determined, unique in the known galaxy. As a rapidly expanding population of Crotalids comes to dominate a region, their prey is completely exhausted in the course of a few decades. The Crotalid population must now migrate to a new location or face extinction, and the creatures instinctually gather in response to their growing hunger. At some undetermined point, the unconscious desires of the Crotalids enable them to move on, not by walking or swimming but by passing through the Immaterium itself.

How Crotalids perform this feat is still unknown, autopsies have revealed no organ or abnormality that might give the beasts the ability to pass through the warp. Certainly no conscious manipulation of the process seems available to the Crotalids themselves, as they can appear on worlds quite

unsuited for them including desert planets and even airless worlds. Nonetheless, migratory packs of Crotalids can appear on worlds up to ten light years from their origin point and have been highly successful in establishing themselves in new environments through this apparently hit-and-miss process. Crotalids have been found all over the galaxy but the densest concentrations of sightings are clustered around the Death world of Lost Hope.

Tracking migratory packs has proved impossible, as has keeping more than three Crotalids together in captivity. However it appears that once a population migrates it will not do so again for several decades, for the impetus seems to be driven by population pressure. Although observation of this phenomena is limited to finding evidence of failed migrations, Crotalids appearing on a world poorly suited to them do not seem able to move on to greener pastures using this remarkable trait. For some, this reinforces the prevalent theories that the Crotalids' ability is not consciously used but an instinctual response to environmental pressures.

A typical migratory pack comprises anywhere up to a hundred or more fully-grown Crotalids and can cause considerable damage. When they first arrive in a new hunting ground, Crotalids are extremely aggressive and will attack anything in sight to establish their dominance. Frontier colonies have been all but wiped out by such unexpected appearances, with livestock and outlying farms paying the highest price in the sudden invasion by large carnivorous reptiles. The pleasure planet of Colonica was entirely ravaged by large numbers of Crotalids multiplying in its picturesque river deltas to the point where they threatened highborn pleasure seekers on the beaches.

Conversely, some Crotalid populations are actively hunted or even farmed on certain worlds. Crotalid meat is tough and unappetizing but their hides and teeth have some value. Hunting Crotalids for sport has some notoriety among more gauche, high society types, but it is more commonly the preserve of desperate men. Bait and traps are the clever ways to kill a Crotalid, preferably by getting it out of the water first.

## Crotalid (Troops) Profile

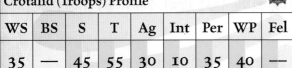

| WS | BS | S | T | Ag | Int | Per | WP | Fel |
|----|----|----|----|----|-----|-----|-----|-----|
| 35 | — | 45 | 55 | 30 | 10 | 35 | 40 | — |

**Move:** 4/8/12/24  **Wounds:** 20

**Skills:** Awareness (Per), Concealment (Ag) +10, Silent Move (Ag) +10, Swim (S) +30.

**Talents:** Crushing Blow, Frenzy†, Furious Assault, Fearless, Heightened Senses (Taste), True Grit.

**Traits:** Crawler, Dark Sight, Natural Weapons. (jaws, claws), Quadruped, Natural Armour (Scaly hide), Size (hulking).

**Armour:** Scaly hide (All 3, Horde 3).

**Weapons:** Jaws (1d10+7 R; Pen 3; Tearing, Primitive) Claws (1d5+7 I; Pen 2; Tearing, Primitive).

### Special Rules

**Horde:** Crotalids can be used as a Horde (see the Horde rules on page 359 of the **Deathwatch** Rulebook). While in a Horde, Crotalids gain the Warp Swimmers†† and Rampage Traits. A Horde of Crotalids also has the Fear 1 (Disturbing) Trait. Alter the Size Trait upward as appropriate for Horde magnitude.

†**Frenzy:** A Crotalid can enter Frenzy automatically without taking an action if it is wounded or able to taste blood within 30 metres.

††**Warp Swimmers:** When in a Horde, Crotalids are capable of travelling through warp space under the right conditions. A minimum sized group of four or more Crotalids is required to make the transition, with increasing numbers adding to the range of the migration. Time and distance are mutable within the warp, thus the distance that a group of Crotalids can traverse whilst migrating is at the GM's discretion. The Horde will instinctively find a world within range to emerge on, but there's no guarantee that it will be suitable for them. The Horde of Crotalid phase in or out together from the warp, taking one Full Action to do so. Succeeding at a **Challenging (+0) Psyniscience Test** will be able to detect the arrival of Crotalids a turn before their emergence from the warp.

## Crotalid Adventure Seeds

**Hunting Expedition:** A hunting expedition packed with planetary nobles has gone deep into Crotalid infested territory in search of some fine trophies. Enemy agents among their multitude of servants do everything they can to isolate the nobles and get them killed, before leaving them to their fate with sunken boats and useless weapons. Finding and rescuing the hapless nobles will have a tight time limit imposed by the hungry Crotalids.

**Strange Visitors:** A migratory pack of Crotalids arrive somewhere acutely embarrassing and potentially dangerous for the current occupants—the governor's fountain park, a fusion reactor's cooling ponds, the sewers under a cathedral. Mass panic and extravagant over-reactions may well cause more damage than the Crotalids ever could before the emergency is over.

**Dangerous Pets:** A Heretek Techno-savant has wired a number of Crotalids for mind impulse control to harness their warp swimming abilities. If his experiments bear fruit he could control a small army of phasing carnivorous lizards able to strike across light years. The hybridised horrors guarding the Heretek's labs include all manner of "enhanced" Crotalid monstrosities.

---

**From the annals of Codicier Taelon**

Some may find my inclusion of the Crotalid in these papers to be a curious one. However, in terms of xenos impact on emergent worlds, few species can match the Crotalid. Consider this testimonial from the colony planet of Fershun IX:

In the summer months we began to see less fish in our nets and by winter the nets themselves were being torn. Come spring we saw the dragons themselves, arrogantly swimming the waters and dragging themselves out on land. Livestock began to vanish and we took up our guns and hunted the dragons down. We began to be afraid of them then, because some people were hurt, some vanished altogether, and there were always more dragons. Come wintertime, we were starving in our huts. Meanwhile, the dragons prowled around outside. By next spring, they started breaking into the huts, looking for meat.

# DIABLODON

Native to the world of Aurum within the Jericho Reach, the Diablodon has managed to find its way across the larger portion of this area of space and beyond. Known within legends and lore of the various tribes and people of Aurum, the Diablodon is a consummate hunter and frightening predator beast. It figures prominently in the natives' culture and the best hunters are those who have managed to best one of these terrifying lizards.

On their native planet, Diablodons are considered to be the ultimate predator. They are descended from the reptile strain of midasaurs. While some midasaurs have been domesticated by the people, many more are not. These range from the small and virtually harmless species, to the massive Diablodons themselves. Found scattered across numerous worlds within the Jericho Reach, Diablodons have been distributed by many Rogue Traders and Free Captains for a variety of reasons: some deliberate and others by accident. They feature popularly within many of the legendary Beast Trades and tournament arenas for obvious reasons.

Diablodons play a significant role in the culture and mythology of the native Aurans. In some of the outlying tribes, the Diablodon is believed to represent the true spirit of the hunter. Dances, performances, and literature have all centred on this terrifying creature. The most prominent role these reptiles play is in the Aurans' Divested Hunt.

The truest test of a huntsman's skill, the Divested Hunt involves tracking, stalking, and then killing one of these great monsters. So voracious and skilful are Diablodons that those who attempt the Divested Hunt rarely return. Once the reptile is found, it must be killed and its carcass ritually prepared. This is easier said than done, for these creatures possess a keen intellect and refuse to be taken down easily.

As terrifying as the Diablodon is, there are many myths and legends surrounding it. On Aurum, the most significant one revolves around the Diablodon as a harbinger of death. In the human cultures on Aurum, the Diablodon is portrayed to herald the dead to the afterlife beyond. Many young hunters also choose to tattoo the Diablodon's image on their bodies, as they believe having the symbol of the monster allows them to channel a small part of its strength and animal cunning. With the return of the Imperium and the Achilus Crusade, this practice has spread throughout some of the regiments of the Imperial Guard, much to the dismay of the Departmento Munitorum.

Diablodons are fearsome looking reptiles. They all have a distinctive crimson hide that has spectacular patterns and whorls streaked into the scales. A typical Diablodon sports a sagittal crest and massive, needle-like teeth. Their eyes are glistening yellow orbs, and their talons are as long and as sharp as an Imperial power sword. Diablodons have a hunched-over stance, walking on their two hind legs. Adults stand as tall as an Adeptus Astartes Dreadnought. They have a distinctive three-toed track that hunters quickly learn to recognise. The talons and claws of a Diablodon are almost always covered in the gore and remains of past victims; so any wounds inflicted by a Diablodon inevitably turn septic unless treated.

Diablodons prefer to dwell within caves or other subterranean places, especially those that are near volcanic or geothermal areas. This preference not only adds to their mystique, but also provides additional protection from potential predators. One of the obvious signs that a Diablodon lair is near, is the grisly pile of leftover carcasses and split bones—the reptile isn't one to finish its meal entirely.

Evidence supports that Diablodons are excellent night hunters, leading some to believe that they possess both excellent night vision and a heightened sense of smell. An unusual trait in Diablodons is the fact that they are not pack hunters—preferring to hunt on their own. In fact, a Diablodon will go out of its way to remove any "competition" from its hunting grounds. While their mating habits are unknown, it's speculated that a Diablodon will only tolerate the presence of another until the female has been fertilised. She will then leave the area and either locate a suitable place to lay her eggs (near volcanic vents, if possible), or return to her own hunting grounds. Members of the Adeptus Biologis suspect that the male is the one who initiates the mating ritual by extending his sagittal crest to lure the female in. However, it's not unheard of for male Diablodons to do this as a means to reduce competition for food sources by attacking the potential mate instead of propagating.

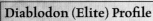

**I: THE ALIEN THREAT**

### Diablodon (Elite) Profile

| WS | BS | S | T | Ag | Int | Per | WP | Fel |
|----|----|-----|-----|----|-----|-----|----|-----|
| 45 | — | (15) 59 | (10) 55 | 35 | 16 | 40 | 36 | — |

**Movement:** 6/12/18/36  **Wounds:** 75

**Skills:** Awareness (Per).

**Talents:** Combat Master, Fearless, Heightened Senses (Smell).

**Traits:** Improved Natural Weapons, Natural Armour (Thick Scales), Natural Weapons (Bloodied Claws and Massive Jaws†), Size (Massive), Unnatural Strength (x3), Unnatural Toughness (x2).

**Armour:** Thick Scales (All 5).

**Weapons:** Bloodied Claws (1d10+15 R; Pen 3; Toxic), Massive Jaws (1d10+15 R; Pen 2; Tearing).

**Gear:** None.

†*Massive Jaws cannot be parried.*

### ADVENTURE SEEDS

**Interruption:** The Kill-team is busy tracking a signal coming from what appears to be a saviour beacon on a desolate planet or moon. As they close in on the signal, they can see that the source belongs to a crashed shuttle or other conveyor, and that it has been there for quite some time. The smell of carrion fills the air, and scattered bones and carcasses litter the area outside a great rent in the side of the craft. Due to a cracked plasma drive, auspex scans are unable to penetrate into the craft. It's dark inside the rusting hulk, but signs definitely point to a Diablodon within. As the Battle-Brothers make their way through the craft in their search for possible survivors, they discover a broken cage within the cargo hold. It appears that the creature escaped and attacked the crew before they could reach their destination. Do the valiant members of the Deathwatch choose to avenge the dead shuttle crew, or do they allow a potentially hostile xeno-beast to roam unchecked?

**Prey:** While on another Mission, the Kill-team discovers that they are being tracked. Whatever is following them, it is stealthy and highly intelligent (as it avoids most common traps and ambushes). The predator does whatever it can to separate the Battle-Brothers from one another and that's when it strikes at them, one at a time. A Diablodon (not native to the planet the Kill-team is on) has decided that they are now its prey. It's odd, however, that it exhibits higher-than-normal intelligence for such a creature.

Brother Codicier,
I have hunted and killed more than my meagre share of creatures within and without the Emperor's great Imperium. Yet I have only rarely encountered anything that matches the intellect and ferocity of the dread Diablodon. My first encounter with one of these fell beasts was while I and my Kill-team were assigned a mission to a small backwater planet named Aurum. During insertion, our gunship was targeted by unseen attackers and we were forced to disembark. While seperated from my Kill-team, I encountered a settlement that had been torn apart with savage fury. The only hint of who or what had committed such an act was a splayed three-toed track in the dirt. Several days later, after my team and I completed our mission, we returned to the site and hunted for the creatures responsible for the death of so many of the Emperor's servants. We quickly discovered that it was the work of a single reptilian beast sporting a massive crest and fierce yellow eyes. It took all our efforts to slay the horror. Brother Robar had the crimson scale hide fashioned into a magnificent cloak as a testament to those who died at the claws of such a terror.

—Brother Callum of the Crimson Fists

# LACRYMOLE

*"The greatest threat is ever the one we know least about, and few xeno-forms epitomise this notion more than the Lacrymole. Their greatest knack, its seems, is convincing us that they no longer exist."*

–Inquisitor Grundvald in an address to the Betacairn Conclave

The Charnel Spectre incident, or the Lacrymole Encounter as it is sometimes known, occurred during the early days of the Achilus Crusade, before the death of Warmaster Achilus and before the true extent of the Imperium's foes had been uncovered. As the Crusade fortified the regions around the Well of Night countless scouts ranged out in all directions. Assessing new worlds for conquest and spying on heretical populations and blasphemous alien empires they sent information streaming back to the Warmaster. Among these reports was the appearance of an ancient space hulk—the *Charnel Spectre*. The *Spectre* was an item of interest to the Inquisition as it had been sighted centuries before and records spoke of it containing the remnants of a relic ship of the Great Crusade; a ship which might have once belonged to the fledgling Inquisition.

A mission was organised; and led by Inquisitor Malas Dyce of the Ordo Xenos and supported by a Deathwatch Kill-team it set off to find the space hulk's location. After months of false leads Dyce and his team finally tracked the *Charnel Spectre*, following its erratic wake in the warp, to the edge of the cursed Credence system just beyond the boundaries of the Iron Collar. There they boarded the vessel and began their search for the relic ship. What they encounter instead was a nest of xenos which had apparently been living on the space hulk and using it as a base for centuries. At first the Kill-team thought they might be facing a Genestealer infestation (common on such ancient space hulks) as clawed shapes moved in the shadows and hissing sounds were heard echoing down the corridors. It was not until it was almost too late that they realised the aliens were shape-shifters.

Laying deadly traps for the Kill-team the aliens had some of their number appear as vile alien beasts, or clawed horrors like the Genestealer, and draw the Battle-Brothers and the Inquisitor and his Acolytes into a hunt. Only then would others pick off lone members of the group from behind (the Acolytes first among these) and assume their forms, then get close enough to strike with surprise. After only a few hours of attack only Dyce and a few Battle-Brothers remained, and the Battle-

Brothers were deeply suspicious that Dyce was an alien imposter. To save himself and return his report, the Inquisitor slipped away from the Kill-team during a firefight and made good his escape from the *Charnel Spectre*, leaving all of his companions behind.

Upon his return Dyce was convinced the aliens encountered on the *Spectre* were the fabled Lacrymole, claiming they were one in the same with those creatures slain by Inquisitor Grundvald and thought put to rest. With no proof however, and the loss of a Kill-team he was derided by his peers and ended his career as a broken and babbling old man whispering of aliens in the dark.

## Lacrymole (Elite) Profile

| WS | BS | S | T | Ag | Int | Per | WP | Fel |
|----|----|----|----|----|----|----|----|----|
| 48 | 23 | 43 | 41 | 51 | 32 | 35 | 35 | 25 |

**Movement:** 5/10/15/30  **Wounds:** 30

**Skills:** Awareness (Per), Climb (S), Concealment (Ag) +10, Contortionist (Ag) +20, Dodge (Ag), Security (Ag), Silent Move (Ag) +10, Shadowing (Ag), Slight of Hand (Ag), Swim (S), Tracking (Int) +20.

**Talents:** Ambidextrous, Blind Fighting, Catfall, Mimic, Rapid Reaction, Swift Attack.

**Traits:** Dark Sight, Fear 2 (Frightening), Natural Armour (6), Regeneration (5), Improved Natural Weapons (Mandibles).

**Armour:** Hardened Hide (All 6).

**Weapons:** Mandibles (1d10+4 R; Pen 4; Razor Sharp, Tearing).

**Gear:** Whatever is normally carried by the creature the Lacrymole has slain and replaced.

### Special Rules

**Xenomorph:** Lacrymole are natural shape-shifters and can take on the shape and appearance of almost anything of roughly equal size to themselves. Shifting takes the Lacrymole a Full Action and may not use its Reaction until the start of its next turn. If the Lacrymole wishes to shift into a very specific shape (such as imitating a specific person), then it will take it at least an hour and even then it must make a successful **Very Hard (–30) Intelligence Test** or minor imperfections will give the shape away to those familiar with the original. In an emergency, a Lacrymole can shift faster and may shift as a Reaction, but only if it passes a **Challenging (+0) Toughness Test**. Failure indicates it shifts on its next turn just as if it was using a Full Action. Finally, the Lacrymole's shape-shifting ability means that it can quickly re-grow things like eyes (or create new ones) and repair damage to limbs or even replace them. As a result Lacrymoles do not suffer limb or eye loss as the result of a critical effect, though they do suffer Critical Damage as normal, and can still be slain by critical results which would result in death.

**Perfect Imitation:** Lacrymole are excellent mimics and can use their Mimic Talent to replicate any sound or noise that they hear. Detecting their mimicry is extremely hard and those trying to do so suffer a –30 penalty to any appropriate Tests.

## ADVENTURE SEEDS

**The Charnel Spectre:** Whispers have reached the ears of the Ordo Xenos about strange disappearances and murders aboard vessels travelling from the Calixis Sector into the Jericho Reach, which seem to bear some of the hallmarks of the shape-shifters discovered aboard the *Charnel Spectre*. The trail which was discovered by the young Inquisitor Rensmi prompted her to try and gain the support of the Calixian Conclave for a full investigation. However the Conclave remains unconvinced on the matter and some amongst its number doubt that the *Charnel Spectre* xenos even exist. Rensmi is determined to shed light on the matter and has requested the aid of a Deathwatch Kill-team to travel to the remote ice world of Tal, where she believes (from notes taken by Inquisitor Malas Dyce) evidence of the aliens exists, hidden in an ancient vault far beneath its frozen surface. Of course if the mythical vault does exist, it may well have some deeper connection to the xenos shape-shifters, and their kind hold secrets best left buried...

**Beacon:** The Kill-team's vessel answers a salvation beacon from an Imperial freighter while on transit from their watch station. When their vessel arrives, they discover only a ghost ship, filled with the bodies of the crew, either chewed bones or having taken their own lives. An extensive search of the vessel turns up no sign of whatever is responsible and only raises more questions, as some crew are found to have killed each other or gone off to die in isolation. Shortly after the Kill-team's vessel departs, members of their own crew start to vanish and odd reports of either dead crewmen walking around or being encountered in two places at the same time start to circulate. The Kill-team must investigate the source of the mystery and perhaps find the creature or creatures responsible. However, they must so quickly as crew morale is deteriorating and fear is spreading like wildfire across the decks.

## Hidden Empires

In the thousands of year the Imperium has endured and Mankind has plied the stars, we have encountered literally tens of thousands of different xenos species. Some, like the Ork or the Eldar, are spread widely, like ourselves travelling between worlds and holding dominion over empires that stretch across whole sectors of space. Others, like the Dusk Stalkers or Catachan Devils, are limited to their worlds of origin, and are unique to these places. The Administratum and the Ordo Xenos have both catalogued many of these creatures, assigning them threat ratings and dealing with them as needs require. What I find more disturbing, however, than the vast number of aliens we know about, are the ones we do not, such as xenos like Inquisitor Dyce's aliens, which we have next to no information on and little understanding of where they come from or what their purpose in the galaxy is.

Moving in the shadows between our worlds, these alien races could be masters of hidden empires and unknown agendas, though we would never know. How many of the stars that glitter in the sky are home to such creatures? Places that man, even in his millennia of exploration, has yet to reach. More worrying still is that for every race like the xenos Inquisitor Dyce encountered (possibly the Lacrymole, or the Simulacra), of which we know almost nothing, there are doubtless dozens more waiting in the dark, unknown and unknowing, for the light of Mankind of stumble across them.

*-Codicier Jaelon*

# LOXATL MERCENARIES

Loxatl are a loathsome race of particularly vile and inhuman xenos that can be found working as mercenaries alongside pirates and renegades. Sightings of them have occurred as far apart as the Maelstrom and the Jericho Reach, but they have been most commonly reported operating in the Sabbat worlds region, in service of Blood Pact armies.

Loxatl resemble slimy skinned reptiles, somewhat larger than a man, that run close to the ground on four crooked limbs ending in wickedly hooked claws. They have broad, fanged heads, with yellow eyes (some varieties have been encountered with red, pupilless eyes), and a flickering purple tongue that constantly tastes the air. By nature they are an aquatic race and out of the water their sight, hearing and sense of smell are impaired. Instead they rely on their uncanny sense of taste and touch to hunt on land.

Loxatl make excellent scouts and trackers, as they can taste the presence of enemies from kilometres away and feel their location through the vibration of their heartbeat or footsteps. Extended dewclaws on their limbs enable them to run across walls or ceilings and climb on any surface, an advantage they fully exploit to strike by surprise from unexpected angles. Their presence is often given away by a distinctive smell of rancid milk and crushed mint, believed to be some kind of chemical secretion exuded in combat. This may be related to the preternatural swiftness and dexterity Loxatl exhibit or a communal warning reflex of some kind.

All Loxatl encountered have used unique weapons known as flechette blasters to Imperial troops. These are carried, along with ammunition bandoliers, on mechanical armatures strapped to their sinuous bodies. The flechette blaster is aimed and fired by a mind impulse device wired into the Loxatl's brain, leaving all four limbs free for climbing at all times. The blasters fire shotgun-like blasts of millions of monomolecular shards that shred through armour and leave terrible wounds in flesh. A common Loxatl tactic is for some members of a group to pin down an enemy while the rest climb into positions to catch the foe in a deadly crossfire.

Loxatl seem to operate in small groups of related kin led by a single matriarch, possibly the only member of the group capable of bearing young. The group communicates with sub-sonic vibrations and, at close range, through iridescent patterning that they are able to flash across their skins. Loxatl are normally grey in colour but seem able to consciously shift their body pattern and colour at will. That they seldom do so indicates how little they rely on the visual spectrum themselves for identifying prey. Las-weapons have been reported to be less effective against Loxatl than solid projectiles, their hides apparently giving them a rudimentary form of photochromatic defence against lasers.

No indications have been found of higher organisation than the kin-related brood of three to twenty individual Loxatl, but multiple broods will work together en masse with a high degree of cohesion. On occasions, a large of number Loxatl broods have used their unique capabilities to cooperatively infiltrate defences and stage surprise attacks, typically to open the way for a full-scale assault by their employers.

The location of the Loxatl home world remains unknown, as are any higher aspirations of the race beyond profit and bloodshed. They seem to have no ships of their own and rely on other xenos for transportation, specifically the Nicassar, Stryxis and Kroot. All encounters between Loxatl and representatives of the Imperium have been bitterly hostile. To date, the Loxatl have shown no evidence of influence by the Ruinous Powers but they willingly serve alongside the Chaos Gods' mortal followers and other enemies of Mankind.

| **Loxatl Mercenaries (Troops) Profile** | | | | | | | | |
|---|---|---|---|---|---|---|---|---|
| WS | BS | S | T | Ag | Int | Per | WP | Fel |
| 30 | 35 | 35 | 30 | (8) 45 | 25 | 35 | 35 | 10 |

**Move:** 8/16/24/48      **Wounds:** 28

**Skills:** Awareness (Per), Dodge (Ag), Climb (S) +20, Concealment (Ag) +10, Search (Per) +10, Shadowing (Ag), Silent Move (Ag) +10, Secret Tongue (Loxatl) (Int), Swim (S) +20, Tracking (Int) +10.

**Talents:** Heightened Senses (Taste, Touch), Talented (Climb, Swim).

**Traits:** Crawler, Dark Sight, Natural Weapons. (jaws, claws), Quadruped, Natural Armour (Slimy Hide), Unnatural Agility (x2), Unnatural Speed, Unnatural Senses (Taste/Vibration 75 metres).

**Armour:** Slimy Hide (All 2, Horde 2).

**Weapons:** Jaws (1d10+3 R; Pen 1; Primitive), Claws (1d5+3 R; Pen 2; Primitive), Flechette blaster (40m; S/3/–; 1d10+6 R; Pen 3; Clip 30; Reload 2 Full; Scatter, Tearing).

**Gear:** 3 flechette blaster reloads.

## Special Rules

**Horde:** Loxatl can be used as a Horde. (See the Horde rules on page 359 of the **DEATHWATCH** Rulebook). While in a Horde Loxatl gain the Tactical Formation and Fear 1 (Disturbing) Traits. Alter the Size Trait upward as appropriate for Horde magnitude.

**Slimy Hide:** The Loxatl's slimy hide gives it additional protection against laser-based attacks, increasing its AP to 4 against las weapons. In addition, the Loxatl receives a +10 bonus to all Concealment Tests due to the chameleonic nature of its skin.

**Unnatural Senses:** Within 75 metres, a Loxatl can locate enemies even if they are out of sight or hidden in some way (by disguise, or a psychic power for example). A Loxatl can taste for known enemies over considerably longer ranges (up to several kilometers at the GM's discretion) by using Awareness, Tracking and Search Skills.

**Wall Runner:** Loxatl count all surfaces as Routine (+20) difficulty for Climbing Tests and move at full speed on even sheer or overhanging surfaces. The GM may simply forego making climbing rolls for Loxatl except under exceptional circumstances such as taking damage.

## LOXATL ADVENTURE SEEDS

**Patrol:** In order to reach their objective, the Kill-team must pass through an area of broken ruins patrolled by Loxatl mercenaries. Stalking or evading the Loxatl through their own hunting grounds without raising the alarm is likely to be a challenging experience. Some outstanding stealth skills or a well-planned distraction will be needed.

**Choice:** Several groups of Loxatl mercenaries are converging on the trail of the Kill-team as they make their way through dense jungle to their extraction point. The Kill-team must decide whether to find a defensible position to stave off the gathering horde, push on to the extraction point, or turn and ambush the individual broods that are on their trail.

**Surprise Attack:** A horde of Loxatl has gathered to launch a surprise attack on a vital defensive position. As the mass of reptilian xenos wriggles forth, some groups split off to hunt down and assassinate leaders while others concentrate on overrunning the garrison itself. Keeping the garrison's leaders alive to rally their men for what follows maybe vital, but without some support the garrison could swiftly fall.

## From the Annals of Codicier Taelon

*The Loxatl are a vicious species that fulfil our worst expectations of xenos. Ongoing efforts must be made to find the point of origin of these creatures so they can be exterminated. The following eyewitness report from the siege of Ubrekka serves to illustrate the extreme loathing and disruption these alien mercenaries can evoke in normal troops.*

***Report begins:

The siege of Ubrekka was in its third month when the situation went awry. We had an outpost line to stop infiltrators getting up to the forward trenches without sounding an alarm. Suddenly, we were losing sentries every night. Come morning, there would be nothing left in the position—there was always plenty of blood, but no bodies. We put out screamers and directional mines, but Guardsmen still kept vanishing, night after night. Before long, our entire company was rattled, and no one volunteered for outpost duty until the Commissars put some backbone into them.

We must have lost a platoon just holding that one stretch of front before command finally sent us some help. They were irregulars of some sort, Throne Agents some were saying—alien hunters. Whoever they were, these specialists wasted no time before they set up sniper teams and waited for dark. That night, we were ordered to fire every flare and activate every luminator the moment we saw or heard any las-fire.

Sure enough, just before dawn, we heard the hiss of long-las rounds and strange, keening cries of pain. The flares went off, and we spotted the Loxatl—their scaly hides allowing them to slip right down the ruined pipeway to get into our lines, right where we'd never think to look for them. I think nearly every weapon in the company opened fire on that pipeway. Las-rounds, heavy bolters and autocannon came in from all sides. In the end, we accounted for a handful of the enemy, but I am quite sure that some managed to escape in the confusion. Emperor's teeth, but those things were quick!***

# II

## RADICALS AND HERETICS

DEATHWATCH

INQUISITOR
THADDEUS HAKK

•

APOSTATE CARDINAL

•

PONTIFEX GUARD

•

MAGOS PHAYZARUS

•

CREATURES OF
TECH-HERESY

# CHAPTER II: RADICALS AND HERETICS

*"Heretics are the worst sort of criminal. They become so willingly, and for that they deserve no mercy."*

–Chaplain Phiron of the Red Hunters Chapter

Despite the harsh but vital despotism of its rulers, the Imperium of Man seethes with anarchy, rebellion and murder, the Pax Imperialis little more than an unattainable ideal on many worlds ostensibly under the sway of the Adeptus Terra. Imagine then the situation in the Jericho Reach, a vast region of populated space, hidden from the Light of Terra for thousands of years. Without the ministrations of the Ecclesiarchy, billions of souls have wandered far from the salvation only attainable at the bequest of the God-Emperor of Mankind. Free of the cruel attentions of the League of Black Ships, populations have borne entire generations of witch-spawn. Without the psychic-choirs of the Astropaths, worlds are both deaf and mute, screaming into the echoing silence of the cold void, never to be heard. Unprotected by the might of the Imperium's armed forces, planets are defenceless against the predations of rebels, heretics and far, far worse.

Before the coming of the Achilus Crusade, the Jericho Reach was a seething mass of violence and heresy. Each world was alone, and while some cleaved to half-remembered impressions of a long lost, "Imperial way," most had long surrendered to their fate. Petty tyrants ruled what small fiefdoms they could wrest from their rivals and those populations forced to suffer under the yoke of their rule knew endless misery and lawlessness. The space lanes were ruled by those few with the means to travel between stars, and none knew whether the coming of such a vessel meant trade or invasion. False doctrines swept the region and untold billions died at the word of one megalomaniac demagogue after another. Sinners did as they pleased, with no recourse to the lores that hold decent men upon the only true path leading to the Golden Throne. Mutation ran rife. In short, the Jericho Reach was a living hell of rebellion and anarchy.

And then, all-out war came. First the Achilus Crusade and then the predations of Hive Fleet Dagon pitched the entire region into total, all-encompassing conflict. Entire worlds were transformed into warzones and the cold void was torn apart as the firepower of whole battlefleets was unleashed. Those worlds subdued by the Crusade's hosts became fortified bastions, while those it battles still to possess are cratered wastelands, carpeted with the dead and the dying. Planets still beyond the Crusade's reach are the mustering places for rebels, heretics and aliens. On both sides, untold hordes are gathered up and fed wholemeal into the endless meatgrinder of war.

On either side of the divide between the Crusade and the enemy, there are those who would see the Jericho Reach submerged beneath a star-spanning tide of blood and anarchy. Human populations under the yoke of both the Imperium and its many foes cleave yet to beliefs declared heretical by their new masters. Many factions look only to their own interests, resenting that any should seek to rule over them. Others beg unclean gods for deliverance from conquerors both human and alien. Some seek only to drown the Jericho Reach in a bloody mire of their own making, giving vent to a hatred and bitterness that would see billions die if they themselves cannot live free.

Radicals are those within the upper echelons of the Imperium's command structure who espouse methods so extreme that they appear more like some twisted plot of the enemy than a sane policy for the advancement of the Imperium's ideals. Some declare that the cyclopean edifice of Imperial rule must be torn down and rebuilt anew, that ten thousand years of the rule of the Senatorum Imperialis have led only to decay and stagnation. Others seek to utilise the tools of the enemy, turning their weapons against them. Though few openly declare themselves of such a mind, these Radicals lurk at every level of the Imperial machine. The Inquisition is especially prone to such creeds, for the servants of the throne are answerable to no man and able to explore any method, creed or philosophy without fear of judgement from anyone but their peers. When grand endeavours like the Achilus Crusade are launched, it is inevitable that men of a Radical mindset are swept along, utilising the mass carnage to further their own ends and enact their own plans. When such Crusades grind to a halt, then such men dare to step forward from out of the shadows, emboldened by the misfortunes of others.

Heretics are those who have renounced faith in the God-Emperor of Mankind, or else perverted the Ministorum's teachings to such a terrible degree that they have been cast out by all of their peers. Some have turned to old gods, those worshipped in ignorance before the Great Crusade united the worlds of Man in adoration of the Emperor. Others have turned to the Ruinous Powers or to alien overlords, practicing unspeakable rituals in veneration of their masters. A few reject all belief as superstition, all gods as falsehood. They claim that the universe is neutral and Mankind has no special place amongst the stars. These last are held in special contempt.

Cells of radicals and cults of heretics exist across the length and breadth of the Jericho Reach. Even within the Inquisition and the highest councils of Warmaster Tetrarchus, there are those who secretly believe that only the most extreme of policies will lead to the Crusade's ultimate victory. Even amongst the multitudes of the faithful, herded daily into the great cathedrals, there are those who merely mouth the holy verses, nurturing the seed of heresy that grows within their heart. Such individuals, wherever they are to be found, are ever watchful for the moment when they can reveal themselves and assume the power promised to them by whatever creed, calling or philosophy they adhere to.

# INQUISITOR THADDEUS HAKK

*"Knowledge endures. It awaits only the light of wisdom to craft it into the vessel of our very survival. It is the ultimate weapon, and I alone amongst our order know how to wield it…"*

–Inquisitor Thaddeus Hakk to Interrogator Sphisid Wor, at the Convocation of Calisi

Thaddeus Hakk is an Inquisitor of the Ordo Xenos and a veteran of almost a century of service to the Imperium. Very little of Hakk's early career is known to his peers, as he came to the Calixis Sector already in possession of the Inquisitorial Rosette. Soon after joining the ranks of the Ordos Calixis, Hakk became embroiled in the machinations of the Ocularians, a Radical faction of the Inquisition obsessed with divining the future and thereby learning what enemies must be faced before they become too powerful to defeat. For over a decade, Thaddeus Hakk moved amongst the unseen and silent courts of the Ocularians, mastering many of the arts of divination and uncovering many dire threats to the future of the sector. One such divination took Hakk beyond the Calixis Sector, through the Maw and into the far reaches of the Koronus Expanse. In a cold tomb on a dead, windswept planet on the verge of the Egarian Dominion, Thadeus Hakk faced the phantom of a long dead race. In so doing, he defeated his foe and undoubtedly saved many lives, but he was changed, his powers of divination gone, torn from him at the climax of that dread combat.

The Inquisitor wandered the Expanse for several years, descending into a madness born of his inability to see into the future. He could not return to his fellow Ocularians or to the Calixis Sector, and so he fell amongst the lowest of the low, the so-called "Footfallen" of the Koronus Expanse. Some say that Hakk forgot that he was an Inquisitor for a time, or else was conducting such secret missions that his filthy, ragged countenance and the black light of insanity shining from his eyes was a highly convincing charade. Whatever the truth, Hakk strayed into places few have ever returned from, and came back possessed of dark knowledge gleaned from carvings pre-dating the birth of Humanity itself.

Somewhere out in the void, in some forbidden crypt, Thaddeus Hakk had found a new source of knowledge. By uncovering the most obscure secrets of the past, he believed, one could uncover the secrets of the future. The further back he delved, the more patterns he perceived in the ebb and flow of history. What had occurred in the past would occur again, he claimed, and the portents were all around if only they could be read. Hakk committed his theories to parchment and dispatched messages on sprint-traders heading back through the Maw to the Calixis Sector. He sought to enlighten his former peers amongst the hidden ranks of the Ocularians, to convince them of this new truth he had discovered. In short, he claimed, if the Ocularians wished to know the future, they must first know the past.

The Ocularians' answer was soon forthcoming, and it was not what Hakk had expected. An unnamed, but undoubtedly senior Inquisitor of the Ocularian faction dispatched a kill-cell to assassinate Hakk, who only just survived. Fleeing Footfall, Thadeus Hakk plunged into the Maw and made for the forbidden Zone 15, the region that is host to the Calixis end of the Calixis-Jericho Reach warp gate. Though effectively outcast from the Ordos Calixis, Thaddeus Hakk still bore the Seal, and soon established himself amongst the senior servants of the Achilus Crusade.

Since his coming to the Jericho Reach, Thaddeus Hakk has taken every opportunity to explore further his radical philosophy, and the region has proved a fertile ground for his theories. He has established a network of Acolytes and contacts, and led dozens of expeditions into the benighted Outer Reach. With the coming of Hive Fleet Dagon, Hakk sought to enact his wild theories, and claims to have uncovered crucial evidence that the Tyranids have visited the galaxy before, perhaps hundreds of millions of years ago. In seeking evidence to verify this theory, Hakk has learned of the existence of the Black Library of the Eldar, and believes that forbidden archive must surely contain the key to how the Tyranids were defeated the last time they ravaged the galaxy. He appears not to have considered that the Tyranids might not have been defeated then at all, and are merely returning to reap another harvest in an eternal cycle of seasonal devastation and regrowth.

In personality, Thadeus Hakk is driven to the point of insanity, yet grim and determined, and utterly focused on his quest for knowledge. He has visited Watch Fortress Erioch several times, and has addressed the Chamber of Vigilance. He fervently believes in penetrating the most hidden depths of the past, and of uncovering every last scrap of knowledge to be found within. His increasing obsession with the Black Library is a matter of some concern amongst his peers, some of whom claim he is likely to bring down the wrath of elder powers if he continues. Perhaps the mysterious Eldar Harlequins are already hunting him, closing on him through the secret passages of the webway.

Inquisitor Hakk equips himself in a manner befitting his mission. He has no interest in finery or overt shows of power, and instead prefers to wear simple, utilitarian clothes. He often wears a battered old armoured vacuum suit, suitable to protect him in the alien environments into which he delves. He equips himself with the tools of the explorer, and is always well armed. Inquisitor Hakk is often accompanied in his expeditions by squads of retained troopers, each a veteran of scores of dangerous missions, as well as a cadre of expert xenologists, archaeologists and historator-savants. He owns several vessels, none of which appear on any registries as belonging to him, and it is thought that he returns to Footfall periodically, perhaps to consult the contents of some hidden repository of forbidden knowledge he is slowly building up. To what end, none can say, but it is certain that the Ocularians want Inquisitor Thadeus dead. Perversely, a small number of Inquisitors, including some former Ocularians, have aligned themselves with Hakk, and a nascent faction— the Antiquarti—has come into existence. Though yet small in number, the Antiquarti are an active force in the Jericho Reach, and one set to become increasingly influential as more forbidden knowledge is uncovered.

Erioch-Pattern Battle Servitor found on pages 374 to 376 of the DEATHWATCH Rulebook). In the field, Hakk should be accompanied by at least a squad of Imperial Guardsmen, several heavy-armed Battle Servitors, and whatever other mission-specific specialists the GM deems appropriate.

## Inquisitor Hakk (Master) Profile

| WS | BS | S | T | Ag | Int | Per | WP | Fel |
|----|----|----|----|----|-----|-----|----|-----|
| 48 | 42 | 37 | 40 | 36 | 52 | 40 | 51 | 41 |

**Movement:** 3/6/9/18  **Wounds:** 18

**Skills:** Awareness (Per) +20, Carouse (T), Ciphers (Alien Markings, Inquisition) (Int), Command (Fel), Common Lore (Imperium, Jericho Reach +20, Koronus Expanse +20) (Int), Deceive (Fel), Dodge (Ag), Evaluate (Int) +20, Forbidden Lore (Archeotech +20, Black Library, Inquisition, Xenos +20) (Int), Inquiry (Fel) +20, Interrogation (Will), Intimidate (Str), Literacy (+20), Logic (Int), Navigation (Surface) (Int), Scholastic Lore (Archaic, Cryptology, Legend, Numerology, Occult) (Int), Scrutiny (Per), Search (Per) +20, Speak Language (Int), Survival (Int) +10, Trade (Archaeologist, Cryptographer, Linguist) (Int).

**Talents:** Basic Weapon Training (Universal), Enemy (Ocularians), Hunter of Aliens, Jaded, Light Sleeper, Melee Weapon Training (Universal), Orthoproxy, Paranoia, Peer (Inquisition, except Ocularians), Pistol Weapon Training (Universal), Polyglot, Step Aside, Total Recall.

**Armour:** Armoured Vacuum Suit (Head, Body 6, Arms, Legs 4).

**Weapons:** Plasma Pistol (30m; S/2/–; 1d10+9 E; Pen 6; Clip 10; Rld 4Full; Overheats) with Red-Dot Laser Sight, Chainsword (1d10+5 R; Balanced, Tearing).

**Gear:** Inquisitorial Rosette, Scanner, Cartograph, Combi Tool, Data-Slate, Elucidator, Lamp, Helmet-mounted Pict Recorder, Helmet-mounted Vox-Caster.

**Retinue:** Inquisitor Thaddeus Hakk is rarely encountered without a group of guards and experts at his side, especially in the field. The exact composition of Inquisitor Hakk's retinue is left to the GM's discretion, but should include at the minimum an Acolyte, a bodyguard and a Battle Servitor (use the profiles for the Imperial Agent, Imperial Guardsman and

## ADVENTURE SEEDS

**Politics:** Inquisitor Thaddeus Hakk is an interesting and entertaining character for the Game Master to introduce into a mission, because he could either be an ally or an enemy, or indeed both at the same time. The Deathwatch are, at least in theory, above such notions of Puritanism and Radicalism within the ranks of the Inquisition, but that does not mean they can't become embroiled in the bitter internecine wars that continually rage within the Orders. The Kill-team could be assigned to accompany the Inquisitor on a dangerous mission into the Outer Reach, only to witness him attempting to recover xenos artefacts the Battle-Brothers can see clearly should be left undisturbed. The Deathwatch may be bound to serve the Ordo Xenos by the Apocryphon Conclave of Orphite IV (see page 305 of the Deathwatch Core Rulebook), but that does not mean they will not intervene in some manner if in the Battle-Brothers' eyes an Inquisitor overstepped the bounds of his mission. The Kill-team might be forced to make a very difficult decision indeed, and one that might drag the Battle-Brothers into a whole new world of politics and betrayal.

**Distress Call:** Another way of using Inquisitor Hakk is to have the Kill-team dispatched in answer to a distress call he has been forced to issue, having over-extended himself on some alien world in the Outer Reach. Perhaps he has uncovered some remnant of a long-dead xenos race and is holed up with his retinue and besieged by ghostly horrors. Alternatively, the Inquisitor could have become cut off behind a tendril of Hive Fleet Dagon and desperately needs the Deathwatch's aid to escape hordes of slavering Tyranids. A further possibility is that in his search for the Black Library, Hakk has come close to discovering an entrance to the Eldar webway and a troupe of Harlequins has caught up with him.

To Codicier Taelon, by the hand of Inquisitor Lord Vibalee

I commit this communication to you that you might be forewarned of the activities of one of my own Ordo. Inquisitor Hakk is known amongst those of the Holy Ordos as an outcast, one who would travel into realms forbidden by mutual decree. He seeks to uncover the secrets of the ancients themselves, and to commune with the unquiet spirits of those whose time has long since passed. I make these accusations in the knowledge that such matters are outside of your immediate concern, yet I cannot sit idly by and watch one who bears the Seal bring doom upon us all, especially in these most calamitous of times.

Hakk's myriad transgressions are too numerous to recount, and so I include only the direst, that you may be warned should he petition the Chamber for aid in his endeavours. It is of course well within your prerogative to render what aid you believe should be granted, and it is not my place to lecture such as you or your brethren on such matters. Nevertheless, I beg that you heed well my warning.

+++On Aurum XX, Inquisitor Hakk infiltrated a native death cult and used his influence to enter a barrow complex forbidden to all but the caste of mortuary-shamans. There he disinterred the shrivelled mummies of a dozen shaman-kings and removed them from their resting place. It was his belief that these corpses were somehow imbued with dark powers, which he would be able to manipulate in the furtherance of his own fell doctrine.+++

+++On the outskirts of the Melancholia system, Hakk located a rogue planetoid of artificial and undoubtedly xenos origins. He seconded a company of Imperial Guard veterans from the Greyhell Front and led them on a boarding mission. There were few survivors, for the boarding force was met by some manner of sentinel deep within the stygian bowels of the planetoid. Several of these survivors have since been tracked down and under extreme excoriation given up their confessions and made their peace with the Emperor. These accounts are wildly divergent in many details, but all agree that at the centre of the planetoid Hakk conversed with a being of impossible age, and went away infused with utterly forbidden knowledge.+++

+++Hakk has ventured into the benighted region of the Hadex Anomaly, and there traded knowledge with the arch overseers of the Ruinous Powers. No such compact can possibly be made with such forces, and I dread to ponder what information the Inquisitor might have offered in return for the knowledge he sought. Although unconfirmed, I have reason to believe that Hakk might have conferred with a Daemon Prince of Chaos, perhaps seeking clues that will aid him in his ongoing search for an entry into the webway of the Eldar.+++

I trust these brief examples of Hakk's crimes will serve as a warning to you and your brethren.

By the Light of the Emperor,

*Inquisitor Lord Vibalee*

# APOSTATE CARDINAL

*"What right have you to preach to us? You who abandoned my people to the night so many long centuries past. You have no such right; it is I who shall preach to you, and teach you the error of your faith in your so-called god!"*

–Last words of Jahoh Faas, Pontifex Maximus of Psili V (executed 798.M41)

The Ecclesiarchy is a vast, galaxy-spanning institution that unites the faithful of over a million worlds in the veneration of the God-Emperor of Mankind. Its cathedrals tower high above the cities of Mankind, every settlement has at least one chapel dedicated to a local saint and even the most ramshackle hab contains a small shrine at which the occupants offer daily praise for the continued beneficence and protection of their masters. While the Ministorum operates on a very high level indeed, gathering tithes from entire sectors, it is in fact a vast conglomeration of individual cults, creeds and local sects, none of which are in total doctrinal harmony with its neighbours. Ordinarily, theosophical divergence is contained by the strong leadership of regional figures, and rarely escalates beyond heated debate. So long as the essentials of the overarching Imperial Creed are maintained, then a huge range of local variation is tolerated. While the high offices of the Ecclesiarchy appear homogenous, this is little more than a veneer that disguises a sprawling mass of variation in modes of worship, social mores, doctrinal points and teachings.

Despite the inherent variation within the Ecclesiarchy, on occasion a local sect diverges sufficiently far from the core tenets of the Imperial Creed that the higher offices declare it heretical. Such an event is comparatively rare, and is most likely to occur when a formerly cut off world is opened up to the greater Imperium once again, perhaps having suffered centuries or even millennia of isolation. During this time, local teachings and modes of worship come to prevail over those passed down from higher authorities, and ancient, half-forgotten, pre-Imperial beliefs resurface after countless generations festering on the outskirts of society. When such a world is welcomed back into the fold of the Imperium, the Ecclesiarchy dispatches purity purges, often headed by the zealous warrior-women of the Adepta Sororitas. Those deemed to have turned their faces from the light of the Ecclesiarchy's true creed are ruthlessly suppressed, entire populations of unrepentant heretics sometimes burning on the pyres. The Jericho Reach, having been isolated from the Imperium for so long, is beset by countless such heresies, and following in the wake of every Crusade advance is an army of preachers, confessors and missionaries, backed up the Battle Sisters ready to purge the heretic with bolter, flamer and meltagun.

Yet the Jericho Reach is vast and only a portion of its worlds has been brought under the iron shod heel of Imperial rule. Dozens of worlds, each host to countless heresies are yet to be returned to the fold, and even on those planets that have been occupied by the Crusade's forces, old beliefs refuse to die. Apostate Cardinals, a general term for any one of many thousands of the demagogues active in the Reach, preach resistance to the Crusade and the enforced conversion that follows close behind it. They whip their followers into a frenzy of hate, sometimes literally, sometimes with words of bile and sometimes with promises of a blessed afterlife for those that die in defence of their faith.

Apostate Cardinals rule over a staggering range of cults and sects. Some are warrior-brotherhoods preaching martial virtues, while others are mendicant or penitent. Many are a bizarre hybrid of pre-Imperial religions, merged in the 31st Millennium with the Imperial Creed, and then diverging throughout the Jericho Reach's Age of Shadow. Some have all the outward appearance of a respectable arm of the Ecclesiarchy but upon closer study indulge in forms of worship abhorrent to right-minded Imperial subjects. Some worship the Emperor, but make all manner of wild claims about his godhead, or deny it entirely. Others worship a range of gods, from a small pantheon to thousands. A few believe that the Emperor long ago turned his face from the galaxy and those who claim to rule in his name are evil or deluded. Others venerate figures that may in fact have their roots in the long-dead Primarchs of the Space Marine Legions, including some that worship gods that may in fact be derived from those Primarchs who turned to Chaos. Some devote themselves to xenos gods, knowingly or not, and at least one appears to welcome the coming of Hive Fleet Dagon as if they themselves are its long lost children who will soon be swept up in glorious union with their creator.

The Ecclesiarchy preaches that the ultimate end of all of these heresies can only be the worship of the Ruinous Powers. It is certainly true that the Gods of Chaos are well able to plant the seeds of heresy in the souls of the followers of these outcast cults, and watch them grow into something twisted and perverted. Warrior creeds are easily turned to the worship of Khorne, while those that seek ancient religious truths are led astray by Tzeentch. Those who preach liberty and the casting off of oppressive social laws and restrictions are rich pickings for Slaanesh, while Nurgle is all too willing to answer the prayers of those who seek deliverance from the inevitability of death. While the Apostates of the Jericho Reach might not yet have fallen prey to the depredation of Chaos, the Ruinous Powers ever hunger for their souls.

## Apostate Cardinal (Master) Profile

| WS | BS | S | T | Ag | Int | Per | WP | Fel |
|----|----|----|----|----|----|----|----|----|
| 35 | 30 | 32 | 36 | 33 | 40 | 38 | 40 | 40 |

**Movement:** 3/6/9/18      **Wounds:** 23

**Skills:** Awareness (Per), Charm (Fel) +10, Command (Fel) +20, Common Lore (Jericho Reach, War) (Int), Deceive (Fel) +10, Forbidden Lore (Heresy) +10 (Int), Inquiry (Fel) +10, Interrogation (WP), Literacy (Int), Intimidate (Str) +10, Scholastic Lore (Occult, Philosophy) (Int), Scrutiny (Per) +10, Speak Language (High Gothic, Low Gothic).

**Talents:** Air of Authority, Battle Rage, Chem Geld, Die Hard, Disturbing Voice, Enemy (Adepta Sororitas, Ecclesiarchy, Inquisition), Frenzy, Hatred (Adepta Sororitas, Ecclesiarchy), Into The Jaws of Hell, Inspire Wrath, Iron Discipline, Master Orator, Melee Weapon Training (Shock), Pistol Weapon Training, Rival (other heretical creeds in the Jericho Reach), True Grit.

**Armour:** Concealed xeno-mesh (Body, Legs 3).

**Weapons:** Ceremonial maul containing concealed shock field generator (1d10+3 I; Pen 4; Shocking).

**Gear:** Ornate robes of office, various blasphemous and highly damning texts.

### Special Rules

**Dark Tirade:** When using his Master Orator Talent, the Apostate Cardinal may spend a Full Action to make a **Challenging (+0) Willpower Test** in order to affect every one of his followers within earshot.

### ADVENTURE SEEDS

**Thrall:** An Inquisitor of the Ordo Hereticus has petitioned the Chamber of Vigilance for aid in apprehending a particularly vile and infamous Apostate Cardinal, who has spread his heresies across a number of worlds spinward of the Hadex Anomaly. The Apostate is known to be amassing a sizable army of followers, and preaching an anti-crusade. The Inquisitor believes that now is the time to strike, as the Apostate does not yet have sufficient interstellar transport capacity to turn his hateful dreams into a reality. The Kill-team is appointed to undertake the mission at the Inquisitor's side, for the Chamber of Vigilance agrees that this blasphemy must not be allowed to continue. However, when the Battle-Brothers finally track their target down, they discover that all is not as it might seem. While the Apostate Cardinal preaches salvation from the tyranny of the Imperium, he is in the thrall of the Tyranid Hive Mind, perhaps having been corrupted by the touch of some previously unknown vanguard organism. Even worse, the Apostate is accompanied by a secret bodyguard of Genestealers, which are only revealed when the Kill-team finally closes on him.

**Deluded:** Word has reached Watch Fortress Erioch of an Apostate Cardinal active on the Dead world of Sagacity. The Kill-team is dispatched to investigate, perhaps stopping off at Watch Station Hestus to exload monitoring data from the station's machine core that might provide an insight into recent events. The Watch Station's logs contain transmission intercepts that suggest the Apostate has recently uncovered the ruins of an impossibly ancient alien tomb structure, and is preaching the imminent return of the "First Gods.' It appears that others have heard the Apostate's words and he has amassed a small body of followers, mostly drawn from the pirates and other outcasts operating beyond the reach of the Imperium's forces. The Apostate intends to enact a ritual that he claims will awaken the First Gods, a ritual in which he intends to sacrifice all of his followers as an offering to his vile deities. Needless to say, the Kill-team must stop the ritual, or else disaster will befall the entire region.

*Some may question the wisdom of assigning such a valuable asset as a Deathwatch Kill-team to silence a single heretic. Like a foul weed, sedition can grow from a single voice, ensnare and choke the toils of loyal servants of the Emperor; even serve as a significant (and unacceptable) distraction to the officers of the Crusade. When the Holy Ordos wish to eliminate a target with extreme prejudice, I consider the best two options available to be the Grey Knights and the Deathwatch.*

*Sometimes, the most dangerous threat of all is an idea. They are often subtle, insidious, and difficult to destroy...*

*— Inquisitor Adrielle Quist*

# Addendum by Codicier Taelon

The following is a cross section of notable Apostates currently marked for extreme measures.

**High Cardinal Jovan, Lord of the Righteous Lost:** Thought to be leading a subversive and insurgent body on several Fortress worlds within the Acheros Salient. Recent intelligence suggests that Jovan's followers have turned a number of high-ranking Imperial Guard commanders to their beliefs, which have striking similarities to those of the radical Hurosian faction active within the Inquisition.

**Vestal Vitium Arista:** Vestal Arista outwardly preaches compassion and mercy, yet this is known to be a front. In reality her followers are cruel and depraved. Arista appears to take great satisfaction in corrupting highly placed Imperial servants with her honeyed words, before engineering their downfall as some twisted mockery of their former creed. The Vestal is known to operate on Tabius Rasa, but the presence of her followers has been detected on Ries and Vespasia in recent years.

**The Oracle of Phonos:** It is not known whether the so-called Oracle of Phonos is a single individual or a ceremonial rank, yet recent readings of the Emperor's Tarot strongly indicate his or its involvement in some unknown yet imminent calamity. The last Deathwatch mission to Phonos coincided with the appearance of Hive Fleet Dagon and failed to return. It is not known whether the mission was lost due to the actions of the Tyranids or some agency connected to the Oracle, and preparations are being made for an investigation mission to ascertain its fate.

**Qessel Uwick, Underlord of Chthonic Splendour:** Qessel Uwick is a self-professed prophet, recently risen to prominence on the world of Octavian. According to intercepts logged by Watch Station Midael four decades ago, he claims to have discovered some existential truth whilst wondering lost in a long-exhausted mining complex, and returned to lead the faithful in a crusade against what he calls the "false existentialism of the feeble human mind." Ordinarily he would not feature prominently on the list of Apostates tagged for extreme measures, yet a number of Inquisitors have petitioned the Chamber of Vigilance to launch a mission against his movement. To date, no mission has been sanctioned, and since Watch Station Midael fell silent, very few details of his activity have been logged.

**Lomann Sarel, Arch Reconvenor of the Hethgard Diaspora:** The Hethgard Diaspora is a movement of the dispossessed and the defeated, the remnants of those who fled before the Crusade when it first came to the Jericho Reach. The Diaspora maintains the religious practices espoused before the coming of the Crusade, and seeks to maintain them in secret even under the yoke of Imperial authority. The Diaspora's practices are believed to rely heavily on human sacrifice, and the so-called Reconvenor is thought to be behind a number of recent attacks on Crusade facilities on Alphos, Pyrathas and Hethgard itself.

# PONTIFEX GUARD

*"One step further and you enter the halls of your ancestors. None may approach my master without my permission…"*

–Pontifex Guard Ryx to the Missionary Eras Vor (deceased)

Few Apostate Cardinals rise to power in the Jericho Reach without the protection of a cadre of highly skilled and trusted bodyguards, ever watchful for the knives of assassins sent by rivals as well as the Ecclesiarchy. Pontifex Guards represent the most devoted of the Apostate's followers, warriors pledged in body and soul to lay down their lives in defence of their master.

Pontifex Guards are the most loyal of an Apostate's servants, and they accompany him everywhere he goes. They are often the only men and women allowed to bear arms in the Apostate's presence, and they are ever ready to deal death to any who approach their master without their permission or with ill intent. They are often gifted with the very finest weapons, armour and equipment that their master can provide, and they are richly rewarded for their service. The exact form of the Guards' reward depends very much upon the character of the cult leader they are protecting, as well as the resources he himself can bring to bear. There are some cadres of Pontifex Guards who are rewarded with noble titles and riches beyond dreaming, each a lord in his own right and the owner of palaces filled with luxuries. Others have rejected such things entirely, leading a life of self-imposed poverty in return for the untold riches that shall be theirs not in this life, but in the next. Many more seek no reward whatsoever, for the only compensation they seek is the act of duty itself. Some Apostate Cardinals appear to exert a formidable control over their guards, whether by the sheer force of their personality or, in some rare cases, because they are gifted of untutored and instinctive psychic powers.

In many cases, the Pontifex Guards form not only a cadre of bodyguards but an inner circle of the Apostate's priesthood. They are his attendants during rituals and ceremonies, and often steeped in the lore of his creed. Their word is obeyed without question by all lower rungs of the religious order, and a single word from one can bring instant execution to anyone who speaks or acts against their master.

Any force seeking to assassinate or otherwise neutralise an Apostate Cardinal is doomed to fail in its mission unless it takes account of the skill and devotion of his inner circle of guards.

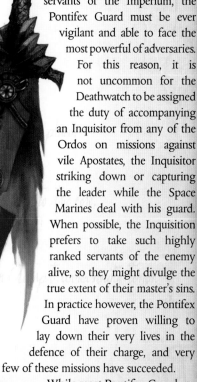

While Pontifex Guards are still just men, they are often gifted not only with rare and powerful wargear but with all but unbreakable faith in their master. Such devotion makes these warriors deadly adversaries indeed. Even when no overt threat is apparent, the Pontifex Guard remain close to their master, for assassins sent by the Imperium and by rivals never tire and are always watching. On the battlefield, the Pontifex Guard form an impenetrable ring of steel around their charge, a bastion through which any who would bring the Apostate to justice must first penetrate.

Given their outright doctrinal heresy, many Apostates have drawn the attention of the Inquisition. The Ordo Hereticus is especially concerned with putting down their false teachings, while the Ordo Xenos seeks to purge those cults that venerate alien gods or overlords. The Ordo Malleus has an interest too, especially in those Apostates who by their actions might unwittingly bring about daemonic incursion. In order to fend off such puissant servants of the Imperium, the Pontifex Guard must be ever vigilant and able to face the most powerful of adversaries.

For this reason, it is not uncommon for the Deathwatch to be assigned the duty of accompanying an Inquisitor from any of the Ordos on missions against vile Apostates, the Inquisitor striking down or capturing the leader while the Space Marines deal with his guard. When possible, the Inquisition prefers to take such highly ranked servants of the enemy alive, so they might divulge the true extent of their master's sins. In practice however, the Pontifex Guard have proven willing to lay down their very lives in the defence of their charge, and very few of these missions have succeeded.

While most Pontifex Guard are armed and armoured similarly across the Jericho Reach, a few groups have been exceptionally well-equipped by their patrons. The Crimson Sentinels of Lomann Serel, for example, have acquired xeno-tech suits of "living armour," able to repair and upgrade themselves after every encounter with a variety of unusual and exotic weaponry. Before being overcome and slaughtered to a man, these foul guardians laid low a number of Space Marines from the Death Spectres Chapter during the Battle of Screaming Shadows in 810.M41.

## Pontifex Guard (Elite) Profile

| WS | BS | S | T | Ag | Int | Per | WP | Fel |
|----|----|---|---|----|-----|-----|----|-----|
| 40 | 45 | 40 | 45 | 45 | 30 | 35 | 40 | 20 |

**Movement:** 4/8/12/24      **Wounds:** 25

**Skills:** Acrobatics (Ag), Awareness (Per) +20, Command (Fel), Common Lore (Jericho Reach) (Int), Concealment (Ag) +10, Dodge (Ag), Evaluate (Int), Forbidden Lore (Heresy) (Int), Intimidate (Str) +10, Scrutiny (Per) +10, Search (Per) +10, Security (Ag), Silent Move (Ag) +10, Speak Language (High Gothic, Low Gothic) (Int), Tracking (Int).

**Talents:** Assassin Strike, Blademaster, Chem Geld, Counter Attack, Crushing Blow, Deflect Shot, Disarm, Double Team, Heightened Senses (Sound), Light Sleeper, Lightning Reflexes, Melee Weapon Training (Power), Nerves of Steel, Pistol Weapon Training (Bolt), Precise Blow, Preternatural Speed.

**Armour:** Carapace (All 6), Storm Shield.

**Weapons:** Power sword (1d10+12 E; Pen 6; Power Field, Balanced).

**Gear:** Ornate ceremonial robes.

### Special Rules

**Ultimate Sacrifice:** The Pontifex Guard are utterly dedicated to the protection of their master, and if necessary will sacrifice their own lives for his. Any Pontifex Guard within 4 metres of an Apostate Cardinal may use his Combat Shield to make a Parry Test as a Reaction to block an attack made against his master. If successful, the Apostate Cardinal may then disengage and make a Run Move as an immediate Free Action.

## ADVENTURE SEEDS

**Bodyguard:** Pontifex Guard make ideal high-level minions for Apostate Cardinals, and the GM should generally use both adversary types together. The guards should be used as a final obstacle which the player characters must overcome before facing down the Apostate Cardinal himself, rather than as a nemesis in themselves. Individually, neither the Apostate Cardinal nor the Pontifex Guard are a huge challenge for even a single Battle-Brother, but given the combination of wargear, numbers, the Cardinal's leadership and an advantage if fighting on their "home turf," they should certainly present a significant threat.

**Surprise!:** Aside from their combat abilities, the Pontifex Guard can also be used to provide a twist at the very conclusion of a mission. Perhaps the Apostate Cardinal and his most trusted guard swap places in a pre-arranged bid for escape, or maybe one of them harbours prodigious psychic powers or carries a devastating exotic weapon, of which the Kill-team had no prior knowledge.

---

### Addendum by Codicier Taelon

Pontifex Guards are to be respected as adversaries, for while they do not benefit from the sacred gene enhancement bestowed upon the servants of the Emperor, they are utterly devoted to their apostate masters and well versed in many of the rites of combat. I have faced such adversaries on several occasions, and each time prevailed only at great cost to the mission.

Once I faced them on the world of Eleusis, whilst engaged upon a mission to identify and destroy a suspected Tyranid infestation. I was accompanying Kill-team Gunnar, moving through a long-abandoned sub-level of mouldering crypts beneath the Shrine City of Saint Kardia's Rest, when we discovered signs of recent conflict. The ancient stone walls were peppered with blast marks, and entire lengths of tunnel were scorched black by what could only be the effect of a flamer discharged at full stream. Residual psychic spoor suggested the involvement of our original targets in the conflict, and so we tracked the signs through many miles of crypts until we discovered their source, and encountered not one, but two enemies deep beneath the world of Eleusis. One was the Tyranid infestation we had come to purge, the other an older foe from ages long past—a resurgent heretic cult, an echo of the twisted faith practised on Eleusis before the coming of the Crusade.

We soon found ourselves fighting a battle on two fronts, for both factions recognised in us a mutual foe. That is not to say that our enemies formed any sort of alliance, for they continued to attack one another even as they assaulted us, and this was their undoing. In a vast subterranean mortuary-chapel, Kill-team Gunnar and I faced a horde of shrine attendants twisted to xenos-worship, a swarm of adherents of the heretic creed, and the very elite of that creed itself, the Pontifex Guard of its apostate figurehead. The scene was one of utter carnage as hundreds fought and died in the chapel nave, while my Battle-Brothers and myself faced off against the guard. We soon determined that they were fighting not for their own lives, but for their master's, who had fled leaving the battle behind him. The Pontifex Guard were fearsome opponents indeed, and possessed of no concern for their own lives. The ensuing battle was fought in the greater chaos of the confrontation between the two factions and while we prevailed, Brother Rozenn fell, while Brother Temiro lost an arm to a blow from a power halberd, though he exacted his vengeance on the heretic that had dealt it. When at last the elite guard were defeated, we left the battle raging behind us and sought to pursue the Apostate Cardinal that the Pontifex Guard had sold their lives so dearly to protect. Alas, he was long escaped, and so we called down the wrath of the Emperor, obliterating the entire tomb complex with an orbital strike from *Thunder's Word* high above. To date, the apostate has not reappeared, and so we pray him and his vile creed burned in the fires of the bombardment.

# MAGOS PHAYZARUS

*"It is not enough that this abomination dares to steal gifts the Emperor intended only for his chosen. In doing so, he destroys that sacred line of legacy, which is all that sustains our future. We will show him the price of his transgressions."*

–Brother Ramiel of the Dark Angels

The heretical Magi of Samech twist and tarnish the pillars of the Adeptus Mechanicus's faith. This desecration encompasses not only the machine, but also the Machine Cult's quest for knowledge. Few better examples of the latter's corruption are to be found than Magos Phayzarus, the Perjurer.

Once a respected scion of Forge Dimeris, Phayzarus specialised in penetrating the datacrypts of human memory. Over time he developed a vast network of cogitators that could extract crude meaning from the electrical readings of a subject's brain. While the other Magi of Dimeris were content to reap the secrets his discoveries revealed, it was not enough for Phayzarus's addiction to knowledge. In the seventh century of M41 he obtained the corpse of a fallen Space Marine and extracted the warrior's Omophagea organ for study. After years of analysis, splicing, and self-experimentation, Phayzarus succeeded in replicating the Omophagea's memory-absorbing abilities by grafting a sample of the organ into his own spine. He did not long enjoy his success before the new tissue began to fail.

Without the divine interaction with the source of the Space Marines' blessings, the Progenoid gland, his ill-gotten gift began to fade. In order to maintain his covetous hold, Phayzarus re-forged himself for a single, unimaginable purpose: to hunt Space Marines. He turned all of Samech's forbidden science to his cause, re-making his body into a self-repairing amalgam of metal and artificial flesh to rival an Adeptus Astartes. Using subsumed knowledge, he acquired powerful archeotech, and ruthlessly documented every scrap of wisdom and every verse of battle doctrine he could absorb from the Angels of Death.

Armed with knowledge and with ingenious technology, Phayzarus now subtly engineers the deaths of Space Marines to feed his dependency. He does not discriminate in his source of sustenance, thieving the gene-seed of Space Marines who follow Chaos and the Emperor alike. This earned him the enmity of the Chaos forces in the Charon Stars, and Samech's Magi ultimately exiled him from their ranks for their own safety. However, information is a valuable currency, and Phayzarus's stolen gifts make him rich. The Apostate Magos is well aware of his many enemies, and surrounds himself with the best protectors and strongest allies his secrets can purchase.

The Achilus Crusade has showered the Perjurer with a fresh source of prey and new waves of bloodshed to hide behind. However, the Deathwatch remains a favoured target for Phayzarus as its teams usually operate in smaller numbers and more isolation than a Space Marine company. In turn, the Deathwatch's loathing for his sacrilege knows no bounds; they can neither forgive nor forget the crimes committed against their Battle-Brothers.

While Magos Phayzarus tries to avoid direct confrontation with the Adeptus Astartes, his addiction puts him in the crosshairs of many Astartes targeters. Over the years he has taken drastic measures to survive and escape such encounters. His profile includes the effects of his numerous physical modifications and implants, and his armoured exo-skeleton: the Bones of Subversion.

## DARK WORKS

Below is a representative but by no means complete list of the murders the Perjurer Phayzarus has engineered.

**M41.599, The Demi-Herald:** The Deathwatch found a xenos ship drifting silently near Watch Station Klaha. Battle-Brothers boarded to investigate. Their transmissions reported quick progress through the empty vessel for two hours. However, upon the third hour, their diminishing vox signals were laced with the sound of bolter fire. When a larger Deathwatch force breached the vessel to provide support, they found the entire Kill-team dead, and stripped of gene-seed. While their armour was slagged and their corpses charred almost beyond recognition, the Progenoid extraction was performed with surgical precision. At the time, the event was thought to be the work of Chaos Space Marines, but later investigation revealed a delicate modification of the plasma drives that only a skilled Magos could have accomplished.

**M41.787, The Weeping Cradle:** In the Acheros Salient's history of blood, few battles have tallied so many Battle-Brother casualties as those to hold and retake Khazant, after the ascension of Lord Militant Tetrarchus. This period saw hundreds of desperate attempts by cut-off Imperial forces to hold their ground against the forces of Chaos. At the engagement recorded as the Weeping Cradle, the Dark Sons fought a gruelling war of attrition against the Word Bearers in a mountain pass to an Imperial spaceport. This engagement was notable for the number of inauspicious events that prevented either side from conclusively ending the battle. Every time one force seemed to gain the upper hand, rockslides, vehicle malfunctions, or information leaks put their victory in jeopardy. Several picts from the site showed an unidentified red-robed figure near the field.

**M41.809, The Redshale Gambit:** A Kill-team under the command of Watch Captain Drucall responded to reports of Enslaver forces spreading through the colony of Redshale on Sovereign. These reports were in error; the populace was in fact in the thrall of a dormant mutagen. The signs of Enslaver incursion were falsified, presumably to lure the Deathwatch into the infected colony. Over half of the designated Kill-team perished when Redshale suddenly erupted into a mob of blood-crazed mutants. Before the Deathwatch could bring the matter fully under control, agents of the Ordo Hereticus arrived and purged the planet of all native inhabitants. Their headstrong zeal erased any chance to learn more about of Phayzarus's infection, making it likely that the Perjurer will be able to use a similar ploy again.

## Magos Phayzarus (Master) Profile

| WS | BS | S | T | Ag | Int | Per | WP | Fel |
|----|----|----|----|----|----|----|----|----|
| 40 | 50 | (10) 55 | (14) 70 | 45 | 65 | 50 | 55 | 32 |

**Movement:** 4/8/12/24  **Wounds:** 35

**Skills:** Awareness (Per) +10, Chem-Use (Int) +20, Common Lore (Adeptus Astartes, Adeptus Mechanicus, Deathwatch, Tech) (Int) +20, Dodge (Ag), Forbidden Lore (Adeptus Astartes, Adeptus Mechanicus, Archeotech, Mutants, Tech) (Int) +20, Logic (Int)+20, Scholastic Lore (Chymistry, Heraldry, Legend) (Int) +10, Tech-Use (Int) +20.

**Talents:** Arms Master, Bulging Biceps, Combat Master, Ferric Lure, The Flesh is Weak (3).

**Traits:** Auto-Stabilised, Dark Sight, Mechanicus Implants, Regeneration (4), Touched by the Fates (3), Unnatural Strength (x2), Unnatural Toughness (x2).

**Armour:** The Bones of Subversion (All 9, total 12 including The Flesh is Weak).

**Weapons:** Conversion Beamer with Suspensor (100m; S/–/–; Special†; Clip 4; Rld 2Full**)**, Energised Talons (2d10+15 E; Pen X; Power Field, Unwieldy), Improvised Reductor (1d10+12 R; Pen 10).

†See page 153 in the **DEATHWATCH** Rulebook for Conversion Beamer's Damage and Penetration.

**Gear:** Auspex, ††Teleportation Net.

### Special Rules

**Hunter of Angels:** The Magos has spared no effort in studying his prey, and has absorbed many memories through his vile addiction. His ill-gained knowledge provides him insight into Astartes attack patterns and tactics. When facing Space Marines, Phayzarus gains the Step Aside and Wall of Steel Talents.

**Adeptus Astartes Anathema:** Space Marines who know the deeds of Magos Phayzarus automatically count as having the Hatred Talent against him.

**Profane Imitation:** Phayzarus's profile is depicted while he is sustained by stolen Progenoid glands. Every 10d10 days Phayzarus must perform his debased sustenance rituals, and in doing so consume an intact Progenoid gland. If he fails to do so, he enters withdrawal and loses his Unnatural Traits. As long as he is not in withdrawal, Phayzarus may consume genetic material to absorb knowledge; this functions identically to the Omophagea organ on page 17 of the **DEATHWATCH** Rulebook.

††**Teleportation Net:** This dangerous fusion of archeotech and empyrean directors flings the wearer through the warp without the need for a teleportarium. A small homing marker is still employed, and must be activated at the target location ahead of time. By spending a Half Action, the wearer instantly disappears into the warp, emerging 1d10 Rounds later near the marker. The device may be activated as a Reaction by passing a **Difficult (–10) Agility Test.** Every time the bearer uses the Teleportation Net, he must make a **Challenging (+0) Willpower Test** or gain 1d5 Corruption Points. The net may also be activated without preparing the homing marker, but this is an act of desperation as it gives the wearer no control over where he re-emerges.

## ADVENTURE SEEDS

**A Lost Brother:** The unnatural powers of Magos Phayzarus began with a single Adeptus Astartes victim. His great theft of the Emperor's gift was less than two centuries ago, so the name of the dishonoured warrior he robbed could be discovered. It may even have been a member of the Deathwatch. Making the progenitor of Phayzarus someone connected to the Kill-team heightens their personal stake in bringing him to justice.

**Trapped:** The Deathwatch responds to the distress signal of a group of high-ranking Imperial Naval officers. Their Naval transport has crashed-landed on a Tau-controlled world populated with xenos auxiliaries. When the Kill-team arrives, they find the officers long-dead. No sooner do they realise someone else has lured them to the planet with the distress signal, than their own transport is crippled. They are the latest quarry in a trap laid by Magos Phayzarus. He subtly reveals the Kill-team's presence to the hostile aliens, turning the hunters into the hunted. Can the Kill-team find a way off-planet while staying ahead of the Sept forces and Phayzarus? Will they recognize the hand of the mastermind sabotaging their efforts and locate him?

**Ambush:** While investigating the disappearance of another Kill-team the Battle-Brothers find the remains of an ambush and worse yet—the harvested corpses of their Brothers. Whether or not the Kill-team recognises the infamous signature of Magos Phayzarus, honour demands they recover the stolen gene-seed and bring the desecrator to justice. However, the Kill-team are not the only ones on the trail of the outcast Magos. A group of Chaos Space Marines are also hunting Phayzarus. If they find him first, any gene-seed in his possession will go to the enemy.

# THE FORGE-DISTRICTS OF SAMECH

The mighty armada defending Samech presents a face of unified defence, but below the rusty atmosphere, reality is quite different. The Forge-Districts of this corrupted Forge world are a fractious collection of squabbling territories, constantly warring over resources and tech patterns. Below are some of the most prominent powers of the Iron Pit.

## FORGE DIMERIS

Forge Dimeris holds that the mind is only an electrical pattern, an inferior machine spirit in organic casing that can be harnessed with the proper tech-rites. Some claim they can create psykers from normal men, and this rumour is perpetuated by the large number of psychic Magi and troops found serving Dimeris. The masters of this Forge-District are also said to pay dearly for Eldar waystones, and to possess the ability to create cogitator algorithms that mimic the personality and knowledge of a living being with unholy accuracy.

## THE IRRADIAL FORGE

Most Districts on Samech are touched by the Ruinous Powers in some way, but the Magi of the Irradial Forge have given their souls over to Chaos with willful abandon. Their Magi pursue the most dangerous secrets of the warp, cultivating alliances with sorcerers and disciples of the Dark Gods. The Irradial Forge is infamous for the corrupt, warp-infused technology that issues from its foundries. It provides a substantial portion of the Reach's Defilers, as well as the most sophisticated daemon-fused warships found in Samech's orbit.

## DESSEN

One of the smallest Districts on Samech, Dessen claims only a few jagged peaks at the broken mountains of the planet's northern pole. The small tech-coven specialises in the mysteries of the photon. Dessen las weapons sell for small fortunes, their hololiths are so lifelike that they can fool the naked eye, and their shadow generators can bring night to an entire battlefield. Owing to its small size, Dessen cannot profit from volume, and instead produces only custom masterworks of artifice that each sell for a staggering sum. Their main clientele are assassins and elite champions of Chaos in the Acheros Salient, but like all of Samech, Dessen will deal with anyone who can meet their price.

## THE LEST DISTRICT

Many Forge-Districts exploit the unusual magnetic tides of Samech, but none as masterfully as the Lest District.
This expertise was driven by necessity. The large District is located in one of the most electro-magnetically charged regions of the planet. Polarised winds and intense lightning storms rage constantly across the cracked terrain. Vegetation stunts and the ground buckles beneath the opposing forces of lodestone deposits and the planet's magnetic tides. Only by taming electro-magnetism were the Magi of Lest able to shield their forges from these forces and change the violent climate from a source of devastation to a layer of defence. The District is also home to one of Samech's largest exploratory contingents, making them a frequently encountered foe of the Deathwatch.

## THE FREE UNION OF VISION

The Union of Vision is ruled not by a technocracy, but by menials. Centuries ago, the slaves and labourers rose up and slaughtered their mechanical masters. However, lives are more easily extinguished than superstition. The people's faith in the machine's divinity has only increased in the absence of Tech-Priests. Like paupers in a gilded manse, the Free Visioners struggle to survive in a metal labyrinth filled with technological marvels they dare not touch. Their talented technomats can repair and operate some of the most basic tools and weapons, and the forge's auto-defences keep it secure. However, the automated factories and hosts of servitors remain silent objects of worship and fear. When substantial repair rituals are required, the Free Union sometimes trade their services as inconspicuous middle men to the neighbouring Districts.

## Addendum from Codicier Taelon

*The libraries of Occludus and Erioch contain uncountable tomes on the blasphemous, and it has become a necessary reflex to suppress the anger that their contents can arouse. However, every time I must delve into the works of the Perjurer Phayzarus, I feel my lips twist in hatred anew. The account below comes from Brother Elnocte of the Dark Sons, survivor of the Weeping Cradle:*

*I did not then know the visage which the spirit of vengeance has now burned into my mind. However, even then the Magos's form was brazenly unwholesome. Like a lumbering carrion beast, he moved from one body to another, the blood of my Brothers flying in the carelessness of his greed. It was only as he drew closer that I realised what sacred prize this vermin dug from neck and chest. A bellow of outrage tore from my lips, and fury brought me to my feet despite my injuries. The despicable creature whirled to face me, and that moment galled more than his scavenging. His ravenous eyes dared betray a flicker of recognition—from memories he had stolen as he stole the gene-seed of my Brothers.*

# IRRADIAL COGITATOR

*"When the box sings a pretty song; When it saves you from all that's wrong; When it adds a sudden price, you bless it once to be cursed thrice."*

—Children's rhyme from the Jericho Reach

The brilliance of Samech's cogitators was legendary long before their fall from grace. And while the Iron Pit's Magi have turned to the forbidden and blasphemous across the ages, their craft with these calculating machines has only grown. Many Districts still trade their cogitators to those that will buy, and their designs range from questionable to horrifically perverse. One of the more troubling sources of such machines is the Irradial Forge. Their cogitators are outwardly innocuous, but their razor-keen intelligence comes not just from fine layers of circuits, but the daemons that course through them.

Some purchasers are completely ignorant of the dark power inside these devices, transacting with unscrupulous middlemen or Free Unioners in the guise of honest traders. Others are versed in or even proponents of dark tech, while still others are simply too desperate to care. An Irradial cogitator is often a bargain too good to pass up, a miraculously efficient machine whose price appears remarkably low. In their nascent stages, an Irradial cogitator's intellect can answer a struggling hive's prayers. Disease, hunger, and pollution are some of the most common problems the beneficent machine seems to cure for its new masters.

While the cogitator's miracles are still endearing it to the local population, it seeks its first apostle. This person will be the seed of fear and worship. He serves as an innocuous voice for the infused cogitator's true wishes, a disciple of its impending divinity. Tech-priests are the obvious choice, but anyone in a position to maintain the cogitator's physical housing, who holds substantial regard for the device's miracles is a candidate. While the first apostle cultivates the population's reverence for the cogitator, it begins to spread its sphere of direct influence as well.

An Irradial cogitator spreads the tendrils of its neural pattern out into technology connected to its location. Installation requires a physical connection and is not possible over vox channels. This limits the rate and range to which an Irradial cogitator can spread its dominion, but that is more than enough to appropriate buildings, hives, or even entire worlds with tightly networked data looms. Using this sphere of control, it reinforces the apostle's message, causing serendipitous boons for the faithful and misfortunes for vocal opponents of the budding cult. Over decades, the Irradial daemonic core builds worshippers and their dependence on it, as they install its code in devices the network does not reach.

The daemon whispers, through its disciple, of rites that must be performed to keep the burgeoning god appeased. Year by year the runes of the Mechanicus become runes of an altogether different religion. Within a few generations the daemon holds as tight a sway over the populace as it does over their technology.

An Irradial cogitator's "body" is an inanimate machine, easily destroyed if it can be located and reached. However, the daemonic spirit within is possessed of malevolent brilliance, and has many abilities that allow it to indirectly influence its surrounding to protect itself.

## Irradial Cogitator (Master) Profile

| WS | BS | S | T | Ag | Int | Per | WP | Fel |
|----|----|----|----|----|-----|-----|----|-----|
| 55 | 55 | — | — | — | (16) 80 | 60 | 75 | 50 |

**Movement:** —                    **Wounds:** —

**Skills:** Awareness (Per), Ciphers (Chaos), Charm (Fel), Deceive (Fel) +10, Lip Reading (Per), Literacy (Int) +20, Logic (Int) +20, Lore: Forbidden (Adeptus Mechanicus, Archeotech, Daemonology, Psykers, The Warp, Xenos) (Int) +20, Lore: Scholastic (All), Speak Language (High Gothic, Low Gothic, Miscellaneous Blasphemous Tongues, Techna-Lingua), Tech-Use (Int) +20.

**Talents:** Combat Master, Feedback Screech, Inspire Wrath.

**Traits:** Daemonic, Machine (1), Stuff of Nightmares, Unnatural Intelligence (x2).

**Armour, Weapons & Gear:** None.

## Special Rules

**Neural Installation:** The Irradial cogitator may control machines upon which its neural pattern has been installed as long as they are within the same star system. A device so possessed uses the Intelligence, Perception, Willpower, Fellowship and Skills of the daemon. It gains all Talents and Traits the daemon possesses, in addition to those the host possesses. Its Weapon Skill and Ballistic Skill are chosen from the higher number of its own Characteristic and the daemon's. The maximum number of devices that can be controlled at any one time is equal to the daemon's Willpower Bonus.

# ADVENTURE SEEDS

In Missions involving Irradial cogitators, the actual cogitator that hosts the daemon is an inconsequential foe. Instead, the environment, human worshippers, and infected machines pose the physical threats.

**Spores:** The Ordo Xenos is on the trail of criminals who trade frozen Hormagaunt mycetic spores as weapons of mass destruction. The Kill-team chases one spore to a populous Hive world, trying to prevent the Tyranids from spreading. The Kill-team does not know that the spore was actually purchased by the planet's last remnants of loyal Imperial citizens, who would rather see their world consumed than in the thrall of a daemon. When the Kill-team arrives, the local authorities are cooperative but distant. The closer the Kill-team gets to completing their objective, the more equipment malfunctions and dangerous accidents threaten their lives. The Irradial cogitator and its worshippers are secretly trying to engineer the mutual destruction of the Space Marines and the Tyranids. If the Kill-team succeeds in purging the aliens, rather than finding gratitude, they find an entire hive turned against them.

**Feud:** Deep in the Charon Stars, the entire planet of Eos has long belonged to an Irradial cogitator. However, the cult of a powerful Daemon Prince threatens the cogitator's domination. The Deathwatch must launch a daring infiltration mission to retrieve a stolen datacrypt of powerful alien weapon patterns in the midst of this daemonic civil war.

**Divided Loyalties:** Pareed is a Hive world of divided faith. Its underhive denizens have kept the Imperial Creed, but the soft nobility and privileged classes embraced the Greater Good many years ago. The Ordo Xenos and the Deathwatch launch a joint Mission to help the faithful retake their world. The Kill-team is responsible for re-taking Hive Autumn. However, the hive's elite have slowly been falling under the sway of an Irradial cogitator. When the Deathwatch's battle against these two-fold heretics is thickest, Tau forces arrive. The Tau's original directive was to supplement their followers, but that may change if they discover Hive Autumn's new faith.

**Caveat Emptor:** As the Kill-team is completing a Mission on a Hive world, they discover information about an Irradial cogitator that has just arrived with a Free Visioner broker. If the Battle-Brothers act quickly, they can prevent the daemonic tech from ever gaining a foothold. However, subtly locating a human is a difficult task for the conspicuous Battle-Brothers. Once the daemonic intelligence and its minions realise the Deathwatch seeks them, they are sure to retaliate.

## Addendum from Codicier Taelon

Below is an excerpt from the logs of Rogue Trader Maximillia Prophet, whose vessel, the *Aurum Infinitas*, had the misfortune to make berth on a planet in the sway of one of Samech's daemonic cogitators:

I wanted to be gone from Crayg the instant we landed there. After long enough trading the void, you develop a sixth sense for when you're not wanted. You recognise a cold paranoia in the natives, and nine times out of ten it is hiding something that is anything but profitable. Unfortunately, my ship was going to burn its drives out if we didn't get the parts my Enginseers needed.

We'd made it about halfway through their list and managed to avoid any trouble; then we went to buy a Mars-pattern cooling unit. The salvage shop obviously wasn't expecting us, because we walked right into the middle of a nightmare. Two dozen people that had no business doing anything together—scribes, technomats, tech-priests, mercenaries—stood in a circle around a piece of tech; Explorator Lux told me later it was some sort of power core. The air was choked with rancid incense, like sweet charcoal, and the braziers illuminated the rows of parts in a yellow light. Even in the putrid glow, I could tell it wasn't machine oil they used to anoint the tech; it was blood—probably their own blood from the dripping cuts on many of their arms. Late in the sleep cycle I can still see the symbols they drew burning against the dark of my eyelids.

Needless to say they didn't welcome our intrusion. We thought we were clear once we fought our way out of the shop. Emperor's bones, but we were wrong. I know now what the lapins must have felt like in the hunts my family used to carry out on our estate. The entire hive seemed to be bearing down on us as our transport sped back to the spaceport. The people were the easy part. They were angry, but they weren't well-armed. Then servo-skulls started to dive bomb us and empty vehicles started throwing themselves at us—that we weren't ready for. I notice my seneschal rid himself of all his familiars after Crayg.

I lost several good crewmen getting back to the *Infinitas*. We tossed every last scrap of tech we'd picked up on that Emperor-forsaken world and had to completely replace the main plasma drive by the time we reached another system— but that was better than installing anything from that damned planet on my ship.

# SAMECH REDEMPTION SERVITORS

Samech is pitted with the scars of strip mining, and its crust shaved thin to feed the hungry forges. While the Forge-Districts trade for raw materials with their unscrupulous customers, they also scavenge their planet's deadly lava wastes for the wrecks and scrap from internal wars and victims of the deadly planet. Each District produces countless models of automatons and servitors for this purpose, but the Redemption Servitor is among the most infamous.

While becoming a servitor is viewed as an immortalizing privilege on some worlds, on many more it is a punishment reserved for criminals and unruly serfs. The Adeptus Mechanicus prize logic and knowledge; even for corrupt offshoots like the Magi of Samech, an un-life as a thoughtless drone is a humiliation worse than death. Lobotomisation and transformation into the grotesque, trash-digging Redemption Servitors is therefore a fate reserved for traitors, weaklings, and hated enemies of those in power. Many say that the feral intelligence of these drones still bears the tormented, malicious echoes of those now trapped in servitude.

Scholars suspect the Redemption pattern originated in the Lest District, where it remains extremely popular. However, the model can be found in use throughout Samech. The pattern involves heavy replacement of the neck, arm, and leg joints with pivots that provide almost 360 degree rotation. The torso is then augmented with four additional limbs, creating a squat arachnid profile. Most models also use epidermal armour plating, although its design varies with the forge of manufacture.

The Redemption Servitor incorporates several pieces of Samech's electro-magnetic wargear, although it is of substantially poorer quality than devices used by Magi. The standard configuration includes a techxorcism cannon—usually installed in the chest and fired through the gullet— for neutralising other technological enemies and scavenging machines that may not be completely inert. In order to reach and disassemble precarious wreckage, the Redemption Servitor contains an auxiliary magnetic repulsion system that allows them to traverse unstable structures, and its spindly limbs are capable of puncturing steel.

These limbs also double as dangerous weapons, which the savage servitor needs little provocation to use. The Redemption pattern's principal drawback is that its programming works as intended. In order to scavenge Samech's wastes effectively, they must be relatively autonomous, with the capacity for self repair and an instinct to seek out valuable technology. Not only does this cause the automatons to kill for the smallest scrap of tech, it has led to a high incidence of the servitors infesting ships bound offworld. This would make Redemption Servitors nothing more than an annoying pest in the Jericho Reach were it not for their savage disposition, and the prominent use of transmuter cores for their power source.

Samech suffers an endemic shortage of traditional power sources, having long ago consumed all its traditional fuel resources. A transmuter core allows Redemption Servitors to operate in the planet's lava wastes without the need for valuable perpetual generators or constant recharging. The core can convert biological matter into electricity, allowing the scavengers

to subsist on corpses and vermin found amidst their salvage. However, transmuter cores are more efficient at converting living matter than dead. This has led to an un-intended preference in the servitors to "feed" on the living rather than the dead. Units low on power often abduct victims to use as bio-sources until they expire.

## COMMON ALTERNATE REDEMPTION CONFIGURATIONS

**Guardian Configuration:** Magi employing Redemption Servitors for specific tasks usually replace their plasma cutters with more formidable armaments. Solid ammunition weapons are a popular choice, as an extended ammo feed can be stored in the servitor's hollow chest cavity. Up to two climbing spindles can also have chain or power weapons affixed without impacting the automaton's climbing ability.

**Retriever Configuration:** Their feeding instincts make Redemption Servitors excellent at live capture, provided the target can be recovered from the servitor afterwards. If one is employed for this purpose, a webber is usually mounted on its exterior, and a primitive auspex package is often added for tracking bio-signs.

**Skulker Configuration:** Despite a lack of physical or pictorial evidence, anecdotes persist of Redemption Servitors equipped for the sheer purpose of causing terror and disruption in Imperial populations. It is claimed that such versions have enhanced vox units that produce a range of unhallowed cries. The units are also frequently described as being rusty and in poor repair.

## ADVENTURE SEEDS

**Artefact:** The Kill-team deploys to a dead world where an unknown xenos race eradicated all life. Somewhere in the crumbling ruins of this hive lies an alien artefact of immense power—perhaps the one responsible for this genocide. A cadre of Samech Magi have also come in search of this valuable weapon, and with them comes a host of Redemption Servitors to search the dead spires. However, something older and even more dangerous remains to guard the artefact. The dark Magi and the Deathwatch both might fall prey to it as they hunt each other in the ruined hive.

**Cultists:** On Eleusis, belief in old, dark gods festers in the shadow of Hive Fleet Dagon. In the necropolis beneath its temples, a clutch of Redemption Servitors scavenge the tainted wreckage of the previous heretical society. One recently replenished itself by taking a talented diviner as its latest bio-source. This seer's predictions have led to many important victories in the Achilus Crusade, making her a valuable resource that must be recovered. The Kill-team is tasked with finding the Redemption Servitor in the infested crypts. Furthermore, at least one religious faction on the rebuilt Shrine world would rather the seer remained un-rescued, and is doing their best to thwart the Kill-team's progress through misdirection and politics.

**Deadly Cargo:** A civilian ship transporting the Kill-team to a Mission recently became infested with Redemption Servitors while conducting unsavoury business in the Acheros Salient. This poses several problems for the Battle-Brothers: they can tell something is quickly damaging the ship and slowly killing the crew, but the captain is doing his best to hide the source, lest the Space Marines question how the creatures got aboard. Once they do realise what they are dealing with, the compact, stealthy nature of the servitors makes direct confrontation all but impossible within the confines of the ship. The Kill-team must find more creative ways to eliminate the creatures. Otherwise the servitors may damage the ship enough that the Battle-Brothers reach their destination too late—or not at all.

**Traits:** Armour Plating, Auto-Stabilised, Dark Sight, Fear (1), Machine (4), Multiple Arms, Unnatural Strength (x2), Unnatural Toughness (x2).

**Armour:** Armour Plating (All 6, 10 including Machine Trait).

**Weapons:** Climbing Spindles (1d10+12 R; Pen 4; Unbalanced), Plasma Cutters (10m; S/2/–; 1d10+8 E; Pen 8; Clip N/A; Rld N/A; Volatile), Techxorcism Cannon (60m; S/–/–; 2d10+6 E; Pen Special††; Clip —; Rld —; Haywire(1), Recharge, Shocking, Special††).

**Gear:** Force shield (Protection Rating: 40; Overload Roll: 1–15), Reclaimation Cavity full of assorted scrap.

## Special Rules

**Reconstruction Protocol:** Although they cannot reproduce, Redemption Servitors are incredibly resilient, possessing distributed redundant logic processors and backup cells. The servitor is destroyed the first time it takes Critical Damage. However, if the human brain and two or more of the spindle limbs remain intact, it can attempt to reconstruct itself using nearby scrap and power sources.

†A Redemption Servitor uses its Perception rather than its Intelligence on the Evaluate Skill.

††The Techxorcism Cannon ignores all armour. If a target hit by this weapon has any cybernetics, his Toughness Test against the Shocking Quality is at a –20 penalty.

### Addendum from Codicier Taelon

Nothing that issues from the corrupt aura of the Charon Stars is harmless, not even their artificial vermin. Although Redemption Servitors share many habits with common pests, it would be remiss to dismiss them as merely nuisances. They are a mechanical plague that can be found from one end of the Jericho Reach to the other, preying on men who are ill-equipped to fend off these foul creations. One of the beasts alone is only a match for a Battle-Brother if he fails to be watchful, but they are often found in groups that can pose an unexpected threat.

Ample specimens have been recovered for analysis. The Crucible Resolviate has provided the following readout of the primary behaviour algorithm in one sample:

```
10. IF POWER LEVEL < .20 THEN ERROR:
INVALID REFERENCE
20. IF ASSESS (INPUT) > THRESHOLD THEN
AQUIRE (INPUT)
30 [DATA CORRUPTED]
40. ACQUIRE *
50. LUMENS <= 100?
60. MOD 40
70. ACQUIRE WHERE MAX (VITALITY (INPUT))
80. [UNABLE TO READ SEGMENT]
```

### Redemption Servitor (Elite) Profile

| WS | BS | S | T | Ag | Int | Per | WP | Fel |
|----|----|----|----|----|-----|-----|----|-----|
| 40 | 55 | 40 (8) | 40 (8) | 55 | 15 | 40 | 20 | –– |

**Movement:** 5/10/15/30      **Wounds:** 25

**Skills:** Acrobatics (Ag), Awareness (Per) +10, Climb (Str), Concealment (Ag) +20, Evaluate (Per)† +10, Search (Per) +10, Silent Move (Ag) +20, Trade (Reclaimator) +20.

**Talents:** Binary Chatter, Concealed Cavity, Electrical Succour, Ferric Lure, Ferric Summons, Feedback Screech, Hoverer (5), Independent Targeting, Melee Weapon Training (Universal), Talented (Trade: Reclaimator), Two-Weapon wielder (Ballistic, Melee).

# SLINNAR WAR MACHINE

Speculation and false information surrounds the plasma-driven constructs dubbed Slinnar War Machines. As their name implies, their origins appear to lie at the spinward edge of the Jericho Reach, in the stellar body known as the Slinnar Drift. Even their link to this proto-star cluster is tenuous, based on little more than whispered stories and an observation that the emission frequency of the War Machines' cores resembles that of celestial bodies in the Slinnar Drift.

What is unerringly agreed upon is that a Slinnar War Machine is an engine of destruction, given life through the sacrifice of a human soul. Although a War Machine is similar in size and shape to a Stealth Suit or power armour, they hold no living pilot. Instead, ancient transference rites must be used to imbue the machine with the soul that becomes its pilot. While operational, a Slinnar War Machine pulses with the light and heat of a star captured in an obsidian cage. This energy can be unleashed in short but incredibly potent bursts. These blasts appear similar to the discharge of a plasma weapon, but contain enough energy to breach nearly any material with minimal diminishment of the beam.

The exact amount of time a transferred life can power the construct is unknown. Speculation ranges from a few years, to a normal human lifespan and beyond. It is certain that War Machines expire eventually, as the possession rituals necessary to activate one have an easily documented aftermath. Many die attempting this dangerous ritual, although the aid of a practitioner versed in both the technological and the arcane can improve the chances of success and survival.

Even beyond this risk, the nature of Slinnar War Machines is a matter of some debate within the Inquisition and fringe groups of Explorators. Many argue that in order to function, the soul transfer must involve some manner of forbidden warp-circuitry, but others counter with force swords as an example of an orthodox parallel. This camp—which includes the Crucible Resolviate— is not so eager to condemn the Slinnar War Machines, and would greatly like to acquire one for study. They dismiss as unfounded rumours claims that the War Machine's own alien spirit eventually overtakes that of the possessor.

The War Machine's reputation is little improved by the desperate and ruthless individuals usually driven to occupy one. Most often these devices are acquired by zealous rebels or power-hungry criminals. Few sane men would ever choose to undergo the possession rites. Although a Slinnar War Machine does offer immense power, it comes only at the high price of one's humanity. War Machines have no voice, and anyone or anything the possessor ever loved is now beyond its burning touch.

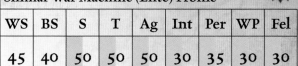

| Slinnar War Machine (Elite) Profile | | | | | | | | |
|---|---|---|---|---|---|---|---|---|
| WS | BS | S | T | Ag | Int | Per | WP | Fel |
| 45 | 40 | 50 | 50 | 50 | 30 | 35 | 30 | 30 |

**Movement:** 5/10/15/30 — **Wounds:** 30

**Skills:** Acrobatics (Ag) +10, Awareness (Per), Common Lore (Jericho Reach), Speak Language (Low Gothic), Swim (S), Survival (Int).

**Talents:** Basic Weapon Training (Choose One), Fearless, Furious Assault, Leap Up, Melee Weapon Training (Primitive), Rapid Reaction, Swift Attack, Target Selection.

**Traits:** Dark Sight, Undying.

**Armour:** Obsidian shell (All 8).

**Weapons:** Integrated Plasma Cannon (80m; S/–/–; 3d10+5 E; Pen 12; Clip —; Rld —, Devastating(5), Reactive), Plasma Scythe (1d10+15 E; Pen 7; Defensive, Felling, Power Field).

**Gear:** None.

## Special Rules

**Ebbing Will:** Over time, the possessor of a War Machine begins to lose his humanity. Every year, the inhabitant must pass a **Challenging (+0) Willpower Test** or reduce his Willpower Characteristic by 1d5. Once his Willpower reaches 0, his will is completely consumed by that of the War Machine. For the next 1d10 years, the construct persists on a dimming plasma core, following its creators' inscrutable agenda until the core finally goes dark.

**Psychic Blank:** Slinnar War Machines are completely immune to Psychic Powers, and psychic energy and effects directed against them (as well as warp powers, possession, sorcery, etc). Also, they cannot be detected by means of Psyniscience or similar abilities. Powers of this type directed at them, even if successfully manifested, simply fail. If they are caught in the effect of a Psychic Power over a wide area, it simply fails to affect them— although it may affect other targets normally. The Slinnar War Machine must spend a Half Action to activate this ability, it is not always "turned on."

**Stellar Core:** The creature radiates searing energy. It does 2d10 E damage, ignoring armour, to anyone who touches it, and its melee attacks do an extra 4 points of Damage and Penetration (already included in its profile). The creature also takes no damage from fire, and halves the final number of Wounds done by plasma, melta, and other heat-based attacks.

# New Weapon Quality: Reactive

Collision with other matter does not stop the fusion reaction of this attack. The blast continues in a straight line out to the Range of the weapon. The firer may attempt to catch one additional target within 2 metres of the first with an additional −10 attack. If the target is further away than that, lining up an accurate shot is simply too difficult.

### Addendum from Codicier Taelon

I once encountered the dark marionettes called Slinnar War Machines in the jungles of Jove's Descent. The constructs' warp signature is enough to support the claims that more than a machine-spirit drives them. They echo with the distortion of a soul—although theirs exuded the loss and pain of purgatory itself. I can only conclude that if these machines do somehow encase a human spirit, that their existence is a tormented one. Thus, on the subject of transfiguration I shall write no more.

During our encounter on Jove's Descent, Brother-Techmarine Lohk took extensive readings of the dense energy that powers the War Machines. By his calculations the core of one of these devices is many orders of magnitude greater than the reactions which drive our own power armour. He was particularly intrigued with the ability of their blast weapons to maintain an energised beam regardless of obstacles. Fortunately, he seems to have ceased his efforts to replicate it after breaching several void seals in the attempts.

# Adventure Seeds

**Intruders:** The Kill-team deploys to rid Spite of nigh-unstoppable "alien" intruders. This elite force has already assassinated three high-ranking officers on the Fortress world. The Kill-team does not have to search long before they clash with a Slinnar War Machine and several Tau sympathisers in the Black Zone. The sympathisers have turned to forbidden technology to eliminate the tyrant Lord Commander Ebongrave, and it is obvious they've had inside help. Ebongrave insists the insurrection is supported by the city-state of Tigris, which lies at the edge of the tectonic scar known as the Sorrow. However, he lacks evidence, and the Prefect of Tigris insists the accusation is mere paranoia and an old personal grudge. This may be true, but the Prefect's aide seems remarkably eager to see the Kill-team on their way. For that matter, Ebongrave's second in command continues to drop suggestions that the Lord Commander's untimely demise might be best for Spite's cities. Can the Kill-team see their way through the paranoia and politics to find their true enemies?

**Partisans:** Atonement is a planet that the Achilus Crusade would just as soon erase from the charts. In the early days of the Crusade, as it secured the Iron Collar, many worlds accepted their rule only grudgingly. Large populations exist of those who swore loyalty at the end of gun barrel. The Crusade opted to separate these undesirable elements from otherwise-loyal populations, and Atonement is one such dumping ground for the unwanted. The planet has since come under Tyranid assault, and only the Deathwatch has seen fit to answer their pleas for help. If the Kill-team can help the disorganised Planetary Defence Force re-secure several strategic locations, the people of Atonement might yet stand a chance. However, not all of the local population was content to wait for aid that might have never come. A small band of former revolutionaries gave up their lives to inhabit Slinnar War Machines so that they could combat the Tyranid menace themselves. Matters are further complicated when the Ordo Hereticus Inquisitor tasked with watching this den of traitors demands the immediate destruction of the War Machines.

**Relic:** Xenos artefact traffickers have unearthed a relic powerful enough that Ordo Xenos have predicted disaster if it is not retrieved. The Kill-team pursues them from Jove's Descent to Shedu, where the Battle-Brothers are a conspicuous Imperial presence in a den of outlaws and recidivists. The local reaction to Space Marines is one of shock and avoidance, and the Battle-Brothers could easily get distracted from their real Objective by a hundred petty crimes. Unsurprisingly, the Deathwatch's quarry realise they are being hunted. They race to acquire a unit of Slinnar War Machines for defence. Meanwhile the local scum do their utmost to keep news of the War Machines and the Space Marines from spreading to the Orks in the desert, lest what passes for civilisation be overrun with Orks looking for a good fight.

# SPIRE SLAYER

*The Soulless sentience is the enemy of all.*

–The 12th Universal Law of the Adeptus Mechanicus

A Spire Slayer is an animated doomsday device. These aptly named weapons have but one purpose: to slaughter the population of an entire hive. Samech's baleful artisans have long constructed these war devices for clientele set on eliminating capital worlds. Although all Slayers possess common attributes to make them fit for their purpose, no two are alike. Each one is commissioned to a particular hive's quirks, and given a form that can easily hide on that particular world. Lastly, each blasphemous masterwork holds an empyrean-matrix that sustains a powerful bound daemon. The daemon animates the mechanical chassis, and contributes many unique and unpredictable gifts to each Slayer. It also provides a Spire Slayer with the murderous ingenuity necessary to engineer millions of deaths.

The majority of Spire Slayers are forged in the shape of gargoyles or statuary, allowing the creator to individualise his work with a terrifying visage, and yet permitting it to hide in plain sight. Speed and agility are critical to a Slayer's success so that it can work its way rapidly through the population and traverse the sprawling hivescape with ease. A slayer's metal shell is capable of sustaining massive amounts of damage; it must be all but disintegrated before the construct ceases to function.

The elegant blades and pinions adorning a Slayer's chassis become deadly instruments of bloodshed once the daemon's essence infuses them. Although each of these creatures relishes personal slaughter, it would only be able to kill a few million victims a year if it hunted the entire population one at a time. A Spire Slayer's activity cycle is characterised by three phases: Waking, Culmination, and Waning.

In the Waking Phase, the Slayer is full of hunger and violence, but lacks the power necessary to cause mass casualties. Its strength grows as it accumulates victims. This takes anywhere from a few months to a few years as it build its power and sates its most pressing violent urges.

When the bound daemon has grown powerful on the souls of its victims and the empyrean conduits which link it to the warp are fully charged, the Spire Slayer enters the Culmination Phase. In this state it is all but unstoppable, with the daemon able to power the devastating gifts imbued at its dark forging. The brand of ruin that a Slayer can wreak is as unique as the abomination itself. Mass warp incursion, plague, and seismic disasters are but a few examples.

In the Waning Phase, the Slayer hunts the survivors of its apocalypse. The majority of its power has been expended; it no longer possesses the omnipotence with which it attempted genocide, but it is still more than a match for even a small army of humans. Furthermore, it has forged a deep link with the hive, and as such has preternatural knowledge of every living creature in its

## ADVENTURE SEEDS

**Stigmartus:** The Chaos-pledged Stigmartus forces have divined a dormant Spire Slayer beneath a populated world in the Acheros Salient. Believing these heretics are searching for alien ruins, the planetary authorities beseech the Deathwatch for aid. By the time the Kill-team arrives, the Stigmartus army has large portions of a hive under their cruel control as they excavate beneath it. It is up to the Kill-team to free the victimised people and stop the Spire Slayer from rising. If they fail, the daemon has no loyalty to the forces that woke it, and begins an indiscriminate reign of death.

**Unwanted Guest:** The Deathwatch receives news of a Spire Slayer upon one of the Jericho Reach's rare pleasure worlds. The planet does not discriminate in its clientele, and deliberately keeps no records of visitors or their whereabouts. The Kill-team is a most unwelcome presence in this decadent garden of vice, and the ruling elite stalwartly refuse to believe a word about a daemonic killer in their paradise. However, the working class who clean and serve in the world's luxurious palaces are disappearing at an alarming rate.

domain. The entire cycle of murder can easily take decades, but a Spire Slayer has nothing but time and fury to expend. Some Slayers quickly fall dormant once the last sentient being has been purged from their hive, or move on to a neighbouring hunting ground. Others still stalk the skeletons of dead worlds— reigning over the desolate fruits of their labour.

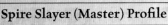

## Spire Slayer (Master) Profile

| WS | BS | S | T | Ag | Int | Per | WP | Fel |
|----|----|------|------|------|-----|-----|----|-----|
| 65 | 20 | (12) 60 | (10) 50 | (12) 65 | 50 | 50 | 50 | --- |

**Movement:** 12/24/36/72 **Wounds:** 80

**Skills:** Acrobatics (Ag) +20, Awareness (Per) +10, Climb (S) +20, Concealment (Ag) +20, Dodge (Ag) +10, Forbidden Lore (Daemons, Warp) Int +20, Security (Int), Silent Move (Ag) +20, Shadowing (Ag) +20, Survival (Int), Swim (S), Tech-Use (Int) +10.

**Talents:** Ambidextrous, Assassin Strike, Combat Master, Crushing Blow, Dual Strike, Fearless, Leap Up, Lightning Attack, Lightning Reflexes, Preternatural Speed, Sprint, Step Aside, Swift Attack, Wall of Steel.

**Traits:** Daemonic (TB 10), Dark Sight, Fear 3, Flyer (12), From Beyond, Machine (2), Multiple Arms, Strange Physiology, The Stuff of Nightmares, Unnatural Agility (x2), Unnatural Speed (x2), Unnatural Strength (x2).

**Armour:** Warded Adamantine Shell (All 9).

**Weapons:** Empyrean-forged pinions (1d10+14 R; Warp Weapon).

**Gear:** Twin Force Fields† (Protection Rating: 35, Overload Roll 01–10).

### Spire Slayer Varieties

There is a great deal of variety in Spire Slayers' abilities, as each one is unique to the creator's artistry and the whims of the daemon within. The profile on this page is representative of some of one such creature. The GM should feel free to substitute other weapons, Traits, and Talents as appropriate. Although the Slayer presented here does not possess Psychic Powers, such abilities would also be appropriate.

**Special Rules**

**Rain of Desolation:** As a Full Action, the Spire Slayer calls down a torrent of toxic, corrosive rain. It lasts for as long as the Slayer retains concentration, plus 1d10 Rounds. Each Round, all creatures and objects exposed to the rain take 1d10+5 E Damage. Armour and cover protect normally, but the corrosion eats away at such protections at the rate of 1 AP every 2 Rounds. Anyone who takes Damage from the rain must also pass a **Difficult (–10) Toughness Test** or take an additional 1d10 E Damage, ignoring Toughness and Armour. The base area for this ability is a radius of 1d100 metres. However, that radius grows with the number of lives the Slayer has taken in the last month (exact effects are at the GM's discretion).

†As normal, the Minoris Spire Slayer can only benefit from one field at a time. However, its twin projectors mean that it continues to be protected if one field overloads.

*One of the few well-documented encounters with a Spire Slayer involved the 105th Brontian Longknives Regiment during the first Blood Trinity encounter in 812.M41. Inquisitional reports from the survivors of the assault document that the enemy was armed with crackling power-halberds and pistols that fired daemonically-charged shells able to puncture even the toughest armour. This indicates that Samech may have manufactured a number of variants of the core design, each individually equipped with particular tools for its grisly trade.*

*—Inquisitor Barnabas*

## The Fate of Sagacity

To: Codicier Taelon
From: Lexographer Raffe

My Lord, by your request I have compiled what fragments my archive contained on the former Hive world, Sagacity:

Like so many worlds swallowed by the Age of Shadow, only fragments remain of the now-barren world dubbed Sagacity. Historical documents from elsewhere in the Reach date the planet's last days as somewhere in early M36, which makes it one of the first systems to fall into what we now call the Age of Shadow. During this period, Sagacity suffered a massive geological event. In the centuries that followed, many traders and mercenaries refused to visit the planet on the basis that it was the hunting ground of a mysterious predator. The few reports I have archived depict a dwindling population living in increased fear and isolation. Riots were common on the rare occasion that space vessels docked, as the inhabitants fought for supplies and passage offworld.

Sagacity's wealth and military strength during the height of the Jericho Sector created many enemies, making it difficult to speculate on whom might have engineered its downfall.

This case bears comparison to records of the lost world Minoris. Accounts of Minoris detail an opulent pleasure world, covered in clear rivers and lush foliage. The planet was a centre of trade and politics while the Emperor smiled on the Jericho Sector, and later of debauchery and heresy as Shadow spread across the sector. Accounts point conclusively to a sudden and deadly change in the atmosphere.

Similar to Sagacity, from this point, legends ensue of a terrible creature hunting the dying population of Minoris until the planet fell into total obscurity. I have found no documents detailing the location of this world; in all likelihood it is lost for all time to the void. However, a chance exists that one of the worlds charted and named by the Crusade is in fact Minoris, and that the instrument of its doom waits to be re-discovered.

*This information casts the Blasphemy on Spite in a new and disturbing light.*

*-Taelon*

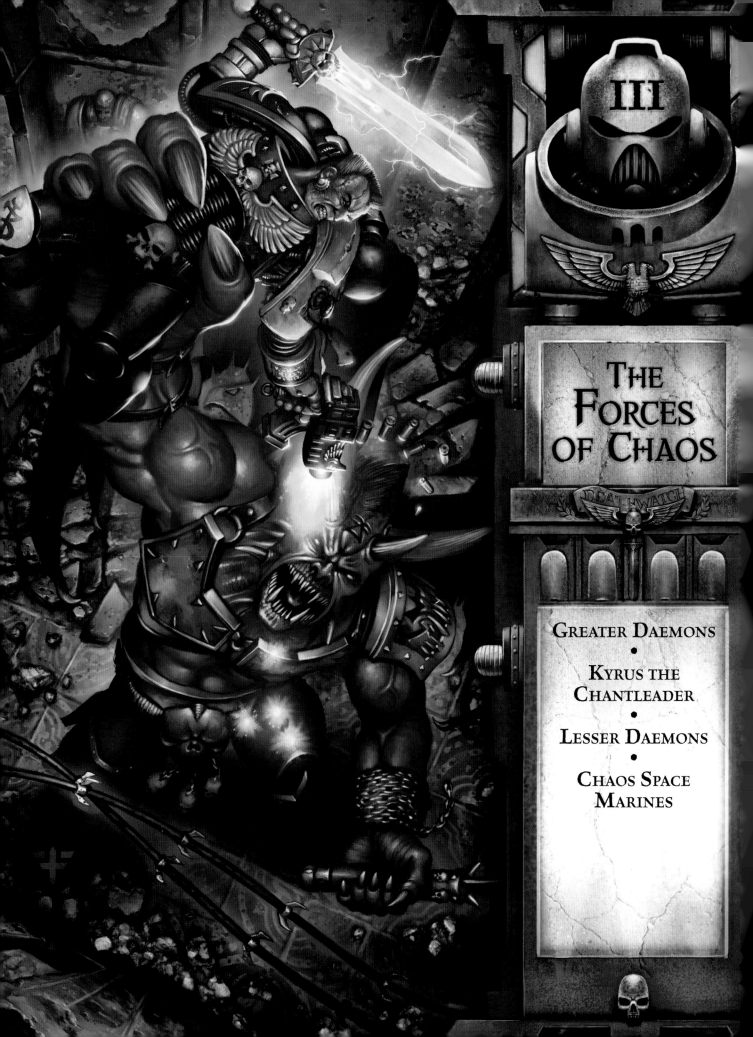

# THE FORCES OF CHAOS

**GREATER DAEMONS**

•

**KYRUS THE CHANTLEADER**

•

**LESSER DAEMONS**

•

**CHAOS SPACE MARINES**

# CHAPTER III: THE FORCES OF CHAOS

*A tide of depravity is upon us. The universe trembles under the hooves of the Daemon horde. Mankind has unlocked the doors of the nether-prison and now must pay the price. The weak and the foolish will be the first to fall. None will be spared the ghastly predations of Khorne, Tzeentch, Slaanesh, and Nurgle, nor a host of lesser evils. A temple of degradation will be built over the ashes of the Emperor's Palace.*

–*The Book of the Last Days*, Chapter I, Verses I-VI

Chaos is the ancient enemy of Mankind, the force that hungers from the Warp beyond. It is the whispered lie that turns brother upon brother, and the hidden hand that steers entire worlds towards war and damnation. Ever since the dark days of the Horus Heresy, the Ruinous Powers have sought no other end than the total enslavement and ruination of Humanity. Perhaps the greatest tragedy is that Chaos is both an unalterable fact of nature, and a product of Mankind's own passions and failures. The impossible dimension of the Warp at once feeds and is fed by the deeds of men, at once causing war, and drawing ever-greater strength from it.

Wherever Mankind has gone in the galaxy, there too has Chaos accompanied him, festering in his heart and just a word away from manifestation. While the void may once have been the domain of alien civilisations, and might one day be again, while Mankind rules the stars, Chaos is there too. At the beginning of the history of the Jericho Reach, the expeditionary fleets of the Great Crusade pushed back the darkness at great cost and planted the flag of the Emperor in the soil of a hundred worlds. Xenos empires were put to the flame, and entire species were consigned to the forbidden histories. Worlds once the crucible of alien life now lent their sustenance to human populations, and soon the fact of the aliens' existence was forgotten entirely. Having established his new realm, Mankind turned his hand to exercising his authority over his domains, of waging war against those in his ranks who refused to follow his ways. The Jericho Reach was subdued, but the Ruinous Powers were ever present.

When the Jericho Reach slipped from the grasp of the Imperium and entered its Long Night, Chaos burgeoned. Without centralised authority, isolated worlds descended into anarchy and barbarism, fuelled by the machinations of the Ruinous Powers. Despots and warlords bereft of outside sources of arms and reinforcements implored the unseen powers of the universe for aid, and it was the Gods of Chaos that in many cases answered. At first, only the inner circles of these foolhardy warlords knew of the true power behind their strength. In time, whole armies were raised in the glory of Chaos, bearing the fell icons and banners of unholy patrons and bellowing their praises openly. At length, Sorcerers

appeared in the ranks, men and women able to exert some control over the raw power of the Immaterium and turn it upon their foes. At the last, the Chaos Gods granted men the ability to call forth the Daemons of the Warp themselves. Man and monster marched to war side by side, and entire worlds knew damnation.

Nowhere in the Jericho Reach is this damnation more apparent than the worlds of the Charon Stars. At one time, the greatest of the regions' planets was the mighty Hive world of Verronus. But during the Age of Shadow, Verronus devoted itself mind, body, and soul to the devotion of the Ruinous Powers. With the Imperium a distant, all but forgotten presence, Verronus and the Charon Stars churned with the fell energies brought into being by an entire planetary population offering praises, and sacrifices, to the malefic beings that dwell in the Warp. Much later, the phenomena known as the Hadex Anomaly came into being, swallowing the Charon Stars and surrounding space, and turning vast reaches of the void into a seething ocean of warping energies through which no truly living being can pass. Some say that Verronus has been transformed into a Daemon world and sits at the heart of the Anomaly, the seat of power not of the long-lost lords of the Jericho Reach, but of Daemon Princes and the greater servants of the Ruinous Powers. It is not known if the Hadex Anomaly is the product of the Warp or something else entirely. Certainly, the phenomenon provides a breeding ground for Daemons of Chaos and some manner of staging ground for the mortal warrior warbands of the Traitor Legions. Where, or indeed when these warbands hail from is a dire mystery, and an entire conclave of the Inquisition is said to have disappeared whilst probing the Anomaly's weirdling depths.

The mission of the Deathwatch is focused upon others than the mortal followers of Chaos, yet the threat can hardly be ignored. The elite alien hunters of the Ordo Xenos are frequently drawn into the battle against the dread powers, for to ignore them is to invite utter ruin. Some servants of Chaos are highly adept at sowing discord and seek to manipulate the efforts of the Crusade to their own ends. Thus Tetrarchus is forced to fight a war on multiple fronts, and even in the face of the dire threat of Hive Fleet Dagon, he must commit ever greater forces to the Acheros Salient and in particular the Cellebos Warzone, simply to hold the hordes of Chaos at bay. Before the Tyranids came to the Jericho Reach, the task of conquering its rebellious worlds was a vast undertaking indeed, especially when that rebellion was fuelled by the worship of Chaos. Now, with the Tyranids devouring world after world, the Crusade is forced to divert vital forces to the battle against the servants of Chaos, forces that would be far better utilised against the inexorable encroachments of the hive fleet.

It is tragic indeed that a region that has suffered so greatly since slipping away from the Imperium should now be lost because its own peoples refuse to submit to the will of the Emperor and unite against the far greater threat. Yet, it is said that the Ruinous Powers care not from whence the blood flows, so long as it flows. Of all the myriad and twisted fates that await the war-torn Jericho Reach, that blood shall **be** spilled is perhaps the only certainty.

# BLOODTHIRSTER

*"Khorne, we beseech thee. We offer you our very lifeblood! Send unto your faithful servants the means of this world's deliverance!"*

—Last words of Venerati Lhorgh

Bloodthirsters are the unholy fury of the Chaos Power Khorne, Lord of Battles and Blood, incarnate. They are the Greater Daemons of the Blood God, each a manifestation of the unreasoning rage and savagery of total war. It is said that there are no more powerful masters of battle in the entire galaxy than the Greater Daemons of Khorne and that none may stand before them. They are the very essence of brutality, every blow ever struck and life ever taken distilled into a single towering form of iron and sinew.

In appearance, Bloodthirsters resemble every fear ever expressed through legends of the devils and daemons that hunger for the souls of men. While most stand around ten metres tall at their hunched shoulders, the mightiest of their kind are the size of a scout Titan. Their feet are cloven and the ground burns at their passing. Their skin is the deep red of encrusted blood. Their bodies are impossibly muscled and covered in iron-tipped barbs. From their backs grow a pair of mighty wings upon which they can soar high above the battlefield and strike their enemies at will. Most hideous of all are their faces, which are moulded in a form resembling a feral, snarling beast with fangs the size of swords.

Bloodthirsters carry two weapons, each the very epitome of its type and responsible perhaps for millions of deaths. The first is a mighty axe, the iconic weapon of Khorne. The blade of this weapon is at least the height of a Space Marine, and its haft several times longer. With it the Bloodthirster may strike down the mightiest fortress gate or cleave in two a super-heavy battle tank. No mundane armour is proof against the Bloodthirster's axe and no opponent able to resist its touch. But the axe does not simply destroy the body, it consumes the souls of those it slays, offering them as sacrifices to the Blood God. What torments these souls must endure in Khorne's realm for all eternity are too terrible to bear.

The second weapon carried by the Bloodthirsters of Khorne is a great whip. This coiling lash is capable of striking down those cowardly foes that seek to engage the Greater Daemon from afar, so that even the most cunning of opponents cannot escape the Bloodthirster's wrath.

Bloodthirsters are not only able to unleash the most fearsome of attacks, they are able to endure them too. Their hide is said to be made not of living flesh but of the hardest iron, cast in hellish foundries of Khorne's infernal bastion in the Realm of Chaos. Only the mightiest of blows has even the slightest hope of causing more than a dent upon the Bloodthirster's iron hide, though few enemies stand any chance of landing such a blow in the first place.

In addition to their warp-cast hide, Bloodthirsters bear sections of armour adorned with the glowing skull rune of their master. These attest to the blessing of the Lord of Battles, who abhors above all else the cowardly use of sorcerous powers on the field of battle. The runes are proof against the most fearsome of psychic attacks, a fact that strikes utter horror into the hearts of the most accomplished of battle-psykers.

But the Bloodthirsters of Khorne are not simply mindless berserker engines of war. They are the generals and ultimate champions of the Daemonic Legions of the Blood God. Countless Lesser Daemons march beneath them in unstoppable assaults against the enemies of their master. Bloodthirsters are masters of every tactic that leads to the spilling of blood. They eschew stealth and guile as the coward's way and direct their forces towards the total defeat of their enemies with stunning brutality. Against such a combination of rage and leadership, none can stand.

The only hope that servants of the Imperium have of not dying at the hands of a Bloodthirster is not to face one. Bloodthirsters are near the very apex of Khorne's servants and as such are incredibly rare. Their only potential weakness lies not in any deficiency of arms or armour, but in the very nature of their existence. As daemons, the Bloodthirsters are made of the raw stuff of the Warp, condensed and distilled and motivated by a will that resides entirely within the boiling depths of the Immaterium. As such, the daemon relies upon the link between the material universe and its own realm remaining strong and constant. Only upon Daemon worlds such as those thought to lie at the heart of the Hadex Anomaly are such conditions known to exist. Beyond these worlds, the Bloodthirsters' grip on existence is tenuous, and they can be banished back to the Realm of Chaos by a foe with the will or purity to do so.

To date, no solid, verifiable accounts have been found that confirm the manifestation of a Bloodthirster upon any battlefield within the Jericho Reach. That is not to say that such manifestations have not taken place, for if they had there would be few surviving witnesses left to give such accounts. Yet, the Deathwatch know that while Chaos has such a grip upon the worlds at the heart of the Jericho Reach, while Lesser Daemons stalk its worlds and while the mortal hosts of Chaos sing the praises of the Ruinous Powers, it is just a matter of time. Surely, upon some blasted battle ground such as Khazant or Vanity, the air will fill with the stench of brimstone and spilled blood and the ground will tremble with the tread of burning, cloven hooves. Then, a Bloodthirster of Khorne shall stride forth, and the slaughter begin.

## Bloodthirster (Master) Profile

| WS | BS | S | T | Ag | Int | Per | WP | Fel |
|----|----|-----|-----|----|-----|-----|----|-----|
| 99 | 40 | (21) 75 | (18) 65 | 50 | 48 | 60 | 75 | 25 |

**Movement:** 7/14/21/42 **Wounds:** 192
**Skills:** Awareness (Per), Command (Fel) +20, Dodge (Ag), Forbidden Lore (Daemons, Warp), Intimidate (S) +20, Speak Language (All known languages).
**Talents:** Ambidextrous, Berserk Charge, Combat Master, Crippling Strike, Crushing Blow, Dual Strike, Frenzy, Furious Assault, Hammer Blow, Heightened Senses (All), Preternatural Speed, Resistance (Psychic Powers), Swift Attack, Thunder Charge, Two-Weapon wielder (Melee), Inspire Wrath.
**Traits:** Brutal Charge, Daemonic (TB 12), †Daemonic Presence, Fear 4 (Terrifying), Dark Sight, Flyer (10), From Beyond, Size (Massive), Unnatural Strength (x3), Unnatural Toughness (x2), Strong Minded, The Stuff of Nightmares, Touched by the Fates (3), Warp Instability, Warp Weapon.
†**Daemonic Presence:** All enemies within 25 metres of a Bloodthirster suffer a −20 penalty to Willpower Tests in the area.
**Armour:** Iron Hide (All 13).
**Weapons:** Axe of Khorne (3d10+21 R; Pen 10; Felling (2), Devastating (3), Razor Sharp, Unbalanced), Whip of Khorne (Range 10m; 1d10+21 R; Pen 8; Snare, Tearing).

### Special Rules
**Emissary for the Skull Throne:** Unless the GM determines otherwise, a Bloodthirster is always accompanied by 2d10 lesser Khornate daemons, such as Bloodletters.

## ADVENTURE SEED

**Uncertain Allies:** The Kill-team is serving alongside a group of veteran Imperial Guardsmen belong to the elite Mortressan Highlanders. These stone cold killers are bloody handed indeed, but the Battle-Brothers have reason to suspect something is awry. Throughout the course of the joint mission the Highlanders become ever more savage and frenzied with each passing battle. While the Kill-team does not know it as yet, the Mortressans have established a warrior lodge dedicated to Khorne, and sold their souls to the Blood God in return for his blessings on the field of battle. How will the Battle-Brothers deal with this revelation when it is discovered? Will they be forced to face both their original foe and their erstwhile allies at once?

### USING BLOODTHIRSTERS

Bloodthirsters are such horrific adversaries that they should only be used against a Kill-team truly ready to face one. This is not simply a matter of the power level of the Battle-Brothers, but of relative rarity. A Bloodthirster should only be encountered at the climax of a campaign, and only after the Battle-Brothers and faced and overcome every other servant of the Blood God. To make things even more dramatic, the Greater Daemon could be fielded as part of a huge, climactic battle and its minions given the Fanatical Devotion or Spawn Horde Trait (see page 136). While entire regiments of Imperial troops might be taking part in this grand battle, ultimate victory or defeat should rest with the Kill-team, and the fate of worlds should be held in their hands. If they defeat the Bloodthirster, its legions will be banished and the world saved. If they do not, they may never live to see the planet transformed into a Daemon World of Chaos.

All Khornate daemons who can see the Bloodthirster gain the Blademaster Talent and Brutal Charge Trait, if they do not already have them.
**Servant of Slaughter:** All Critical Effects involving gore or blood (such as requiring an Agility Test not to fall over) do not apply to creatures of Khorne.
**Supreme Warrior:** When using the All Out Attack Action, Bloodthirsters may make a single melee attack that may not be dodged or parried. A Bloodthirster may perform this attack a number of times per combat equal to his Intelligence Bonus (normally 4).

## Addendum by Codicier Taelon

*I have witnessed the aftermath of a battle in which a Bloodthirster was said to have taken part, long before my service in the Deathwatch. While serving with the Death Spectres on the lost world of New Muin, my company received pleas for aid from the local defence forces and made haste to intervene. We were too late, for upon making planetfall we found only a plain of blood-soaked bones so vast it stretched from horizon to horizon. Not a single living soul walked the surface, every one having been offered up to the Blood God. Being gifted of the psyker's art, I could hear their screams upon the ether, countless millions calling out for deliverance that would never come. In truth, I know that a single company could not have altered the fate of New Muin and an attempt to have done so would have been a grave waste. Yet, those screams still come to me, upon the field of battle when the stink of blood is in the air and cries of rage come unbidden to men's lips…*

# GREAT UNCLEAN ONE

*"And there shall come seven plagues, and in them you shall read his works, writ in black bile and red ruin across the land. And he shall come amongst you; all shall feel his touch, and wither. In righteous joy, he bestows these gifts. Rejoice!"*

–Imperial Astropath Sythia Zale, moments before her execution

Great Unclean Ones are the harbingers of Nurgle, god of rot and ruin—his greatest servants, bearers of his most sacred plagues and poxes. They are squat mountains of ruptured, roiling flesh, covered in open sores that weep with streams of pus. They burst through the veil with an ear-shattering howl of glee, delighted to walk the earth once more, spreading their bounty.

The Greater Daemons of Nurgle are not subtle. Their appearances on the mortal plane are heralded by disease and desolation on a planetary scale. If an incursion is left unchecked, whole worlds can go dark: their populations reduced by six-sevenths, their feeble leaders filthy and raving, their very cities collapsing around them. Through it all waddles the beaming, bile-slicked plague-father, bestowing his blessings, borne along on a living tide of chortling, chattering Nurglings. Great Unclean Ones are beings of decay and entropy made manifest, and before them the works of man are but castles made of sand, perched on the edge of a storm-wracked sea.

In battle, Great Unclean Ones wield enormous blades and maces of iron, crude, corroded cleavers and immense plague flails—each one dripping with pestilence.

Those that survive the wave of desolation that accompanies a Great Unclean One often become its faithful slaves. Wracked by disease, bloated by corpse gasses, stripped of their loved ones and surrounded by the dead and dying, many plague thralls give themselves over to their suffering, venerating and worshipping the very ailments that brought them low. Perversely, those who embrace Nurgle's foul contagions are made stronger by them, their ravaged bodies inured to pain, their rotting forms all but impervious to greater harm. The thriving colonies of bacteria gestating within their bloated bodies grant unholy regenerative abilities to their hosts, sealing gaping wounds in seconds and expanding ever-outward, until the creatures that were once men remain little more than disease-wracked shells, foetid human cauldrons of pox and pestilence.

Great Unclean Ones are always accompanied by—and infested with—thousands of gibbering, diminutive Nurglings, pint-sized daemons of mischief and malice who caper about madly, tongues lolling, their fat bodies supported by improbably spindly legs. Great Unclean Ones dote on these scabrous sprites, bouncing them on their knees and scratching behind their malformed ears. Even the rotting hulks of their bodies are colonized by Nurglings; these tiny creatures dwell in the burst carbuncles and rank wounds that cover a Great Unclean One, and particularly love to nest within its great, rent belly, burrowing deep inside the steaming intestines that hang in long, gore-slicked loops from its body. A Great Unclean One looks upon this cackling horde with munificence and paternal love, and Nurglings are quick to defend their "father" when he is threatened. Unwary foes are often dragged down by the murderous wave of shrieking, biting daemons that billows forth from the body of a Great Unclean One the instant it is attacked.

Natural-born carrion creatures also number among the Greater Daemon of Nurgle's faithful friends. Rats, vultures, worms, crows and sky-blackening clouds of flies trail in its jolly wake, hideously multiplied in both size and number.

Great Unclean Ones typically take the form of gargantuan, immensely fat humanoids, hot intestines dribbling out of huge tears in their enormous bellies. Their horrific girth is supported by two impossibly small and atrophied-looking legs, and their bulbous heads are crowned by the enormous antlers of a stag. Their suppurating, sore-covered bodies are host to every disease ever catalogued by man, and many more besides, and their stench can be detected from miles away. In perverse contrast with their appearance, their manner is jovial and kind; they are the very picture of mirth and good cheer. Even surrounded by the pitiful moaning of the sick and dying, they smile with pure-hearted benevolence, and their long, pus-coated tongues dangle from toothy face-splitting grins.

To look upon a Great Unclean One is to gaze upon the face of decay, to realize that all things must break down, must collapse and congeal, must rot and rust and fall to ruin, that the great works of man will one day vanish from the universe, and the stars themselves must one day die.

## Great Unclean One (Master) Profile

| WS | BS | S | T | Ag | Int | Per | WP | Fel |
|----|----|----|----|----|----|----|----|----|
| 64 | 42 | (18) 65 | (21) 77 | 40 | 61 | 43 | (12) 61 | 35 |

**Movement:** 4/8/12/24  **Wounds:** 273

**Skills:** Awareness (Per), Scrutiny (Per) +10, Search (Per), Forbidden Lore (Warp, Daemonology) (Int), Deceive (Fel), Speak Language (All known languages).

**Talents:** True Grit, Strong Minded, Bulging Biceps, Crushing Blow, Die Hard.

**Traits:** Crawler, Daemonic (TB 14), †Daemonic Presence, Dark Sight, Fear 4 (Terrifying), From Beyond, Regeneration (5), Size (Massive), Unnatural Strength (x3), Unnatural Toughness (x2), Unnatural Willpower (x2), Warp Instability.

†**Daemonic Presence:** All enemies within 25 metres of a Great Unclean One suffer a –20 penalty to Willpower Tests in the area.

**Weapons:** Tooth and Nail (1d10+21 R; Pen 2; Felling (2), Toxic), Plague Blade (2d10+21 R; Pen 6; Felling (2), Toxic).

### Special Rules

**Cloud of Flies:** All those within 5 metres take a –10 penalty to Weapon Skill and Ballistic Skill Tests as choking clouds of buzzing, biting flies attack every exposed inch of flesh.

**Lord of Decay:** Great Unclean Ones often know a number of psychic powers; the GM should select any appropriate powers from the **DEATHWATCH** Rulebook and the Chaos Psychic Powers section on page 127.

## ADVENTURE SEEDS

**Aftermath:** The Kill-team is sent to investigate the mysterious aftermath of a horrific industrial accident on an intensely-polluted Hive World. A chemical factory within one of the hives exploded, collapsing part of the structure and sending toxic fumes throughout the hive. Accidents of this nature are regrettable but far from uncommon, and ordinarily of concern to the rulers of the Hive world only in terms of lost production. This time, however, the contagion seems to be spreading, as level after level of the hive goes dark, all communication cut off. In reality, the accident was engineered by the secret servants of Nurgle to disguise the manifestation of a Great Unclean One, who now rules over the diseased cultists and gang members of the lower hive.

**Prophecy:** Deep within the vaults of Watch Fortress Erioch, the Kill-team discovers an ancient and long-forgotten prophecy warning of a Great Plague, destined to sweep through the Jericho Reach, reducing world after world to festering charnel houses of disease and decay. The prophecy seems to point to a great architect behind this plague, a creature that—if left unchecked—will soon put its dire plan into motion…

**Lord of Corruption:** A Great Unclean One may inflict Righteous Fury. However, instead of rolling an additional 1d10 Damage, the victim instead suffers 1d10 permanent Toughness Damage.

## Addendum by Codicier Taelon

*The stench. It is seared into my memory, above everything else. Dispatched to investigate the disappearance of another Kill-team near a small mining colony, we arrived on-world on a hot summer's day, and the smell nearly made me collapse. The entire colony had succumbed to some sort of great contagion; the white walls of their hab-units were slicked with blood and slime, and the bodies of the dead and dying were everywhere. My fears were confirmed when I encountered a group of survivors near the entrance to the mineshaft: they had given themselves over completely to the dark gods, chanting psalms and hymns to the leader, a figure they called "The Rotting King". Bolters took care of these plague-maddened miners, but deep within the bowels of that foetid mine we gave battle to their ruler—a hideous greater daemon of Nurgle. Despite the support of a Dreadnought and a double-strength Kill-team, I survived the battle with barely half of my Battle-Brothers intact… and many of those who lived would never be the same. I was lucky; my enviro-sealed armour kept the worst of the contagion at bay, and my body was strong enough to endure the rest. Even so, I was quarantined in Watch Fortress Erioch for a month before I was declared free of taint.*

SEALED
DATA

# KEEPER OF SECRETS

*"Better to pluck out your eyes and fight blind than to look upon such a vile, blasphemous monstrosity."*

–Chaplain Trakus, White Scars Chapter

Keepers of Secrets are the Greater Daemons of Slaanesh, the so-called Prince of Chaos. Like their master, these Greater Daemons are the ultimate despoilers, revelling in the corruption of their foes. Keepers of Secrets seek not only to lead astray, but to debase their victims, reducing once proud champions of Humanity to twisted vile things, barely recognisable to their erstwhile kin. To turn a pure and innocent soul to the worship of Slaanesh is the ultimate delicacy for the Keepers of Secrets, the further the fall and the deeper the corruption, the sweeter their satisfaction.

In appearance, these Greater Daemons vary enormously, although all are possessed of a bizarrely alien and utterly disturbing countenance. In size they range from several times the height of a man to ten or more metres. Their limbs are lithe and often multi-jointed, enabling swift and unpredictable movement. They typically have four or more arms, one pair terminating in cruelly pointed claws and the other in razor sharp pincers or blades. Most vile of all are the daemons' faces. Some are strangely bovine, while others are elongated and alien. A few are almost human, androgynous and terrifyingly beguiling.

Only the staunchest of mortal beings to set eyes upon these beasts sees their true form. Keepers of Secrets are enshrouded in an aura of scintillating illusion, entrapping the souls of even the strongest of foes. The beguiled drops his weapon and stands dumb-founded in the midst of raging battle, his arms spread wide as his doom approaches. Those not dragged down in the cruel embrace of the Daemonettes that invariably accompany the Greater Daemons are crushed beneath its hooves, cut in two by its blade or blasted by its sorcery. The most unfortunate may meet another end entirely, and not one that sane men would dwell upon.

While the greatest of the Keeper of Secrets weapons is its beguiling nature, they commonly bear mighty warp-forged blades with which to strike down those few not ensorcelled by their infernal beauty. Such blades are commonly several metres long and encrusted with fell runes that burn the eye and sear the soul. The weapons phase in and out of reality, bypassing armour and slicing through the flesh within. At their touch, the soul is drained from the body to be carried away to the dread Realm of Chaos, there to be tormented for all eternity by the cruel caresses of Slaanesh's servants.

In combat, the Keepers of Secrets display speed and guile that few can defeat, made all the harder to combat by the beguiling aura that assails their foes. They are impossibly fast, their form shifting and blurring as they dart and in and out, every touch dealing blessed torment. In addition to their speed, the Keepers of Secrets bring prodigious sorcerous powers to bear on their enemies, blasting them with the raw energy of the warp or reducing them to gibbering fools. They are capricious and cruel, preferring where possible to twist and corrupt rather than simply kill. Foes become playthings, their souls the prize in a monstrous game of corruption and

defilement. Nothing is sweeter to a Keeper of Secrets than to deliver to its master the soul of one of Humanity's greatest champions. They will stay the killing blow indefinitely if they see a chance of doing so, wearing the enemy down body and soul until ready to strike.

On the field of battle, the Keepers of Secrets are rarely encountered alone. They are invariably accompanied by swarms of prancing Daemonettes, the Lesser Daemons of the Prince of Chaos. These cavort and dance across the killing fields, singing the praises of their master and dealing death to the armies of men. Worst of all, the Daemonettes often avoid killing the enemy's greatest champions and leaders, slaying or corrupting lesser troops as a delectable taster of the glorious spectacle that is the coming of the Keeper of Secrets. The champions are taunted and teased by the Daemonettes until the battlefield is carpeted with twitching dead. And then, the Greater Daemon appears, and the main course begins.

Ever since the launching of the Achilus Crusade, the servants of the Ordo Malleus have maintained a watch for the presence of the Keepers of Secrets within the Jericho Reach. Of late, an unnamed Inquisitor has made several visits to the Brass Tower at Watch Fortress Erioch, conferring with the Inquisitor of the Chamber. Several recent readings of the Emperor's Tarot have foretold of the coming of such an adversary to the region, and the attentions of the Chamber of Vigilance are turning towards this gravest of threats.

## Keeper of Secrets (Master) Profile

| WS | BS | S | T | Ag | Int | Per | WP | Fel |
|----|----|----|----|----|-----|-----|-----|-----|
| 81 | 42 | (18) 65 | (14) 72 | (12) 69 | 65 | 75 | 75 | (14) 75 |

**Movement:** 8/16/24/48      **Wounds:** 180

**Skills:** Acrobatics (Ag), Awareness (Per) +20, Charm (Fel) +20, Command (Fel) +20, Deceive (Fel) +20, Dodge (Ag) +20, Forbidden Lore (Daemons, Warp) (Int), Intimidate (S) +20, Invocation (Will) +10, Psyniscience (Per) +20, Scrutiny (Per) +20, Search (Per), Speak Language (All known languages).

**Talents:** Counter Attack, Crippling Strike, Heightened Senses (All), Lightning Attack, Lightning Reflexes, Psy Rating (8), Preternatural Speed, Sprint, Step Aside, Sure Strike, Swift Attack, Wall of Steel.

**Traits:** Aura of Acquiescence, Daemonic (TB 14), †Daemonic Presence, Dark Sight, Fear 4 (Terrifying), From Beyond, Improved Natural Weapons (Daemonic Claws), Multiple Arms, Size (Massive), Unnatural Fellowship (x2), Unnatural Strength (x3), Strong Minded, The Stuff of Nightmares, Touched by the Fates (3), Warp Instability, Warp Weapon.

**†Daemonic Presence:** All enemies within 25 metres of a Keeper of Secrets suffer a −20 penalty to Willpower Tests in the area.

**Weapons:** Etherblade (2d10+18 R; Pen 8; Unwieldy; Warp Weapon), Daemonic Claws (1d10+20 R; Pen 4; Warp Weapon).

### Special Rules

**Aura of Acquiescence:** All Greater Daemons of Slaanesh are enshrouded by a beguiling, soporific aura that renders even the most chaste and devout of the Emperor's servants into beings of ravening depravity or reduces the strongest men to drooling wrecks. All enemies within 5m suffer a −20 penalty to all Weapon Skill, Ballistic Skill, and Willpower Tests (including Focus Power Tests involving Willpower) against the Keeper of Secrets. This effect stacks with Daemonic Presence.

**Spirit Swallower:** Every time the Keeper of Secrets inflicts Damage on a living creature (i.e., not against foes with the Daemonic or Machine Traits), it immediately recovers an amount of Damage equal to one half (rounding up) the Damage it has inflicted. This healing ability may not take the Greater Daemon above its starting number of Wounds. In addition, if the Keeper of Secrets inflicts Damage upon a player character that survives the encounter, the character suffers 3d10 Corruption Points.

## Adventure Seeds

**Extraction:** The Kill-team has been assigned to extricate a senior Imperial Commander and his noble clan from a world that is about to fall to the advance of Hive Fleet Dagon. The world has only been in Imperial control for a couple of years, and the newly installed leadership has become corrupted by a deeper taint ingrained in the populace. The new ruling class has fallen entirely to the worship of Slaanesh, and it is through their lax devotion to their duties that the world's defences have collapsed and the Tyranids have attacked so easily. The Kill-team only discovers the nobles' true allegiance as the world falls. At that point, the Imperial Governor reveals his patron, a Keeper of Secrets, who rends apart the thin veil of reality and manifests in the midst of the fighting. The Kill-team must defeat this foe, either rallying what few local defences can be diverted from the battle against the invading Tyranids, or perhaps engineering events so that both sets of adversaries must face one another while the Kill-team executes the traitor governor and exfiltrates.

### Using a Keeper of Secrets

Just like the rage-fuelled Bloodthirsters of Khorne, Keepers of Secrets should only be introduced into a campaign once the Player Characters have reached a decent level of experience. Such Greater Daemons are mercifully rare, but their appearance on the battlefields of the Jericho Reach can only be a prelude to a full scale Daemonic Incursion. One way of introducing the Keeper of Secrets into a Deathwatch campaign is to have its influence felt long before it makes an actual appearance on the battlefield. Corrupted forces, both allied and enemy should provide a clue that all is not as it should be, and this corruption should manifest closer and closer to the Battle-Brothers until a trusted (non-Adeptus Astartes) NPC is revealed to be beguiled. At that point, the Kill-team may be forced to intervene to halt a summoning ritual that would open a catastrophic breach into the Warp and bring about the doom of an entire world.

## Addendum by Codicier Taelon

*The archive stacks contain a sealed sub-layer, established three millennia ago by a predecessor and accessible to those of the Librarius. This archive is warded with twelve data sentinels, each of which is keyed to initiate a full-sequence meta-warning should it be accessed by anyone not authorised to do so. Upon activation, each ward displays the direst warning against proceeding further that I have yet seen in the archive. These warnings were compiled by long-dead Librarians of our order, and warn of the consequences of viewing the data concealed behind the final ward. They speak of accounts and vid-logs of the Greater Daemons of the so-called Prince of Pleasure, words and images that, according to the warnings, are sufficient to sear the soul and reduce the greatest of our Order to gibbering fools. To date, I have not had cause to penetrate past the Twelfth Seal, a fact for which I thank the Emperor and the Primarch.*

# LORD OF CHANGE

*"Yesss! Just as planned!"*

–Spoken by Xi'aquan, Lord of Change, in its death throes

Lords of Change are creatures borne from some impossible nightmare, immense birdlike daemons with shimmering skin, wicked curved beaks and multicoloured, spectrum-shattering wings. Those who gaze upon these twisted prisms of pure magic begin to feel their sanity shred and reason slip away. Faced by a being of change incarnate, bedrock beliefs crumble and twist, and the mind seeks firm purchase in vain.

Treachery, deceit, capriciousness: these are the hallmarks of the Lords of Change. Tzeentch's greatest servants weave scheme upon scheme, a dense tangle of intermingling threads, so convoluted and eon-spanning that none can grasp their true purpose.

A confrontation with a Lord of Change is likely to occur when and where the creature wills it. Few have ever managed to get the drop on these servants of Tzeentch, for the Changer of Ways is the master of destiny itself, and his greatest servants possess a portion of that power.

Lords of Change tend to work behind the scenes, pulling puppet strings from the shadows. So subtle are these manipulations, and so skilled, that often the playthings of a Lord of Change remain unaware that they are in the thrall of a deadly Daemon. Secret cults, heresies, revolutionaries, and even planetary governors have all fallen under the thrall of a Lord of Change at one point or another. Even Tzeentch's bitterest foes can be manipulated into fulfilling the Great Deceiver's ends—under his greatest daemons' careful guidance, brother can be turned against brother, friend against friend, and the most zealous of Inquisitors can stumble from the path of righteousness. To confront a Lord of Change is to wander through a fog-shrouded mire of lies, ever unsure that one's actions are correct, one false step away from sinking irrevocably.

On the rare instances that a Lord of Change is bested, its schemes sundered and its plans laid to ruin, it will fight like a cornered animal, drawing upon its incredible sorcerous powers to fell its foes directly where deceit and deception have failed. Lords of Change are the greatest Sorcerers in the galaxy, and their mastery of magic is without peer. The mightiest psychic powers and spells employed by feeble human psykers and Sorcerers are the idle cantrips of a Lord of Change, for a Greater Daemon of Tzeentch is a creature of undiluted warp energy and the mortal world quakes at its touch. With the merest flick of an elegantly tapered claw, bodies mutate and writhe, buildings twist and melt, and beings of madness and horror spring forth, cackling, from running rivers of flesh. Nothing that is done cannot be undone; nothing that is made cannot be unmade. To prevail against a Lord of Change, one's convictions must be firmer than the foundations of the earth.

Lords of Change are deceptively delicate-looking. Their long, spindly bodies are topped by a savage, cruel bird's head. Great feathered wings extend from their shoulder blades, glittering and glinting with a thousand impossible colours. Their bones are hollow, and despite their enormous size, they barely seem capable of supporting their own weight, often leaning upon immense staffs, etched with innumerable eldritch signs and sigils.

Their appearance, however, is yet another ruse: Lords of Change are fearsome fighters, serpent-quick with skin like iron. They are also lore-masters, and possess a thorough knowledge of the great feints and fighting techniques of the galaxy. To fence with a Lord of Change is to invite one's own ruin; many overzealous warriors have been felled by their vicious claws, cruel curved beaks and terrible, reaping staves, disemboweled before they could even lift their blades.

Though a Lord of Change boasts many human slaves among his infernal retinue, it can also call upon a dreadful menagerie of Lesser Daemons when its back is up against the wall. The amorphous, spindle-limbed Pink and Blue horrors writhe with the boundless, ever-shifting energy of unbridled Chaos, warping the world around them as they gibber and shriek.

The tubular Flamers of Tzeentch resemble hideous living columns, studded with still-melting mouths and faces and festooned with long, spindly arms. The gouts of magical, multi-coloured fire they spew from their mouth-like hands burn, freeze, blister, mutate and vaporize their enemies.

High above, drifting on the currents of the aethyr, sail the manta-like Screamers of Tzeentch, twisted rays that trail slashing tendrils below their long, flat, strangely sinuous bodies. These tentacles are razor sharp, capable of flaying the flesh from even the most heavily-armoured foe.

## Lord of Change (Master) Profile

| WS | BS | S | T | Ag | Int | Per | WP | Fel |
|----|----|----|----|----|----|----|----|----|
| 54 | 53 | (18) 65 | (12) 65 | 54 | (21) 78 | (12) 65 | (16) 81 | 54 |

**Movement:** 8/16/24/48  **Wounds:** 180

**Skills:** Awareness (Per), Blather (Fel) +20, Ciphers (All) (Int) +20, Command (Fel) +20, Common Lore (All) (Int) +20, Charm (Fel) +20, Deceive (Fel) +20, Forbidden Lore (All) (Int) +20, Intimidate (S) +20, Logic (Int) +20, Psyniscience (Per) +20, Scholastic Lore (All) (Int) +20, Scrutiny (Per) +20, Search (Per), Speak Language (All known languages) +20.

**Talents:** Blademaster, Combat Master, Lightning Attack, Resistance (Psychic Powers), Swift Attack, Strong Minded.

**Traits:** Daemonic, †Daemonic Presence (TB 12), Dark Sight, Fear 4 (Terrifying), Flyer (10), From Beyond, Size (Massive), The Stuff of Nightmares, Improved Natural Weapons (Claws and Beak), Unnatural Strength (x3), Unnatural Intelligence (x3), Unnatural Willpower (x2), Warp Instability.

†**Daemonic Presence:** All those within 25 metres of a Lord of Change realise that they are merely the playthings of capricious gods, beginning to doubt their every conviction. All characters suffer a −20 penalty to Willpower Tests in the area.

**Weapons:** Claws and Beak (Natural Weapons; 1d10+12 R; Tearing), Staff of Tzeentch (2d10+14 I; Tearing, Warp Weapon).

## Special Rules

**Master of Plotters:** All Daemons of Tzeentch are master schemers, their very essence a primal form of deceit and treachery, and the Lords of Change are the greatest masterminds of all. No matter the circumstances, a Lord of Change is always ready to turn the tables on its adversaries. Once per combat, the Lord of Change may add his Intelligence Bonus to any one Test.

**Supreme Sorcerer:** Lords of Change know all Psychic Powers from the **DEATHWATCH** Rulebook (and may know more; if you have access to **ROGUE TRADER** or **DARK HERESY**, the Lord of Change knows all Lesser, Greater, and Ascended Psychic Powers as well, plus the Lesser and Greater Arcana of Sorcery), and may use them as if it had a Psy Rating of 9. A Lord of Change does not trigger any psychic phenomena. In addition to these powers, Lords of Change may also use the Psychic Power Bolt of Change (see page 127) and any other psychic powers from page 127 that the GM deems appropriate.

**Spawn of Fate:** Lords of Change are the architects of destiny itself, capable of weaving together or severing the very strands of fate. Though a Lord of Change does not have access to Fate Points, whenever anyone in combat with one spends a Fate Point, the Lord of Change regains 1d10 lost Wounds. However, when an individual is forced to permanently burn a Fate Point in the presence of a Lord of Change, the Greater Daemon immediately suffers 2d10 wounds ignoring Toughness.

## ADVENTURE SEEDS

**Long-term Plan:** A Lord of Change has slowly, patiently lured the Kill-team to a world of his choosing, subtly manipulating events in order to further its own mysterious agenda. Last-minute rescues, inexplicable delays, and even friendships and rivalries have all been twisted to serve the Greater Daemon's own ends. All that remains is for the Lord of Change to tip the final domino—the Kill-team itself. Will the player characters fall victim to the plan, or will they figure out that their mission is a sham before it's too late?

**Archenemy:** The Kill-team's current mission (unbeknownst to them) threatens one of the best-laid plans of a vicious and vindictive Lord of Change. The daemon will stop at nothing to prevent the Kill-team from succeeding, and as allies desert them and unexpected problems pile up with alarming rapidity, the player characters begin to suspect that all is not as it seems…

### Addendum by Codicier Taelon

I only saw the daemon briefly; a towering, winged figure in the distance, a brief glimpse before it vanished—but suddenly everything made sense. What should have been a routine sweep for Tyranid vanguard organisms on the rim of the Jericho Reach had become a waking nightmare. Plagued for weeks by an endless string of problems (technical failures, a shipboard mutiny, inexplicable astrological phenomena, delayed or waylaid orders), it seemed the very universe was conspiring against us.

Finally, we were forced to set down on a lifeless world in order to gather enough raw materials to effect repairs. While surveying for metals within a sun-scorched canyon, a flash of multicoloured wings caught my eye. It stood nearly 500 metres away, poised on a cliff overlooking the far side of the canyon, an immense staff clutched in its birdlike claws. Its gaze seemed to bore deep within me, and I am ashamed to say that I took a step backward. Before I could raise my bolter, it vanished with a sickening, stomach-churning pop.

What its purpose may have been in stranding us there I may never know, but I shudder to think we played any part in advancing its vile schemes.

# KYRUS THE CHANTLEADER

The Deathwatch data-vaults aboard Watch Fortress Erioch record that Kyrus the Chantleader emerged from the Hadex Anomaly in 801.M40 and orchestrated a series of devastating raids on worlds near the heart of the Jericho Reach. A Chaos Space Marine formerly of the Word Bearers Legion, Kyrus has made a number of dark pacts with the Ruinous Powers. These pacts have granted Kyrus the favour of Khorne, Slaanesh, Nurgle, and Tzeentch, and the Chaos Space Marine has led large numbers of Lesser Daemons from all four dark gods in several engagements along the length and breadth of the Reach. The daemon armies of Kyrus the Chantleader are a persistent danger to the Achilus Crusade in the Acheros Salient. Many senior Inquisitors of the Ordo Malleus consider him a much larger threat, citing a number of reports indicating that the daemon forces he surrounds himself with are particularly powerful for their kind.

Captured agents of the Stigmatus have claimed that Kyrus hails from a Daemon world within the Anomaly, a bleak and twisted planet that serves as a battleground for the dark gods' rivalries. This nameless place is said to have a large native population of mutants and outcasts, all now turned to the worship of the Ruinous Powers by Kyrus and his followers.

Kyrus has been blessed with many gifts from his dark masters, including the ability to manifest massive black wings and two mighty weapons; the pistol dubbed Hateblazer is an ancient plasma weapon of uncertain origin, and he wields a daemon-infused chain axe named Corruptis.

| Kyrus the Chantleader (Master) Profile | | | | | | | | |
|---|---|---|---|---|---|---|---|---|
| WS | BS | S | T | Ag | Int | Per | WP | Fel |
| 55 | 48 | (12) 53 | (10) 54 | 46 | 46 | 47 | 51 | 49 |

**Speed:** 5/10/15/30 **Wounds:** 41

**Skills:** Awareness (Per) +10, Charm (Fel) +20, Command (Fel) +20, Deceive (Fel) +20, Dodge (Ag) +20, Interrogation (Int), Intimidate (S) +20, Lore: Forbidden (Chaos) +20, Lore: Forbidden (Warp) +20, Security (Int), Tactics (All) +10

**Talents:** Air of Authority, Blademaster, Counter-Attack, Combat Master, Crushing Blow, Fearless, Hammer Blow, Into the Jaws of Hell, Iron Discipline, Lightning Attack, Master Orator, Swift Attack, Whirlwind of Death.

**Traits:** From Beyond, Size (Hulking), Unnatural Strength (x2), Unnatural Toughness (x2).
**Armour:** Corrupted power armour (Body 10, Arms and Legs 8, Head 8)
**Weapons:** Hateblazer (30m; S/–/–; 2d10+8 E; Pen 8; Overheat), Corruptis (1d10+16 R; Warp Weapon)

## Special Rules

**Blessing of Chaos:** Kyrus is protected by the pacts he has made with the Ruinous Powers; this acts as a Force Field (see page 166 in the DEATHWATCH Rulebook) with a rating of 33 (this also accounts for his exceptionally high number of starting Wounds) that does not overload.
**Dark Wings:** Kyrus may grow a pair of massive, bat-like wings sprouting from his back at will. He has the Flyer (15) Trait.

## Addendum by Codicier Taelon

*I have received a troubling report that may be related to the difficulties the Crusade is facing in the Acheros Salient. According to my sources, the agri-world of Sulyvan (part of the Alphis Minor system) has been entirely wiped out by a daemonic incursion. The planet is now dead, twisted by the powers of the warp into bizarre and unsettling configurations... it is said that entire continents are consumed by balefires, oceans have been turned into seas of gore, and mountains simply vanish and re-appear in misshapen forms. The planet's moon is pristine and untouched with one startling exception: a kilometres-long blasphemous symbol of the Ruinous Powers, carved from a precise application of orbital lance strikes. I suspect this is another visitation of the traitor Chaos Space Marine known as Kyrus the Chantleader.*

# BLOODLETTER

The Lesser Daemons of Khorne are known as Bloodletters, and it is they who form the core of Khorne's vast battle forces. Bloodletters are amongst the deadliest warriors in the galaxy, possessing immense strength in their sinewy limbs and savage in the ferocity of their brutal charge into battle. Their skin is the colour of blood, and the coppery scent of gore surrounds them like a shroud.

Bloodletters are uncommonly disciplined daemons, able to form complex formations on the battlefield and manoeuvre for the best advantage. Such formations do not last once the Bloodletters engage the foe, however, as the daemons are too focused on competing for Khorne's glory in the brutal frenzy of combat.

Bloodletters are armed with great two-handed weapons known as hellblades. Legends claim that the souls of angry daemons form the core of the hellblades, and that each razored edge is sharpened by pure hatred. No mortal-forged armour can withstand the assault of a hellblade, and the carnage wrought by these wicked weapons has broken the wills of uncounted mortal foes over the millennia.

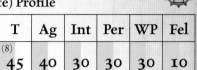

## Bloodletter (Elite) Profile

| WS | BS | S | T | Ag | Int | Per | WP | Fel |
|----|----|----|----|----|----|----|----|----|
| 55 | 30 | (8) 45 | (8) 45 | 40 | 30 | 30 | 30 | 10 |

**Speed:** 4/8/12/24  **Wounds:** 25

**Skills:** Awareness (Per), Climb (S) +20, Dodge (Ag), Intimidate (S) +20, Psyniscience (Per), Speak Language (any one), Wrangling (Int) +10.

**Talents:** Battle Rage, Combat Master, Crushing Blow, Fearless, Frenzy, Furious Assault, Swift Attack.

**Traits:** Brutal Charge, Daemonic (TB 8), †Daemonic Presence, Fear (2), From Beyond, Improved Natural Weapons, Natural Weapons (Claws) Strange Physiology, Unnatural Strength (x2), Warp Instability.

†**Daemonic Presence:** All enemies within 10 metres of a Bloodletter suffer a −10 penalty to Willpower Tests in the area.

**Weapons:** Hellblades (1d10+12 R; Balanced, Warp Weapon), Claws (1d10+10 R; Pen 2).

### Special Rules

**Horde:** When Bloodletters form a Horde, they gain the Disciplined and Blood Soaked Tide Traits.

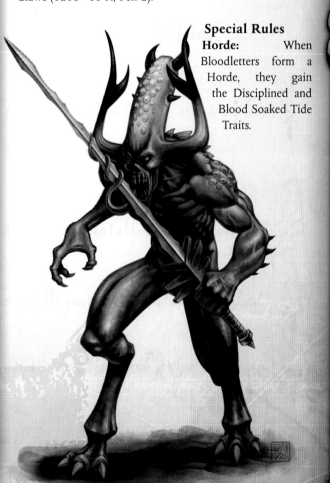

## Addendum by Codicier Taelon

Before I was seconded to the Deathwatch, I encountered a force of Bloodletters on the damned planet of Pyroxis III. Alongside my Battle-Brothers of the White Scars Chapter, we had been despatched in answer to a distress beacon located in a deep-core mining operation centre, the only resource which made the Pyroxis system valuable in the slightest. Boiling out from the vast pit of the mine came a horde of howling, blood-red daemons waving black swords. My Battle-Brothers and I fought valiantly, though I saw far too many of my fellow White Scars cut down with merciless glee by the daemon's hell-forged blades. In the end, we prevailed at great cost, and our triumph over the daemons I credit entirely to Santovis, our Company Champion. Although he did not survive the battle, his unflinching example lent such strength to our arms that we could not fail.

It remains unclear as to the nature of the presence of that daemon horde upon such an isolated and relatively unimportant world. Some have conjectured that the ways of daemonkind are fickle, and some such incursions as the battle upon Pyroxis III are simply a wild, freak chance occurrence. However, I suspect that the very isolation of Pyroxis III was the cause of its doom; men often forsake their faith in such circumstances, and it is not difficult to imagine the miners believing themselves apart from the Imperium, and thus, no longer under the Emperor's protection. The same inner corruption is evident across the Jericho Reach, and remains a challenge for myself and the rest of the Deathwatch. The arrival of the Achilus Crusade may be this region's final hope to escape the final fate of Pyroxis III.

# DAEMONETTE

Slaanesh has many servants, but the most numerous of them are the Daemonettes. Created to fulfil the Prince of Pleasure's every whim, Daemonettes are his courtiers and courtesans, his warriors and messengers. Slaanesh is fickle and capricious, oft likely to send out legions of Daemonettes to destroy any source of frustration.

In appearance, a Daemonette is both alluring and repulsive, with slender, lithe bodies and an androgynous glamour that is heightened by the captivating musk that pervades the air around them. A Daemonette's skin is luminously pale and smooth, and the daemon's hands are replaced by long, dextrous claws covered in iron-hard chitin. These claws can bestow a gentle caress or a fatal slash with equal skill. Daemonettes move swiftly upon languid, long legs and bird-like feet, able to dart across the battlefield with uncanny grace. A Daemonette's bewitching opal eyes can capture the attention of any mortal who gazes upon them, and the Daemonette's face is a genderless mask of cruel beauty. Regardless of their appearance, Daemonettes possess a powerful gift from their master, an aura that always makes them appear as an object of ultimate beauty and desire in the eyes of their enemies, no matter what race, gender, or morality such a foe may possess.

Daemonettes are often found seducing a chosen victim with promises of glory and self-fulfilment. They are instrumental to Slaanesh's more delicate machinations, and Daemonettes are often sent to undermine the will of Slaanesh's enemies or tempt them from their chosen path in order to remove such opposition. Daemonettes whisper into the dreams and nightmares of a victim, taunting and teasing him with visions of ambition and the darkest desires. Many such victims become lured into self-obsession, paranoia, and insanity, irrevocably placed upon an indulgent road towards their own destruction.

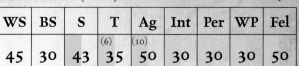

## Daemonette (Elite) Profile

| WS | BS | S | T | Ag | Int | Per | WP | Fel |
|----|----|----|----|----|-----|-----|----|-----|
|    |    |    | (6) | (10) |     |     |    |     |
| 45 | 30 | 43 | 35 | 50 | 30 | 30 | 30 | 50 |

**Speed:** 5/10/15/30 **Wounds:** 20

**Skills:** Awareness (Per), Charm (Fel) +20, Dodge (Ag) +20, Psyniscience (Per), Speak Language (any one).

**Talents:** Fearless, Lightning Attack, Lightning Reflexes, Sprint, Step Aside, Swift Attack.

**Traits:** Daemonic (TB 6), †Daemonic Presence, Fear (2), From Beyond, Improved Natural Weapons, Natural Weapons (Claws), Preternatural Speed, Strange Physiology, Unnatural Agility (x2), Warp Instability.

†**Daemonic Presence:** All enemies within 10 metres of a Daemonette suffer a −10 penalty to Willpower Tests in the area.

**Weapons:** Claws (1d10+6 R; Pen 6; Razor Sharp).

**From: Daemonhunter Ahmazzi, Ordo Malleus:**
**To: Codicier Taelon, aboard Watch Fortress Erioch, Jericho Reach:**

The lesser daemons of Slaanesh are a particularly insidious threat to the Imperium, for their machinations are subtle and twisted. I have lost many friends, many acolytes and throne agents over the centuries, and not a few were victims of the Daemonettes; seduced and led astray, ultimately little more than playthings for these foul daemons. Too late, I discovered the daemon's deception and arrived to find my acolytes' quarters dark and empty, more akin to a tomb than a residence. All that remained were blasphemous runes drawn in the blood of my former allies. The failure is mine; I did not properly prepare my acolytes for such an encounter.

I have learned many things in my career with the Ordo Malleus, but the most important lesson I have learned is that all things related to a daemon are false; place no trust in any daemon's words, no matter how alluring it may seem.

# PINK HORROR

Possibly the most bizarre of all daemons, Pink Horrors are the Lesser Daemons that serve Tzeentch. These daemons possess no head, only a squat pink-hued body with long, gangly arms and legs. Leering faces are normally found upon the centre of their chest, but can disappear and reappear anywhere on their body seemingly at random.

Pink Horrors are often found gathered in cavorting, gleeful mobs, dancing about the field of battle whilst humming a cacophonous, random tune. Cackling with mad abandon, these Horrors attack by launching a barrage of arcane bolts composed of ever-changing colours that can mutate almost any foe into unrecognisable blobs of gelatinous flesh.

These daemons are relatively weak in hand-to-hand combat compared to other Lesser Daemons, having only their claws and fangs to rely upon. However, Pink Horrors are pernicious foes and are particularly difficult to destroy due to the blessings of their creator, Tzeentch, being mostly immune to the effects of many enemy weapons. When they are finally slain, the daemon's most unique form of defence becomes evident; the Pink Horror splits into two halves, which reshape themselves into smaller copies of the original. These two new daemons are known as Blue Horrors (thanks to the vivid colour of their hides), and are competent foes in their own right. In contrast to the Pink Horror, Blue Horrors are morose, whining, and petty.

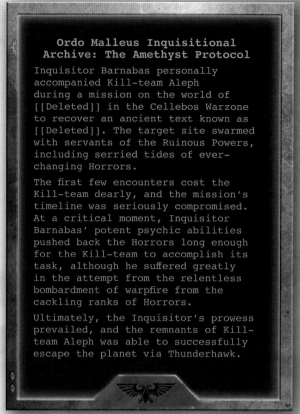

Ordo Malleus Inquisitional
Archive: The Amethyst Protocol

Inquisitor Barnabas personally accompanied Kill-team Aleph during a mission on the world of [[Deleted]] in the Cellebos Warzone to recover an ancient text known as [[Deleted]]. The target site swarmed with servants of the Ruinous Powers, including serried tides of ever-changing Horrors.

The first few encounters cost the Kill-team dearly, and the mission's timeline was seriously compromised. At a critical moment, Inquisitor Barnabas' potent psychic abilities pushed back the Horrors long enough for the Kill-team to accomplish its task, although he suffered greatly in the attempt from the relentless bombardment of warpfire from the cackling ranks of Horrors.

Ultimately, the Inquisitor's prowess prevailed, and the remnants of Kill-team Aleph was able to successfully escape the planet via Thunderhawk.

**Blessing of Tzeentch:** Pink and Blue Horrors are blessed by their patron. This has the same effect as a Force Field (see page 166 in the **DEATHWATCH** Rulebook) with a Strength of 20 that does not overload.

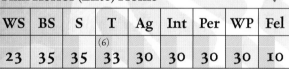

## Pink Horror (Elite) Profile

| WS | BS | S | T | Ag | Int | Per | WP | Fel |
|----|----|----|----|----|-----|-----|----|-----|
| 23 | 35 | 35 | (6) 33 | 30 | 30 | 30 | 30 | 10 |

**Speed:** 3/6/9/18          **Wounds:** 18
**Skills:** Awareness (Per), Dodge (Ag), Psyniscience (Per), Speak Language (Any one).
**Talents:** Fearless.
**Traits:** Daemonic (TB 6), †Daemonic Presence, Fear (2), From Beyond, Improved Natural Weapons, Natural Weapons (Claws), Strange Physiology, Warp Instability.
**†Daemonic Presence:** All enemies within 10 metres of a Pink Horror suffer a –10 penalty to Willpower Tests in the area.
**Weapons:** Warpfire (30m; S/3/–; 1d10+10 E; Pen 6), Claws (1d10+5; Pen 2).

## Special Rules

**Blue Horrors:** When a Pink Horror is slain, it vanishes and is replaced by two Blue Horrors (the Blue Horrors appear within 1m of the Pink Horror when it was slain, assuming there is room). Blue Horrors act as independent creatures and have the same statistics as a Pink Horror with the following changes: reduce Wounds to 9, reduce Strength to 20, reduce the damage of the claws to 1d10+3. When using Pink Horrors as a Horde, this rule applies differently; reduce all damage dealt to the Horde's Magnitude by one half, rounding up.

# PLAGUEBEARER

The Lesser Daemons of Nurgle are shambling, pustulent creatures known as Plaguebearers. These daemons have gangling, bony limbs, their bodies swollen with decay, so much so that glistening innards are exposed rents in their skin. They possess a single, cyclopean eye and a single horn rising above their haggard, drawn faces, their bodies covered in filth and parasites. Despite the Plaguebearer's unusual appearance, they are supernaturally resilient to harm, the gifts of their master having inured them to all pain. Plaguebearers are constantly surrounded by clouds of droning flies and chant monotonous hymns, their gait a staggering lope. Their sonorous voices attempt to keep count of the number of noxious plagues unleashed by Nurgle; an impossible task, for the Grandfather of Plagues constantly invents new strains of viruses.

Plaguebearers carry rusted, heavy blades known as plagueswords. These weapons are infused with foul infections and toxins that can make the merest scratch fatal. These daemons are solemn, cruelly efficient warriors in battle, hideously effective at any war of attrition. They also serve as the Tallymen of Nurgle, eternally bound to record all of their dark god's pestilential creations. Many believe that Plaguebearers are in fact created by such diseases, incubating within plague victims and feeding upon their dying energies, only to later fully emerge from their heaped bodies.

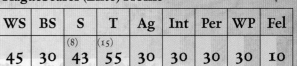

## Plaguebearer (Elite) Profile

| WS | BS | S | T | Ag | Int | Per | WP | Fel |
|----|----|----|----|----|----|----|----|----|
| 45 | 30 | (8) 43 | (15) 55 | 30 | 30 | 30 | 30 | 10 |

**Speed:** 3/6/9/18  **Wounds:** 30

**Skills:** Awareness (Per), Psyniscience (Per), Scholastic Lore (Numerology) (Int), Speak Language (any one).

**Talents:** Crippling Strike, Fearless.

**Traits:** Daemonic (TB 10), †Daemonic Presence, Fear (2), From Beyond, Improved Natural Weapons, Natural Weapons (Claws), Regeneration (1), Strange Physiology, Unnatural Strength (x2), Unnatural Toughness (x2), Warp Instability.

†**Daemonic Presence:** All enemies within 10 metres of a Plaguebearer suffer a –10 penalty to Willpower Tests in the area.

**Weapons:** Plaguesword (1d10+13; Pen 1; Felling 1, Toxic), Claws (1d10+8; Pen 2; Toxic).

### Special Rules

**Cloud of Flies:** All those within 5 metres take a –10 penalty to Weapon Skill and Ballistic Skill Tests as choking clouds of buzzing, biting flies attack every exposed inch of flesh.

## Report from Watch Captain Brand

*Brother Librarian,*

*When you asked me to share anything I knew about the enemies we regularly confront in the Reach, one incident in particular came to mind. I led a Kill-team on a mission for Inquisitor Quist, the details of which I am not at liberty to discuss. The course of our mission took us to an orbital station above a world in the Acheros Salient—we found the station to be dead in space, with only silence answering our vox-hails. My Battle-Brothers and I scoured the station starting from the uppermost decks, but we found nothing... only empty cells and eerily quiet corridors. In the lower decks our auto-senses registered movement, and my Kill-team's Apothecary warned us of rapidly increasing toxin levels. We discovered the crew of the station jammed into a relatively small chamber, their bodies bloated with pestilence, all having been slain by a particularly virulent virus. Not long after this discovery, we faced a group of daemons, each with a single rheumy eye and a black, twisted horn. These daemons were extremely difficult to destroy, and massed bolter fire was needed to take them down one by one, with the last falling to a blow from my powerfist... although it nearly seemed as if more than one swing would be necessary, for these daemons are seemingly immune to any pain or discomfort, even from missing limbs or wounds that would otherwise despatch an enemy. Eventually, we purged the station by opening that chamber to vacuum, then re-sealing it and cleansing each room with flamers.*

# CHAOS SPACE MARINE SORCERERS

*"It is by the Changer of the Ways that I have power, it is by Magnus the Red that I have life!"*

–Ahriman of the Thousand Sons

Chaos Space Marine Sorcerers are some of the most depraved and demented individuals encountered by the forces of the Imperium. During the events of the Horus Heresy, many of them came from the ranks of the Thousand Sons Legion, which had a greater proportion of Astartes with the psyker mutation.

While human Sorcerers are a menace to the integrity of the Imperium of Mankind, there are Sorcerers who are a far greater threat: those Space Marine Librarians who abandoned their duty to the God-Emperor. With the abilities they command through their psychic training, combined with their new powers gifted by the Gods of Chaos, a Chaos Space Marine Sorcerer is a power to be reckoned with. Given an array of gifts and powers, the Sorcerer can cause agonising pain, curse individuals, and summon daemons from the Immaterium to temporarily stalk the material realms.

One of the more potent abilities that are granted to Chaos Space Marine Sorcerers is the ability to call upon the power and essence of daemons in order to fuel their spells. Psychic power that is derived directly from the Warp is dangerous, but the greatest of psychic feats can only be accomplished through the use of daemonic energies. Sorcerers who make such pacts bargain some service or favour in exchange for a portion of that daemon's own essence. By forging a conduit into the Warp through this pact, the Sorcerer is capable of unleashing gouts of destructive energy. The grandest of such Sorcerers have dozens of these pacts made to power their spells and abilities. However, dipping into the well of such power comes with its own price, as the Sorcerer battles constantly to retain control over his own soul.

In the 41st Millennium, Chaos Space Marine Sorcerers are rooted out and hunted down by every branch of the Adeptus Terra, the Holy Inquisition, and the Adeptus Astartes. Psykers are actually tolerated (however slightly) more than Sorcerers—who are hunted down and eliminated with extreme prejudice.

While many of the more powerful Space Marine Sorcerers do in fact come from the Thousand Sons Traitor Legion, there are others who hail from loyalist Chapters—succumbing to the lure of Chaos and turning against liege and lord. Chaos Space Marine Sorcerers, like their ordinary human brethren, are independent souls who often form the nucleus of a Chaos Cult, festering within the confines of society. The most devious of them will often end up abandoning their so-called "children" and leave them as lambs to the slaughter, making their escape to sow more destruction while the forces of the Imperium rain down upon their erstwhile followers. Yet Chaos Space Marine Sorcerers have their own ends beyond mere mayhem and bedlam. They stalk the realms of man in order to collect all manner of arcane knowledge and power. Many Chaos Space Marine Sorcerers are esoteric and

extremely selfish madmen. Once they have supped from the cup of knowledge offered by the Chaos Gods, and glimpsed unachievable realms beyond mortal comprehension, they are forever driven to expand their power and knowledge to an impossible level.

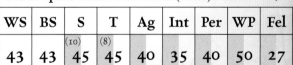

## Chaos Space Marine Sorcerer (Elite) Profile

| WS | BS | S | T | Ag | Int | Per | WP | Fel |
|----|----|------|------|----|-----|-----|----|-----|
| 43 | 43 | (10) 45 | (8) 45 | 40 | 35 | 40 | 50 | 27 |

**Movement:** 5/10/15/30      **Wounds:** 30

**Skills:** Awareness (Per), Climb (S), Command (Fel) +10, Dodge (Ag) +10, Intimidate (S) +20, Literacy (Int), Lore: Forbidden (Daemonology, Psykers, The Warp) (Int), Lore: Scholastic (Legend, Numerology, Occult) (Int) +10, Psyniscience (Int) +20, Scrutiny (Per), Speak Language (Low Gothic) (Int), Survival (Int), Swim (S).

**Talents:** Astartes Weapon Training, Bolter Drill, Die Hard, Fearless, Hatred (Loyalist Space Marines), Heightened Senses (Sight, Sound, Smell), Jaded, Killing Strike, Quick Draw, Rapid Reload, Size (Hulking), Swift Attack, True Grit.

**Traits:** Dark Sight, †Mark of Chaos, Unnatural Strength (x2), Unnatural Toughness (x2).

**Psy Rating:** 5

**Psychic Powers:** Choose two of the Chaos Psychic Powers found on page 127.

**Armour:** Astartes Power Armour (Head 8, Arms 8, Body 10, Legs 8).

**Weapons:** Force Sword (1d10+19 R; Pen 7; Balanced, Special), Astartes Bolt Pistol (30m; S/3/–; 2d10+5 X; Pen 5; Clip 12; Rld Full; Tearing), Astartes Combat Blade (1d10+14 R; Pen 2).

**Gear:** 4 bolt pistol magazines, Sorcerer Robes, Pendant or Emblem with mark of sworn Chaos God.

†**Mark of Chaos:** The Sorcerer possesses one of the following Marks of Chaos. This Mark appears somewhere on his body and is also emblazoned upon his armour—Nurgle, Slaanesh, or Tzeentch. See page 363 of the DEATHWATCH Rulebook for information on how these Marks work. The Sorcerer may only ever possess a single Mark and may not change that Mark.

## Addendum from Codicier Taelon

*I have only crossed paths with two of these depraved creatures in my travels through the Jericho Reach, from different Warbands. Perhaps the greatest insult is that these twisted souls once followed the same path that I walk— and it is also the most gravest of warnings. This is what happens when one falls to the lure of Chaos and forgoes one's oaths of loyalty and fraternity. It was on a mission to cleanse a research outpost of the Adeptus Mechanicus that I had the opportunity to confront one of my fallen Brothers. Apparently, he was searching through the memory coils and data-stacks of the outpost in a desperate attempt for some snippet of lore that was lodged within. When I encountered him, furious energies were unleashed, but in the end, he tore a hole in space–time and escaped to a hidden craft. I can only speculate on what circumstances would turn a noble and honourable Astartes onto the path of Chaos.*

*-Taelon*

# KHORNE BERZERKERS

The blasphemies of those Space Marines that turned their back upon the Emperor reap a foul and bitter harvest among the Traitor Legions. Here the most fervid worshippers of the Ruinous Powers can be found: once proud and noble Adeptus Astartes that have fully embraced the very thing they fought against. These are the most utterly damned of the servants of Chaos, fallen Space Marines sworn body and soul to the ruination of the Imperium they once helped to build.

Khorne Berzerkers are Chaos Space Marines that have dedicated their lives to Khorne, the Blood God, skull lord of battles, patron of murder, slaughter and bloodshed in all its forms. The most infamous Khorne Berzerkers are the Chaos Space Marines of the World Eaters, the insane, undying remnants of the Legion that swore themselves to Khorne and followed Warmaster Horus to the Imperial palace itself.

The World Eaters were renowned for their savagery even before they fell to the dark gods. Their actions over the ten thousand years since their betrayal of the Emperor beggar description. They are joined by followers of the Blood God drawn from all across the Traitor Legions and members of the Adeptus Astartes that have fallen to Khorne's lure down the millennia.

It is a small step from martial pride or righteous fervour to battle fury or unthinking bloodlust, and many peerless warriors flock to Khorne's ranks. All of these fierce souls undergo psycho-surgery to transform themselves into ravening warriors of unchecked rage—perfect candidates to become a Khorne Berzerker.

Such warriors become part of a brotherhood so feral and bloodthirsty that they are apt to set upon their allies or even each other at the slightest provocation. Khorne Berzerkers are highly distinctive on the battlefield and wear blood-red armour decorated with brass that is usually shot scarred and hacked in many places. Skulls hang from chains around their waist and shoulders, along with tattered streamers of hide flecked with gore.

Khorne Berzerkers are savage fighters who revel in the bloodiest of hand-to-hand combats. In their eagerness to offer blood and skulls to Khorne they carry many vicious close combat weapons into battle. Often they wield deadly axes as these are the preferred weapons of Khorne, although the chainsword is almost equally favoured. Khorne Berzerkers relish their role as the sacred destroyers of the Blood God with a fanatical fervour and will fight on even with the most terrible wounds. Their delight in death and pain is so strong that they have been known to fall on their own chainswords as sacrifices to the Blood God.

Khorne Berzerkers are often encountered during boarding actions with Chaos vessels. The close quarters fighting aboard ships, with no possibility of escape, is ideally suited to the frenzied fighting style of the followers of the Blood God. Khorne Berzerkers are also found as leaders of renegade bands, where they become bloody handed tyrants that rule over their miserable underlings with an iron fist. In truth the worshippers of the lord of battle have little patience with planning and leadership, preferring to simply lead by example and slaughtering any who does not keep up.

Khorne Berzerkers seem drawn to the bloodiest battlefields and appear in greatest numbers there. A decades-long siege or a titanic battle involving millions of men is meat and drink to them. In these circumstances, entire warbands of Khorne Berzerkers will appear so that they can participate in the butchery. They build towering pyramids of skulls and lavish blood sacrifices on crude battlefield shrines in praise of their god. Should their allies slacken or falter, these weaklings' skulls will be added to the pile.

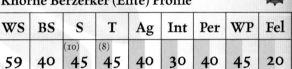

| Khorne Berzerker (Elite) Profile | | | | | | | | |
|---|---|---|---|---|---|---|---|---|
| **WS** | **BS** | **S** | **T** | **Ag** | **Int** | **Per** | **WP** | **Fel** |
| 59 | 40 | (10) 45 | (8) 45 | 40 | 30 | 40 | 45 | 20 |

**Move:** 5/10/15/30      **Wounds:** 30

**Skills:** Awareness (Per), Command (Fel) +10, Dodge (Ag) +10, Forbidden Lore (Daemons, Warp) (Int), Intimidate (S) +20, Literacy (Int), Scrutiny (Per), Speak Language (Low Gothic) (Int), Survival (Int), Swim (S).

**Talents:** Ambidextrous, Astartes Weapon Training, Berserk Charge, Diehard, Fearless, Frenzy, Furious Assault, Hatred (Loyalist Space Marines) Heightened Senses (Sight, Sound, Smell), Jaded, Lightning Attack, Quick Draw, Rapid Reload, Resistance (psychic powers), Swift Attack, True Grit, Two-weapon wielder (Melee), Whirlwind of Death.

**Traits:** Dark Sight, Fear 2 (Frightening), Size (Hulking), Unnatural Strength (x2), Unnatural Toughness (x2).

**Armour:** Astartes power armour (Head 8, Arms 8, Body 10, Legs 8).

**Weapons:** Astartes Chainsword (1d10+14 R; Pen 4, Balanced, Tearing) or Berzerker Axe (1d10+18 R; Pen 4; Tearing), Astartes Bolt Pistol (30m; S/3/–; 2d10+5 X; Pen 5; Clip12; Reload Full; Tearing) or Astartes Plasma Pistol (30m; S/2/–; 2d10+6 E; Pen 6; Clip10; Reload 3Full; Overheat).

**Gear:** 2 bolt pistol magazines, frag grenades.

III: THE FORCES OF CHAOS

**Slaughter:** A Kill-team arrives at their mission to find a band of Khorne Berzerkers already engaged in slaughtering their target. If the Deathwatch intervene the Berzerkers will turn on them immediately, and logic dictates they let the two sides fight it out and then finish off the survivors. But can the Kill-team really stand by while the followers of the Blood God do their work for them? Some Inquisitors would certainly interpret inaction as aiding and abetting the enemy.

## Addendum by Codicier Taelon

The data archives have only sporadic reports of Kill-teams that have had the misfortune to encounter Khorne Berzerkers. Perhaps the most graphic is a restricted work, a testimonial from one Brother Horvan during the dying years of the Angevin Crusade in the Thirty-ninth Millennium. At this time the last of Yu'Vath Hell Worlds in the Adrantis Nebula were being cleansed and Brother Horvan led a Kill-team at the forefront of the final operations.

--------------

Testimonial begins:

"...We purged the traitor slaves without mercy and their xenos masters fled before us. We found those few of them left gathered in a great hall wherein there was a great tree sculpted in fantastical fashion from bone and brass. The Yu'Vath slave minions clustered about this monstrous thing and called out to it in their foul tongue, seemingly beseeching.

As we strode forth to cleanse the last of these pestilential aliens it was suddenly as if we were held back by an invisible force. At the same time the walls of the chamber seemed to recede out of sight so perhaps it was only distance that held us back, all the while tricking us that the tree and the Yu'Vath were still close by. It seemed then as if a brazen sky spread above us and a gusting stench of old blood swept over us.

Still we strove to reach our prey but could come no closer. As we watched, seething with fury, armoured figures stepped forth from the tree and the Yu'Vath fawned and abased themselves before them. These savage apparitions were dark parodies of true Space Marines, clad in blood-red power armour and girt all about with skulls and foul icons that hurt the eye. They bore chain axes and swords in profusion and when they beheld the grovelling aliens they laughed.

Only then did these warriors seem to perceive us and as they did so they rushed forward in a joyous fury. While before we had seemed held apart, now we seemed thrust together and the bloody warriors were among us in an instant. We took hard blows in the battle that followed even though we outnumbered this new foe. Every one of them fought to the last breath and had to be dismembered to finish them off. As the last fell, the vision faded and we found ourselves back in the hall once more, though of the warriors and the Yu'Vath there was no sign."

# NOISE MARINES

A Space Marine's senses are vastly more acute than an ordinary human's, their bodies and minds honed to perfection for waging war. The very intensity of the experience of battle can break down the indoctrination and conditioning of some Battle-Brothers. They can become lost in an orgiastic lust for battle, beyond commands or orders as they indulge themselves in wanton carnage. Others succumb to the temptations of forbidden pleasures denied to them in their cloistered existence: power, wealth, approbation. These fallen Space Marines eventually come to pledge themselves to the Chaos God Slaanesh, caught in the silken bonds of the Prince of Pleasure.

It pleases Slaanesh to transform any such new servants into Noise Marines. This breed of traitors was first created from the Space Marine Legion of the Emperor's Children when they fell into worship of the Chaos powers during the Horus Heresy. Their depredations during the Heresy were foul and bestial in the extreme, most commonly directed against the most innocent and defenceless victims they could find.

As Noise Marines dedicate themselves fully to the Chaos God Slaanesh, they are gifted with mutations peculiar to him. A Noise Marine's hearing becomes a thousand times keener than a normal man's and able to distinguish the subtlest difference in pitch and volume. The Noise Marine's whole mind becomes warped around this vital input, every sound inducing extreme emotional reactions that make all other sensations seem pale and worthless.

Louder, more discordant sounds provoke a more extreme emotional reaction, creating a feedback loop of addiction. Soon only the din of battle and heightened screams of fear of the enemy can stir a Noise Marine to full force. In this heightened state, the Noise Marine's mind ceases to function and he becomes only a vessel for the sensations ignited by the music of the apocalypse. He is enraptured by the screams of the dying as they dance a bloody jig upon the path of destruction. Every new explosion and death cry raises him higher still toward full daemonhood and ultimate release. Noise Marines howl of the eternal glory of their lord Slaanesh, assailing the ears and mind with their messages of corruption and vice.

Noise Marines wear twisted suits of power armour painted in a variety of garish colours, as they have become so jaded that only the most extravagant colours and patterns still register on their senses. Noise Marines arm themselves with a variety of daemonically-forged weapons that produce thunderously loud, discordant blasts. These often work by amplifying the Noise Marines' constant psychic cacophony of babbling, screaming, prayers to Slaanesh into murderous harmonies able to burst organs and break bones. Psykers are particularly vulnerable to the Noise Marines' assault, their senses bludgeoned and overwhelmed by the incessant psychic barrage.

Some Noise Marines wear an intricate arrangement of pipes and tubes around their facemasks to act as voice amplifiers. They use these to project the wearer's terrifying battle screams and howls of pleasure, creating a paralysing wall of sound as they stride into battle. Their roaring song

of hatred and destruction can quail the boldest heart. Other Noise Marines use weapons that unleash harmonics to rip their target apart. Noise Marines play these instruments at a manic pace, working up and down through clashing chords and sliding through scales so that their weapons seem to constantly howl with agony or scream with delight.

The most potent Noise Marine weapons focus a thrumming bass note that rises to an explosive crescendo, harnessing a cataclysmic harmonic that detonates at the target point with an ear-splitting concussion. Victims are sent into violent spasms as the sonic backlash scrambles their nervous system, breaking their own bones as they contort horribly beneath the shockwave. Armour provides little defence as it resonates in sympathy with the deadly frequency, liquefying the flesh of the wearer. Even battle tanks can be shattered by the atonal assault as their armour plates shiver into fragments and their hapless crew members burst like over-ripe fruit.

### Noise Marine (Elite) Profile

| WS | BS | S | T | Ag | Int | Per | WP | Fel |
|----|----|----|----|----|----|----|----|----|
| | | (10) | (8) | | | (8) | | (6) |
| 43 | 43 | 45 | 45 | 50 | 30 | 49 | 45 | 35 |

**Move:** 6/12/18/36 **Wounds:** 28

**Skills:** Awareness (Per), Command (Fel) +10, Dodge (Ag) +10, Forbidden Lore (Daemons, Warp) (Int), Intimidate (S) +20, Lip Reading (Per), Literacy (Int), Performer (Fel) +10, Psyniscience (Per), Scrutiny (Per), Speak Language (Low Gothic) (Int), Survival (Int), Swim (S).

**Talents:** Astartes Weapon Training, Diehard, Fearless, Feedback Screech, Hatred (Loyalist Space Marines) Heightened Senses (All), Jaded, Lightning Reflexes, Litany of Hate, Quick Draw, Rapid Reload, Swift Attack, True Grit.

**Traits:** Dark Sight, Fear 2 (Frightening), Size (Hulking), Unnatural Strength (x2), Unnatural Toughness (x2), Unnatural Perception (x2), Unnatural Fellowship (x2).

**Armour:** Astartes power armour (Head 8, Arms 8, Body 10, Legs 8).

**Weapons:** Astartes Chainsword (1d10+14 R; Pen 4; Balanced, Tearing), or Astartes Chain Axe (1d10+18 R; Pen 4), Astartes Bolt Pistol (30m; S/3/–; 2d10+5 X; Pen 5; Clip12; Reload Full; Tearing), Noise Marine Blastmaster (150m; S/2/–; 1d10+12 E; Pen 6; Clip —; Rld —; Devastating [1], Storm), or Noise Marine Doom Siren (30m; S/–/–; 1d10+12 E; Pen 9; Clip —; Rld —, Flame), or Noise Marine Sonic Blaster (100m; S/2/4; 1d10+9 E; Pen 4; Clip —; Rld —; Storm, Tearing).

**Gear:** 2 bolt pistol magazines, hallucinogen grenades.

### Special Rules

**Psychic Cacophony:** The mind-numbing psychic assault created Noise Marines affects enemies within 75 metres (the GM may increase of decrease this range to account for special circumstances). All opponents of the Chaos God Slaanesh within range automatically suffer a –10 penalty to their Willpower and must take a Willpower Test at the beginning of each of their turns. If the test is passed no further effects occur that turn. If the test is failed, the individual suffers a –10 penalty to all other tests made that turn due to distraction, bleeding ears and the like. If the test is failed by two degrees or more, the victim also suffers one level of Fatigue. Individuals with a Psy Rating that fail their Willpower Test that may not manifest their powers in the same turn. Psychic Cacophony is a mind-affecting psychic-based effect, so any Talents, Traits, Equipment or other rules which offer resistance to warp-based attacks or psychic powers will apply.

## ADVENTURE SEEDS

**Relay:** A band of Noise Marines have seized control of an Imperial communications relay and are using it to pump out their corrupting babble across the air waves. The command disruption being caused is bad enough but the weak-willed are being reduced to little more than zombies by the attack. The communications relay must be recaptured if possible, failing that it must be destroyed.

**Sirens:** On a water planet, the prevailing winds play sonorous notes across a gigantic array of natural rock formations that rise above the waves. An insane band of cultists are working to modify the formations to craft sounds that will resonate through reality and create a breach into the warp.

**Ceremony:** Noise Marines have rounded up tens of thousands of victims for a mass sacrifice to the greater glory of Slaanesh. These poor wretches will be tortured and starved over many days before they are finally massacred in an orgiastic festival to sate the Prince of Pleasure. Mass casualties among the prisoners will serve the Ruinous Powers just as readily as the ceremony going ahead, so the Kill-team must devise a way to destroy the Noise Marines with a minimum of collateral damage.

## *Addendum by Codicier Taelon*

*Let the wise give regard to this warning from the hand of Inquisitor Heurang Rex of the Ordo Malleus.*

An investigation of the catacombs at the Inquisitorial archives on Solipis for data on the so-called "Noise Marines" has revealed one salient detail worthy of words of warning. Recordings of these debased individuals have been found to retain dangerous mimetic properties. This discovery derives directly from the corruption of one of my acolytes, a Lexographer named Tannis. While sorting through the data-stacks it appears that Acolyte Tannis stumbled across a forgotten pile of audio slates. Examination of the security logs for the catacombs shows that after his initial discovery, Acolyte Tannis returned in secret to listen to the audio slates with increasing frequency.

On the sixth such occasion Acolyte Tannis exhibited an outbreak of spontaneous mutation of diverse and foul characteristics, subsequently running amok in the catacombs, causing considerable damage until he was caught and killed. Cautious investigation of the audio slates revealed they dated from a 37th Millennium repression of cultists at Kranor's Star. Heed this warning, four millennia of silence did nothing to dissipate the power of these daemon-born curses and the taint lived on, waiting only for a vulnerable ear to hear them once again.

# OBLITERATORS

*"Through the application and harnessing of the Immaterium, the very force of creation itself, we can remake ourselves. Flesh and bone are weak, yet through technology and the pacts we have with these so-called Infernal Forces, we can remake ourselves."*

–Heretical Teachings of Arch-Magos Erzahd Boge

Perhaps one of the most strange, and certainly amongst the most powerful of foes, Obliterators are shrouded in mystery. Walking armouries bulking even larger than Chaos Space Marines encased in Terminator Armour, Obliterators are masses of twisted flesh melded with weaponry, who look as if their flesh is in a state of flux. Obliterators are inhuman, grotesque arcano-cyborgs whose very flesh and blood can transform into white-hot plasma, titanium-fused bones, or internal organs that generate lethal amounts of electricity. Their brains are as much machine as living flesh.

Obliterators are unique amongst the force of Chaos as they have no allegiance to any particular warband. Entire planets have been laid to waste, whole civilisations perished just to provide a handful of these monsters with the archeotech they so covet, in an effort to gain the promise of future support. Yet, for all their power, the origins of the Obliterators remain open to much speculation and debate.

Often thought to once have been Techmarines of the Emperor's elite Adeptus Astartes, Obliterators are known to be obsessed with the merging of the material and the immaterial, the organic and inorganic. Using knowledge gleaned from their pact with the Ruinous Powers, and with the techno-arcane methods of the Dark Mechanicus, Obliterators have managed to blur the line between man and machine. They are both: one and the same.

There is talk within the ranks of the Adeptus Mechanicus and the Holy Inquisition that Obliterators are the result of centuries of research into the blending of flesh and metal—something the Tech-Priests strive for in their own existence. It's their belief that someone within the ranks of the Mechanicus succeeded through the application of the power of Chaos. However, some (a minority) dismiss such ideas. Instead they believe that Obliterators have contracted some form of daemonic virus that puts their flesh into a permanent state of flux and mutation. It's their belief that many who contract this virus perish as their bodies eventually rebel against the changes wrought upon it. They think that the Obliterators are those who have managed to exercise a manner of control over the flux—they are able to fashion weapons and armour from within their very bodies by tapping into the transmuting power of the virus. Thankfully, this view is much dismissed as there are many flaws—the least of which is that the abilities exhibited by Obliterators in no way act the way a virus should behave.

Aside from their abilities, there is much speculation about the nature of the pact between Obliterators and the Gods of Chaos. Obliterators do not sport any obvious marks of allegiance to any particular Chaos God. They also do not bear the colours of any Traitor Legion or one of the myriad renegade warbands. Many Chaos Lords will go to extreme lengths to secure the fickle aid of even a single Obliterator.

Obliterators is exceedingly rare, and while their exact numbers can only be guessed at, it's apparent that they are among the least numerous of assets employed by the forces of Chaos. They exist outside the structure of the warbands and Legions, and move about from one to the next, exchanging their expertise and power for the chance to claim ancient archeotech or exotic and esoteric wargear from their enemies.

One of the key abilities that Obliterators possess is to manifest a variety of heavy weapons from within their own bodies. As they stalk across the battlefield, they morph their weaponry from lascannons, to plasma cannons and multi-meltas, to specialised weaponry such as the exceedingly rare combi-weapons. Additionally, they can eject spikes and blades from within to engage the foe in close-combat. The only limitation seems to be that an Obliterator is not able to create anything such as a grenade or other type of explosive. Those who study these creatures believe that their weapons are inherently part of their physiology—they could no more create a thrown explosive any more than a mortal man could eject his own heart from his chest.

If more than one Obliterator is in a particular area, they tend to congregate together. Forming an "Obliterator Cult," these creatures will seek to unearth some arcane knowledge or lost technology cache they may have found. The motives of these Cults are just as mysterious as the members themselves.

## Obliterator (Elite) Profile

| WS | BS | S | T | Ag | Int | Per | WP | Fel |
|----|----|----|----|----|----|----|----|----|
| 45 | 50 | 50 (10) | 55 (10) | 35 | 30 | 40 | 45 | –– |

**Movement:** 4/8/12/24      **Wounds:** 40

**Skills:** Awareness (Per), Forbidden Lore (Archeotech, Warp, Daemonology, Traitor Legions) (Int), Intimidate (S), Tech-Use (Int) +20.

**Talents:** Ambidextrous, Crushing Blow, Fearless, Independent Targeting, Mighty Shot, Swift Attack, Two-Weapon wielder (Melee and Ranged).

**Traits:** Auto Stabilised, Daemonic, Fear (2), Natural Armour (Warped Mechanical Flesh), Regeneration (2), Size (Hulking), Sturdy, Unnatural Strength (x2), Unnatural Toughness (x2).

**Armour:** Warped Mechanical Flesh (12 All).

**Weapons:** Power Fist (2d10+22 E, Pen 9, Power Field, Unwieldy), Eviscerator Chainblade (1d10+22 R, Pen 5, Tearing, Unbalanced); Lascannon (300m; S/–/–; 6d10+12 E; Pen 10; Clip X, Rld X); Multi-Melta (60m; S/–/–; 4d10+8 E; Pen 13; Clip X, Rld X, Blast (1)); Plasma Cannon (150m; S/–/–; 2d10+13 E; Pen 10; Clip X, Rld X, Volatile, Blast (1)), Twin-Linked Plasma Gun (100m; S/2/–; 1d10+11 E; Pen 8; Clip X, Rld X, Volatile, Twin-Linked), Twin-Linked Meltagun (20m; S/–/–; 2d10+10 E; Pen 13; Clip X, Rld X, Twin-Linked), Twin-Linked Flamer (20m; S/–/–; 2d10+4 E; Pen 3; Clip X, Rld X, Flame, Twin-Linked).

**Gear:** None.

## Special Rules

**Walking Arsenal:** Obliterators can form a number of weapons from their bizarre flesh, which is an unholy fusion of the organic, the mechanical, and the daemonic. As a Half Action, an Obliterator may manifest a ranged weapon or melee weapon from the selection listed above. It is assumed to possess the necessary training to use any weapon it can create and its weapons have no need to be reloaded. The Obliterator may have 2 weapons formed at any given time and can fire a heavy weapon single-handed.

## ADVENTURE SEED

**Cult:** Agents of the Inquisition have reported that a small cult of Obliterators has been sighted on a nearby planet. They appear to be combing through some ancient xenos ruins. The Watch Commander assigns the Kill-team the mission to capture one or more Obliterators alive. They are then to transport them to a secret Inquisitorial outpost where a team of Tech-Adepts await. It is their hope that they can study one of these creatures up close. However, no one has ever managed to capture a living Obliterator before. Complications ensue during transport to the facility as a Chaos warband strikes at the Battle-Brothers in an attempt to free the Obliterator (in the hope that it will be grateful and assist them at a later time).

## NEW TRAIT: THE PROTECTION OF CHAOS

If the GM wishes, he may increase an Obliterator's threat by adding the Protection of Chaos Trait: The Protection of Chaos is a Force Field (see page 166 in the DEATHWATCH Rulebook) with a rating of 35 that does not overload.

## AN ELITE ENEMY

Because of their ability to create heavy weapons at a whim, Obliterators are more than a match for a single Battle-Brother. Additionally, because they need never worry about ammunition and they are encased in the equivalent of Terminator Armour, they are very difficult to take down unless the Kill-team works together. Thankfully, they are exceedingly rare to encounter.

### Addendum by Codicier Taelon

Obliterators are the foul amalgamation of the techno-arcane processes of the Adeptus Mechanicus and the warping power of Chaos. These once-loyal Techmarines have become something else entirely. I have only ever encountered one in my time as a Space Marine. During that encounter, the creature went to extraordinary depths in order to secure a carved stone chest that was said to contain the remnants of a xenos ruler. Having slaughtered the investigating archeo-team, it was then confronted by a dozen soldiers of the Mechanicus: the Skitarii. I noted with some interest that there seemed to be some manner of hatred or rivalry between the Skitarii and the Obliterator. The nature of this animosity can only be guessed at—perhaps it stems from their connection to their mysterious Machine God. However, eventually the Obliterator had broken and killed the last warrior and turned to walk off from the dig site. That was when my Battle-Brothers and I intervened. Had we known that this foul corruption had planted a series of melta charges in the ruins, we would have been more expedient in our attack. As my eyes cleared from the flash that overloaded my suit's auto-senses, I saw the Obliterator's black form disappearing into a waiting shuttle hidden in the brush.

# PLAGUE MARINES

A Space Marine's body is hardened against every conceivable form of attack, not least against deadly biological weapons and engineered plagues of all kinds. Nonetheless a Space Marine can be laid low by certain warp-spawned infections and diseases, their fantastic constitution betraying them and trapping them in a fevered nightmare between life and death. Lingering in the wracking torture of their own ravaged bodies can force even a Battle-Brother's resolve to weaken enough to make him cry out to the Chaos God Nurgle, the Plague Lord, for succour.

Amongst the most dedicated followers of this debased cult are the Chaos Space Marines of the Death Guard Legion, who fell to Nurgle in the dark days of the Horus Heresy, trapped aboard their ships in the warp as unnatural diseases ravaged their ranks. Over the centuries many other Chaos Space Marines have had cause to dedicate themselves to the Great Corruptor as they stood at the threshold of death. The Maggot Lord welcomes all his children with open arms, instilling in them a kind of morbid energy that is terrible to behold.

Plague Marines are Chaos Space Marines that have dedicated themselves completely to Nurgle. They are greatly beloved of the Lord of Pestilence. Few mortal beings have sufficient vitality to bear the full weight of the many blessings that Nurgle bestows, but the toughened flesh of a Chaos Space Marine is almost limitless in its capacity for the most deadly parasites and plagues. A lone Plague Marine can carry literally thousands of known and unknown viruses and bacteria to infect the battlefield, their bellies churning with maggots, worms and other foul putrescence.

Plague Marines are easy to recognise by their rotted appearance and stink of decay. Dark clouds of flies buzz and swirl all around them as they hobble forward on twisted limbs. Their armour and weapons are pitted and corroded, disgustingly slick with the slime and ooze that drips from pocked carapaces covered in sores. Many Plague Marines appear bloated with distended organs poking out through rents in their armour, their limbs deformed by parasites and disease.

Despite their rotting appearance, Plague Marines are truly fearsome opponents. Their strength is undiminished and, through the blessings of Nurgle, their decaying brains are completely inured to the agony of their physical corruption. In battle this makes them virtually unstoppable as they are all but immune to the pain inflicted by the most terrible wounds in their deadened flesh.

The Plague Marines of Nurgle are armed with rusty, filth-encrusted weapons blessed with some of the Lord of Decay's most virulent diseases. A wound inflicted by a Plague Marine's weapon will fester and become gangrenous within seconds, poisoning the victim's blood and rotting away their flesh. Their bolter rounds carry payloads of virulent pus and infected bone; the teeth of their chainswords are ripped from the mouths of plague victims.

Even the noisome clouds of flies that follow Plague Marines everywhere are a hazard in their own right. The warp-spawned pests swarm across faceplates, clog respirators and bite at exposed flesh unmercifully as if commanded by a sinister volition. A battleground fought over by Plague Marines quickly becomes a toxic wasteland that can be deadly for years to come. A thorough purgation with flamers is recommended in any area where Plague Marines have been present.

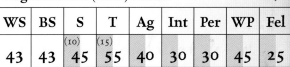

## Plague Marine (Elite) Profile

| WS | BS | S | T | Ag | Int | Per | WP | Fel |
|----|----|----|----|----|-----|-----|----|-----|
| 43 | 43 | (10) 45 | (15) 55 | 40 | 30 | 30 | 45 | 25 |

**Move:** 5/10/15/30      **Wounds:** 36

**Skills:** Awareness (Per), Command (Fel) +10, Dodge (Ag), Forbidden Lore (Daemons, Warp) (Int), Intimidate (S) +20, Literacy (Int), Speak Language (Low Gothic) (Int), Survival (Int), Swim (S).

**Talents:** Astartes Weapon Training, Crippling Strike, Fearless, Hatred (Loyalist Space Marines), Heightened Senses (Sight, Sound, Touch), Jaded, Quick Draw, Rapid Reload, Swift Attack.

**Traits:** Dark Sight, Fear 2 (Frightening), Size (Hulking), Stuff of Nightmares, Toxic (1d10)†, Unnatural Strength (x2), Unnatural Toughness (x3).

**Armour:** Astartes power armour (Head 8, Arms 8, Body 10, Legs 8).

**Weapons:** Astartes Chainsword (1d10+14 R; Pen 4; Balanced, Tearing), Astartes Bolt Pistol (30m; S/3/–; 2d10+5 X; Pen 5; Clip12; Reload Full; Tearing), Astartes Bolter (100m; S/3/–; 2d10+5 X; Pen 5; Clip 28; Reload Full; Tearing), Plague Knife (1d10+10 R; Pen 2; Toxic).

**Gear:** 2 bolt pistol magazines, 4 bolter magazines, 3 Blight grenades.

## ADVENTURE SEEDS

**Ritual:** Epidemics have been ravaging a hive world, killing billions and turning millions more into plague zombies. Adepts have narrowed the source of the diseases to a region of the underhive previously thought too toxic to sustain life. A warband of Plague Marines and their disease riddled supplicants are holding court there, preparing a ritual to summon a Great Unclean One, a Greater Daemon of Nurgle, to complete the ruin of the world.

**Plague Raid:** A pious gathering of Imperial faithful on a Shrine world is being targeted by Plague Marines determined to shame the false Emperor and show His followers how poorly they are protected. They plan to attack in a sudden raid and unleash horrifying diseases into the multitudes of pilgrims before they can be stopped. Once the blessings of Nurgle have been duly dispensed, the Plague Marines can then withdraw and let the epidemic do its work. If the Plague Marines can't be intercepted, untold thousands will be consigned to grisly deaths.

**Epidemic:** Outbreaks of a deadly and virulent disease that is wiping out crews on ships and way stations can be traced back to xenos traders. The traders are selling artefacts which have no ill effect on xenos, but carry a contagion lethal to humans. Tracing the artefacts to their source reveals them to be manufactured by a Plague Marine coven in wilderness space. Eliminating the xenos traders is essential of course, but tracking down the Traitor Space Marines has an even higher priority. Can the Kill-team conquer their natural instincts long enough to pursue the true threat?

### Special Rules

**Cloud of Flies:** All those within 5 metres take a –10 penalty to Weapon Skill and Ballistic Skill Tests as choking clouds of buzzing, biting flies attack every exposed inch of flesh.

†**Toxic (1d10):** This Trait applies to all Plague Marine attacks including ranged ones.

## Addendum by Codicier Taelon

*Truly the deadly virulence of Plague Marines is perhaps the most insidious weapon in their arsenal. Consider this report culled from the log of the Rogue Trader Evar Worak, found when his vessel, the Summer Reign, was boarded after being found adrift.*

------------

*719842.M41*

*As we passed outsystem from Heraklion, an unknown ship was spied on the augur scopes and I ordered full speed as a precaution. Sure enough the newcomer fell in with us and set an intercepting course. It was big, a renegade ship by her rig and certainly too large for us to fight. I altered course to slide past her before she could trap us insystem and we started to outstrip her. Seeing this, the renegades loosed a brace of torpedoes after us, seemingly a pointless gesture but as I altered course again to avoid their tracks, the weapons came about themselves and followed!*

*We fled before them, twisting and turning but the seemingly implacable devices relentlessly closed the distance. Seeing the inevitable conclusion to the race I brought us broadside and let fly at the things. Though the batteries shredded one torpedo, the other one bored on through the barrage and the close-in turret fire, to sink itself in the flank of my beautiful ship. A boarding torpedo of course, and we fought like devils to keep the enemy away from the engine rooms. We had to fight like devils because what came out of that torpedo was surely spawned by daemons. Monstrous, putrid things they were, shaped like Space Marines but filled with an indescribable foulness. Wherever their weapons struck, men fell shrieking, black veins of corruption spreading through their bodies before our very eyes.*

*Our weapons seemed to barely harm them, blasts and bolts sinking harmlessly into flesh and armour that had become a twisted amalgam of both. But we outnumbered them many times over and through bloodshed and sacrifice we dragged them down one by one, though each might cost us a hundred. We slew them all, burned the bodies and cast them out of the 'locks, but now I fear it was not enough.*

*We outran the renegade ship, but some taint has been placed upon our own. The crew are falling to disease, more of them by each hour and the chirurgeons are helpless to prevent it. Emperor protect us.*

# POSSESSED CHAOS SPACE MARINES

*"As I brand my flesh, so I brand my soul. As I prepare for the essence, I remember that I am the elite. For soon I will become the Possessed."*

–S'Trakh, Possessed Chaos Space Marine of the Word Bearers Legion

The Possessed are demented Chaos Space Marines who harbour a singular gift: they allow their bodies to serve as vessels for the daemons of the empyrean. For them, merely serving the Gods of Chaos is not enough; as such, they willingly become hosts to these otherworldly beings—gaining additional abilities and powers in the process. However, such a bargain is not without severe risk. Possession is usually agonising and excruciating as the daemon within morphs and warps the flesh to better serve their needs. Their brethren look on jealously as the flesh melts, and the muscle and bone underneath pop and crack with contortions, such pain eventually driving the Possessed mad—many afterwards describe the sensation as a "joyous moment."

Within some of the most fanatical of Traitor Legions and Chaos warbands, such as the Word Bearers, Brothers of Livos, Fire Reavers, and others, the Possessed are seen as superior to the "normal" Chaos Space Marines. They are seen as the closest to the mad Gods they serve—or at least as close as one can get without succumbing to spawndom or attaining princehood. Those who willingly offer themselves up for possession spend months conducting dark rituals upon themselves: debasement, scarification, and worse. They prepare their body so it can harbour the dark energies and become a daemonic host. This is not a solitary event, for many prepare themselves for mass possessions. Such events are marked with great celebration—orgiastic feasting and depravity the likes of which would drive sane men mad. Others are sometimes marked with solemn and droning hymnals of impurity, depending on the warband's rites.

The Possessed Chaos Space Marine is easy to distinguish amongst his brethren. He features a grotesque visage and mutated body. Many of the Possessed have vicious claws, outlandishly warped musculature, tentacles that wave about, warped faces, twisted bodies, whipping tails, spines, spikes, antlers, horns, and other types of physical abnormalities, as the daemon within reconstructs the body to its own perverted whims. Some have massive bodies (larger for a Space Marine), razor-sharp claws and talons, fangs, or other "natural" weapons that can easily rip through the power armour of a Space Marine (or even through the awesomely tough Terminator Armour).

While harbouring the daemon within them, the Possessed are granted great speed, strength, and stamina. They are able to shrug off wounds that would outright kill any mortal warrior and slow down a normal Space Marine. It is for this power that many Chaos Space Marines will willingly go through the process of possession and undergo such traumatic transformations. However, despite all their ritual and preparation, the life of a Possessed can be cut horribly short. Regardless of their strength and will, in spite of their

awesome augmentations and transformations, sometimes the bodies of the Chaos Space Marines are unable to contain the potent energies of the daemonic essence. When such failures occur, the body mutates horribly and spontaneously beyond all recognition as it's consumed from within by the dark fire of Chaos.

While a Possessed has awesome physical powers that are granted to it by the daemon within, they have other uses aside from being able to tear through the enemy. Due to the inhuman senses of the Daemon trapped within them, the Possessed is able to latch onto the warp presence of other creatures. This makes them superb trackers and scouts, able to unerringly track down and hunt enemy positions and potential victims without being seen. Additionally, this ability also allows Possessed aboard the fleets of Chaos Space Marines to aid the Sorcerers with warp navigation. It is without a doubt that the use of this unique ability is what allows many ships of the Chaos fleet to surprise their enemies and arrive from the warp in places where none thought to look.

| Possessed Chaos Marine (Elite) Profile | | | | | | | | |
|---|---|---|---|---|---|---|---|---|
| WS | BS | S | T | Ag | Int | Per | WP | Fel |
| 43 | 43 | (12) 55 | (8) 45 | 40 | 30 | 30 | 45 | 15 |

**Movement:** 5/10/15/30  **Wounds:** 40

**Skills:** Awareness (Per), Climb (S), Command (Fel) +10, Dodge (Ag) +10, Intimidate (S) +20, Literacy (Int), Lore: Forbidden (Daemonology, Psykers, Warp) (Int), Psyniscience (Per) +10, Scrutiny (Per), Speak Language (Low Gothic) (Int), Survival (Int), Swim (S), Tracking (Int) +10.

**Talents:** Astartes Weapon Training, Bolter Drill, Die Hard, Fearless, Hatred (Loyalist Space Marines), Heightened Senses (All), Jaded, Preternatural Speed, Quick Draw, Rapid Reload, Swift Attack, True Grit.

**Traits:** Brutal Charge, Daemonic, Dark Sight, Fear 2 (Frightening), Improved Natural Weapons, Natural Weapons (Warp claws), Size (Hulking), Unnatural Strength (x2), Unnatural Toughness (x2).

**Armour:** Astartes Power Armour (Head 8, Arms 8, Body 10, Legs 8), Protection of Chaos†.

**Weapons:** Warp claws (1d10+12 R; Pen 4).

†The Protection of Chaos is a Force Field (see page 166 in the **DEATHWATCH** Rulebook) with a rating of 35 that does not overload.

## ABILITIES OF THE POSSESSED

The GM should select one of the following abilities for each Possessed as a result of his possession by the daemonic entity. Note that Stinger, Pincer Claws, and Rending Weapons replace the Possessed Marine's warp claws.

### Stinger

The Possessed is blessed with a stinger. This can either be similar to those of the terrifying Daemonettes, or take on some other form. (1d10+14; Pen 2; Felling (1), Toxic)

### Pincer Claws

One or both of the Possessed's hands are now pincer claws, like those of a crab. Needless to say, this claw prevents the Chaos Space Marine from making use of any gear requiring the use of hands. (1d10+14; Pen 3; Tearing)

### Rending Weapons

Sprouting fangs, horns, spines, or spikes, the Possessed is able to use these horrifying features to rend armour as easily as flesh. (1d5+14; Pen 5; Razor Sharp)

### Feel No Pain

Due to the essence contained within the body of the Possessed, he is inured to pain and physical discomfort. The Possessed ignores all levels of Fatigue and ignores any Critical Effects that relate to pain (GM's option), but not to limb loss or other damage types. The Possessed Marine gains 10 Bonus Wounds.

## AN ELITE ADVERSARY

Possessed Chaos Space Marines are an Elite-level enemy. While they will be a challenge to many individual Space Marines, an uninjured Kill-team will be able to take one down without too much difficulty. However, unless they are in a squad of their fellows, Possessed will rarely attempt to take on a fully armed Kill-team directly.

At the Gm's discretion, Possessed Marines may have any Mark of Chaos (see page 363 in the **DEATHWATCH** Rulebook).

## Power Aura

Through some little-understood warp method, the daemon within is able to surround the Chaos Space Marine and his weapons with a powerful energy field. This means that all melee weapons are treated as having the Power Field Quality and increase their Penetration to 8.

## Powerful Legs

The Possessed's legs have twisted into a form that allows him to leap further and run faster than ever before. Treat the Possessed as having +5 to Movement (e.g., a "standard" Possessed would have a Movement of 10/20/30/60).

### Addendum by Codicier Taelon

I find that the Universe is indeed cruel, but this only serves to reinforce my faith in my Primarch and the Emperor. Today I mourn the loss of two Brothers with whom I have fought side by side for many years. For the past several weeks we were investigating the mysterious deaths of personnel within the ranks of the Imperial Guard. Clearly we had a dangerous predator in our midst— although I must admit that I was unprepared for the form such a creature would take. This killer seemed well-trained in stealth and deception; somehow able to pinpoint the exact location of its victim and eliminate them. We knew that it was only a matter of time before the creature would target us. As it turns out, I was to be the next victim. When this depraved attacker was revealed, I was surprised to find out it was one of the fallen Space Marines, but one who had perhaps fallen further than others. This was one of the Possessed, a group of Chaos Marines who choose to allow a daemon to dwell within them. In exchange for their soul's corruption and eternal damnation, they receive the powers of the daemon; one of which is the ability to unerringly track targets through the warp. As members of my Kill-team lay dying, as this creature's form lay broken—the malfeasance within fleeing— it was almost as if reason suddenly returned to him. I honoured him with a swift death, unlike the ones he gave his victims.

# WEAPONS OF CHAOS

*"Strike the first chord... tap the rune of power... eternal bliss that only the Prince of Pleasures can provide!"*

–Noise Marine Chant

The followers of Chaos have many weapons at their disposal in their never-ending war against the inexhaustible armies of the Imperium of Mankind. Listed below are a selection of some of the more commonly encountered weapons used by Chaos forces across the Jericho Reach.

## NOISE MARINE WEAPONS

The weapons employed by the dreaded Noise Marines use a combination of light and sound designed to stimulate the sensations of both the wielder and the unfortunate victim. Because the Slaanesh-worshipping traitors' minds are so twisted and distorted, only the most deafening and raucous noises stir their senses.

### SONIC BLASTER

A Sonic Blaster unleashes wave after wave of crippling and distorted harmonics of sound to rip targets apart. Many Noise Marines equipped with such weapons use them with manic intensity. They run up and down through the various chords and sliding scales so that these devices perpetually howl with a mixture of agony and ecstasy.

### DOOM SIREN

The Doom Siren is a dreaded weapon fitted to some Noise Marines. A complex arrangement of pipes and tubes that fits around the helmet to act as amplifiers, the device projects the Noise Marine's horrific battle screams and terrifying howls of ecstatic pleasures into a manic wall of destruction across the field. The Doom Siren drives the screeched song over enemies and vehicles in an orgiastic scream of death and destruction.

### BLASTMASTER

Focusing a thrumming bass note that builds to a crescendo of explosive intensity, the Blastmaster is a heavy weapon employed by Noise Marines. This sound is capable of bursting and rupturing organs. Armour offers little protection as it tends to act as a resonator, enhancing the already deadly frequencies, liquefying the bones and organs of those encased within. Armoured vehicles are similarly wrecked, as they crack and shatter under the atonal assault.

The Blastmaster has two settings: by altering the frequency being used, the weapon can either fire off a withering hail of discordant noise, or a single, massive infernal blast.

# PLAGUE MARINE WEAPONS

Giving their loyalty to the Plague Father, Nurgle, Plague Marines are living contagions of disease and death. Many of the weapons employed by these plagued beings likewise transmit horrific and deadly maladies. Listed below are some of the more wicked devices of death designed to please Nurgle and bring about both death and suffering.

## BLIGHT GRENADES

Bloated and swollen with disease, the Plague Marines long to share their pathogens with those who are hale and hearty. Cultivating these contagions into explosive devices designed to wound and infect over a large area, Blight grenades expose those who are injured by the corrupted pieces of plague-ridden shrapnel to the most deadly of toxins. These contagions can penetrate cracks in armour, cause flesh to boil and slough away, and fill the air with blinding spores, all the while keeping the victim alive until the very end—so they can better enjoy the gifts of the Lord of Decay. Some versions of Blight Grenades resemble maggot-filled shrunken heads.

## PLAGUE KNIVES

Corroded and diseased blades that have been blessed by the great Nurgle, plague knives are sure to deliver their blighted corruption to any who are even scratched by them. These are one of the ways the dreaded Plague Marines deliver their "benedictions" across the galaxy.

# OTHER WEAPONS

The weapons detailed below are not specific to any type of band or group. They are found amongst all the dreaded forces of the Ruinous Powers.

## BERZERKER AXE

Found mainly within the ranks of the Khorne Berzerkers, these chain axes are often thought to be possessed by a daemon of rage.

## TABLE 3-1: CHAOS WEAPONS

| Name | Class | Range | ROF | Dam | Pen | Clip | Rld | Special |
|---|---|---|---|---|---|---|---|---|
| Berzerker Axe | Melee | — | — | 1d10+4 R | 4 | — | — | Tearing |
| Blastmaster (Explosive Crescendo) | Heavy | 250m | S/–/– | 3d10+10 E | 8 | — | — | Blast (5), Devastating (2) |
| Blastmaster (Hail of Noise) | Basic | 150m | S/2/– | 1d10+12 E | 6 | — | — | Devastating (1), Storm |
| Blight Grenades | Thrown | SBx3 | S/–/– | 3d10+5 I | 0 | — | — | Blast (†), Devastating (3), Toxic |
| Doom Siren | Basic | 30m | S/–/– | 1d10+12 E | 9 | — | — | Flame†† |
| Plague Knife | Melee | — | — | 1d10 R | 2 | — | — | Toxic |
| Sonic Blaster | Basic | 100m | S/2/4 | 1d10+9 E | 4 | — | — | — |

†If the grenade does any Damage, then, each round after the first, check for another target at random (friend or foe) within d5 metres to see if any Damage is caused to them (rolling for new Damage to represent the mutated virus). Continue until Damage is not taken or after d10 rounds have passed.

†† This weapon follows the rules for the Flame special quality except that it does not set targets on fire.

# CHAOS PSYCHIC POWERS

Listed below are some of the more common Sorcerous powers granted to Chaos Space Marine Sorcerers. These powers are often in addition to their own formidable psychic powers.

## BOLT OF CHANGE

**Action:** Half Action
**Range:** 50m x PR
**Sustained:** No
**Description:** The Sorcerer hurls a roiling ball of coruscating energy at the target. This blast is formed of the raw magic of primal Chaos, and its touch brings rapid mutation and death. Victims of the Bolt of Change are torn apart as their bodies rebel against the blasphemous energies that warp them. The bolt does 1d10 x Psy Rating E damage. Additionally, a victim of the Bolt of Change must pass a **Challenging (+0) Willpower Test**. Failure by 5 degrees or more indicates that the victim is either violently torn apart by the uncontrolled power or mutated into a mewling spawn of Chaos that rapidly expires. (In either case, the victim instantly dies unless he burns a Fate Point, which also prevents mutation in the case of a Battle-Brother.) If the victim passes the Test, or fails by less than 5 degrees, there is no additional effect.

## DOOMBOLT

**Action:** Half Action
**Opposed:** No
**Range:** 20 metres x Psy Rating
**Sustained:** No
**Description:** Doombolt is a common destructive power utilised by a great many Sorcerers to strike down their foes. Doombolts are corrosive bolts of dark energy, formed from the coalesced spite and loathing of the Sorcerer. The psyker must nominate a single target within range and line of sight; if the Focus Power Test is successful, then the target has been successfully hit. For every Degree of Success after the first, the psyker scores an additional hit. The number of extra hits scored in this manner may not exceed twice the psyker's Psy Rating. The first hit must strike the initially-chosen target, while any subsequent hits may strike either the initial target, or any other targets within two metres, providing all of the targets are within range and line of sight. This may be dodged exactly as if it were a Full-Auto Attack. Each bolt has the following profile: 1d10+10 E, Pen 8.

## NURGLE'S ROT

**Action:** Half Action
**Opposed:** No
**Range:** 5 metres + Psy Rating radius
**Sustained:** Yes
**Description:** The grandest and most infamous of Nurgle's contagions, Nurgle's Rot is known by many names and has appeared on countless worlds, leaving entire populations desolated by this terrible daemonic pathogen. Nurgle-devoted Sorcerers take on all manner of diseases, serving as host to the creations of the Lord of Plagues. From this seething mass of decay and entropy, these devotees of pestilence summon forth the psychic echo of this paragon of plagues, inflicting it upon those nearby.

The infectious gift of Nurgle is cast outwards to embrace all who stray too near to the Sorcerer. Creatures within range of the Sorcerer while this power remains in effect suffer 1d10 + Psy Rating damage, with the Toxic (1d10) quality. The damage from this power ignores Armour unless it is environmentally sealed.

While this power remains in effect, the air within the power's range is filled with a thick, acrid fog and swarms of massive bloated flies. Any creature within range that is not devoted to Nurgle suffers a −5 penalty to Intelligence, Perception and Fellowship Tests as the foul vapour and buzzing flies hinder their concentration and drive them to distraction. This effect is in addition to any normal Psychic Phenomena.

## WARPTIME

**Action:** Half Action
**Range:** You
**Sustained:** Yes
**Description:** The Sorcerer surrounds himself with a field of dimensional instability, warping the passage of time. The Sorcerer gains a bonus to his Weapon Skill and Ballistic Skill equal to his Psy Rating +10, and he may re-roll one damage dice every Round.

## WIND OF CHAOS

**Action:** Half Action
**Opposed:** Yes
**Range:** 5 metres x Psy Rating
**Sustained:** No
**Description:** Reaching deep into the corruption within his soul, the Sorcerer unleashes a wave of energy that leaves devastation in its wake. Depending upon the devotions of the Sorcerer, the nature of this outpouring of corrupt power varies—those devoted to Nurgle produce a stream of bilious filth, while a rain of hypnotic light or glittering golden light characterises the powers of a Slaaneshi Sorcerer. Every Sorcerer's Wind of Chaos is subtly different, coloured by their own prejudices and insanities.

The Sorcerer produces a torrent of foul energy in a 30 degree cone out to the power's range, similar to a weapon with the Flame Quality. Creatures caught within the spray may oppose the Focus Power Test with an Agility Test. Any creature that does not successfully avoid the power's effects suffers 2d10+ Psy Rating Energy damage with the Felling (2) and Warp Weapon Qualities, plus a single additional Quality determined by the Sorcerer's alignment.

If used by a Tzeentchian Sorcerer, Wind of Chaos gains the Flame quality. If used by a Slaaneshi Sorcerer, Wind of Chaos gains the Shocking quality. If used by a Nurgle Sorcerer, Wind of Chaos gains the Toxic quality. If used by an Undivided Sorcerer, Wind of Chaos gains the Tearing quality.

## Addendum by Codicier Taelon

The following archival entry I discovered open on my data-terminal. Having thoroughly checked every access log, I am confidant that no intruder entered my cell while I was at prayer, and a sub-level meta-probe revealed no remote access had taken place. I can only assume that the Omega Vault itself recovered this account and presented it for me to read.

It started as a violet shimmer in the night skies, a captivating spectacle that grew more dazzling with each appearance. The multitudes flocked in ever-greater numbers to behold the lights, and some even started to claim that they foretold of the return of the long-lost Emperor.

Soon such tales were sweeping the land, and there was little I and the council could do to impose order. As the lights grew so bright they were visible even in the daytime, all order collapsed. The entire population took to the streets in adulation, singing the praises of the returned Emperor who the rabble-rousers promised them would soon walk in their midst. Each supplicant contested with the next to sing the praises of the Emperor ever louder, until the spires shook with the cacophony of a million incoherent voices.

On the twelfth day, the entire sky was engulfed by the seething violet lights, great tendrils of the ether coiling through the clouds to quest across the wastes. One such tendril came to rest in the grand square, in the very midst of the greatest congregation of supplicants, whose voices were now raised in such unholy din that that their own ears gushed with blood.

And then the square was engulfed in such a mighty radiance that thousands were blinded in an instant. I myself watched from atop my palace bastion, and even at a distance of almost a mile was struck dumb by the scintillating light. The multitudes collapsed to their knees and silence finally descended as a silhouette appeared amidst the light. A figure stepped forth, tall and proud and suggestive of every virtue legend ascribes to the Emperor.

And then the figure was resolved for all to see. He bade the supplicants to raise their heads and look upon his countenance. But it was not the gold-girded form of our long-lost master who stood there before us. It was some manner of fiend, its features cruel and lascivious and its eyes almond-shaped and black. A vile tongue quested forth from a mouth lined with a million lamprey teeth. Its body was adorned with fragments of armour wrought into impossibly complex forms, and its skin, where it showed through the armour was as white as ivory. None could fathom its gender, for it was both male and female, and neither.

By the Emperor, it was beautiful.

Every one of us gave ourselves utterly to that perfect fiend and we are blessed to serve in its exquisite host. The warp is come to my world, the entirety of which I willingly give unto my new master. My people I pledge body and soul to the perfect glory of the Empyrean, and we shall spread word of that perfection across the void.

My soul belongs to Chaos, and soon so too shall everyone in this entire region. This is my oath, in the name of my master, Slaan'ulari, Caller of the Perfect Storm and Lord of the Exquisite Host.

SEALED

DATA

# IV

## ADVANCED ADVERSARIES

DEATHWATCH

USING HORDES IN
DEATHWATCH

•

NEW HORDE TRAITS

•

MASSED BATTLES

•

TURNING POINTS

# CHAPTER IV: ADVANCED ADVERSARIES

*"They came without number and without remorse. They came from every side and at every hour. They came hungry for our blood, and they just kept on coming. Every one that came... we killed."*

–Battle-Brother Glarus of the Crimson Fists

Nothing exemplifies the strength and power of the Space Marines like their ability to deal with a foe that vastly outnumbers them. In fact it is very rare that a Battle-Brother will ever face his enemies in equal numbers, more often encountering scores of foes for each member of his Kill-team team at any one time. Of course this is what a Space Marine expects on the field of battle and he trains to work in small units, or even alone, against these large enemy formations, knowing he is worth any number of lesser warriors and willing to prove it with whirling chainsword and hammering bolter fire. It is a well known adage that there is less than one Space Marine for each world in the Imperium, so it is easy to imagine just how thin the Chapters are spread and how vastly the enemies of man outnumber

them. It is little wonder then that as a Battle-Brother becomes a veteran of many battles, campaigns and wars, it will be atop the bodies and blood of countless foes.

In DEATHWATCH, the players will often find themselves outnumbered by their foes, sometimes many times over, or they might find themselves facing a foe which would be little danger to them individually but in large numbers can pose a threat to even a heavily armed and armoured Space Marine. For both these instances the DEATHWATCH Rulebook includes rules for Hordes (see page 359) which allow the GM to turn any kind of foe into a mob or combat formation of dozens, hundreds or even thousands of individuals, making it far more deadly and harder to kill. This section builds upon these Horde rules and offers advice to the GM on when and how to use Hordes in his games, as well as Horde tactics and how Hordes can be used intelligently to make them even more deadly. It will also cover unusual kinds of Hordes such as Psychic Hordes or Vehicle Hordes and provide guidelines for Horde versus Horde combats. Finally this section also provides a number of new Horde Traits which the GM can apply to his Hordes giving them special abilities that represent the myriad kinds of Hordes the players might face and the different ways in which they will fight in combat.

## USING HORDES IN DEATHWATCH

Hordes are a great way of making an individually weak foe, such as a mutant or Grot, into a real danger for the players. In addition to making these kinds of foes harder to defeat, it also increases their Attacks and Damage and thus in many cases gives them a chance of actually hurting a Battle-Brother by getting past their impressive armour and Toughness. Hordes are also an excellent way to impress upon the players the power of their characters as they mow down scores of foes or wade into mobs of enemies hacking them down left and right. This can then also make the appearance of single powerful foes, such as Genestealers or Tau battlesuits, even more notable as they stand out from the throngs of lesser enemies and test the player's abilities one on one.

Pretty much any kind of enemy can be turned into a Horde simply by giving it a Magnitude and applying the special Horde rules from the rulebook, however some foes make better Hordes than others and some can become very deadly indeed. As a general rule, if the GM thinks that an individual foe is a match (or more than a match) for one of the Battle-Brothers, then it should generally not be encountered as a Horde (this is not to say the foe could not be encountered in large numbers, only that the normal rules should be enough to make such an encounter challenging). For anything below this level of power, however, Hordes work well. The GM can even build up to a Horde to give it greater impact when it does arrive, such as having the players easily dispatch numerous small groups or lone Termagants, before a wave of them descends on the Kill-team in their hundreds.

To create an Endless Horde, the GM sets the Horde's Magnitude as normal, depending on the amount of foes which can realistically get at the characters. This could range from as small as 20 or 30 in confined spaces such as a bunker or void ship, to 60+ in open cities or blasted battlefields. The Horde then fights normally using all the standard rules for Hordes governing its number of attacks and damage it can deal, with the two following exceptions:

• Damage inflicted on the Horde only lasts for its following round, at the end of which it is restored to its starting Magnitude (even if it was reduced to 0 Magnitude) as fresh warriors rush in to fill its ranks.

• Endless Hordes need never test morale and will never break or run away—there are just too many of them to be defeated by "a handful" of casualties.

## EXAMPLE

*The Kill-team is holding out in the ruins of an Imperial firebase against a Tau battlegroup numbered in its thousands, while they wait for an orbital barrage to even the odds. The GM decides that there are so many Fire Warriors in the Horde that it counts as Endless and assigns it a Magnitude of 60, given the ease at which they can bring their numbers to bear. In the players' turn they manage to reduce the Fire Warrior Horde's Magnitude to 45 with their attacks, so in the Fire Warrior's turn it makes return attacks at this reduced Magnitude, working out attacks and damage based on a Magnitude of 45. At the end of its turn however it returns to a Magnitude of 60.*

## HORDE TRAITS IN DEATHWATCH

The Horde Traits presented here are designed to work alongside those from the Traits section of the DEATHWATCH rulebook. For completeness, the five Horde Traits in the rulebook fall into the following categories:

- Trained Traits
- Disciplined (DEATHWATCH page 130)
- Fighting Withdrawal (DEATHWATCH page 132)
- Fire Drill (DEATHWATCH page 132)
- Wild Traits
- Blood Soaked Tide (DEATHWATCH page 130)
- Overwhelming (DEATHWATCH page 133)

# NEW HORDE TRAITS

*"A lone hormagaunt is little more than target practice; a hundred, however, is a different beast entirely..."*

–Battle-Brother Darstan, 10th Company Storm Wardens

No two kinds of Hordes are exactly the same and depending on the nature of the creatures which make up their numbers they will fight and behave in very different ways. Some Hordes may be unruly mobs that come at the Battle-Brothers in a mass of teeth and claws, while others will be disciplined ranks of well trained foes which attack in methodical precision under the guidance of officers and commanders. Some Hordes are even stranger than these and consist of foes which gain special properties when gathered in large numbers, bending the laws of reality and tearing holes in the Materium with their very presence. Some of these differences will come through as a result of the creature profile on which a Horde is based, however in many cases Hordes possess abilities and effects which only become apparent when they gather in large numbers. This is where the GM can use Horde Traits to represent the distinct natures and fighting styles of different Hordes.

Horde Traits are divided into three broad groups (Trained, Wild and Unnatural) to help the GM decide which kinds of Hordes they might be appropriate for. There are no absolute rules as to which Traits can be used with which Hordes and the GM can apply any of the Horde Traits presented here to any Hordes he might create, using his own common sense and best judgement. In fact, it is also entirely possible that two Hordes of the same type may have different Traits depending on their level of training, the exact type of creature they are or their commanders (i.e. one well trained Traitor Guardsman Horde might have the Volley Fire Trait while another fighting alongside it with less discipline might not). The GM may also give his Hordes more than one Trait, though this is unusual and should be reserved for the most dangerous or elite kinds of Hordes. It would be a very unusual Horde indeed which had Traits from more than one of the categories below (Trained but Wild Hordes tend to be rare indeed).

## TRAINED HORDE TRAITS

Many kinds of warriors in the 41st Millennium have been extensively trained to fight together in large formations, and excel in situations where they have the support of their comrades. A trained Horde usual operates under a commander and exercises discipline and fire control on the battlefield, its every move a carefully measured tactical response to its enemies, following ancient rules of warfare laid down by veterans and tacticians of its race. When encountered in strength and under solid leadership, a trained Horde can be a fearsome foe indeed and use its weapons and warriors to their most devastating effect. Tau Fire Warriors, Imperial Guardsmen and Eldar Guardians are all good examples of trained Hordes.

### Focused Fire

A well trained unit of soldiers can lay down a devastating curtain of fire by overlapping their firing arcs, working in dedicated fire teams and choosing common targets from amongst their foes. This Trait represents the Horde's ability to maintain fire discipline and selective targeting even in the heat of battle, which greatly increases their chances to score telling hits against their enemies. A Horde with the Focused Fire Trait can add its Magnitude to its Ballistic Skill when making ranged attacks up to a maximum bonus of +30. Note that this bonus is an increase to Ballistic Skill and not a modifier to hit and so can be in addition to any other beneficial modifiers the Horde might gain for close range or automatic fire.

### Reform

As a trained combat unit takes damage and its warriors fall in battle, others move up to take their place and cover their position. In this way such a formation can maintain its strength even in the face of casualties and keep up a constant level of fire upon its foes. This Trait allows a Horde to regenerate some of its Magnitude each turn under the close tutelage of its commanders. A Horde with the Reform Trait can recover 1d5 Magnitude at the start of each of its turns as a Free Action. If the Horde is led by an able commander, he can make a **Challenging (+0) Command Test** to increase this number by 1, plus an addition 1 for every degree of success. This test counts as a Half Action for the commander.

### Rally

Discipline is paramount in a well trained military formation, and soldiers are drilled constantly to stand their ground and do their duty regardless of casualties they might suffer. Some units however have more resolve than others and are better at following their orders to the bitter end regardless of the cost in lives. This Trait allows a Horde to hold its ground even in the face of overwhelming casualties and almost certain defeat. A Horde with the Rally Trait can ignore its first failed break test (such as by being reduced by 25% or by 50%). If the Horde is led by a commander then this Trait makes his troops easier to command given their level of discipline and he gains a +10 bonus on all Command Tests when dealing with the Horde.

### Tactical Formation

A drilled combat unit knows how best to protect itself from area attacks such as artillery, grenades and flamers by spreading out and maintaining a good battle formation. When used to full effectiveness, these tactics can greatly reduce the damage from such weapons and make them no more deadly than massed lasgun fire or suppression fire from heavy bolters. This Trait protects a Horde against attacks from blast weapons and flame weapons which would normally do much more damage against tightly packed troops. A Horde with the Tactical Formation Trait reduces additional hits from weapons with the Blast quality or the Flame quality by 1 to a minimum of 1. This reduction applies to each individual attack made from such weapons, regardless of how many attacks occurs against the Horde each round. An able commander can also increase the effectiveness of a Tactical Formation by using a Half Action and making a **Challenging (+0) Command Test**. If successful the reduction is increased to 2 (still with a minimum of 1 damage from each attack).

### Volley Fire

In much the same way that a unit can focus its fire by judicious use of selective targeting, it can also increase its rate of fire by creating gun lines and swapping out soldiers to reload while fresh ones take their place, keeping up a constant fusillade of fire. This Trait allows a Horde to increase its rate of fire and make extra ranged attacks. A Horde with the Volley Fire Trait may make one more ranged attack than normal. For example, a Horde with a Magnitude of 30 would normally make 3 ranged attacks each round, while the same Horde with the Volley Fire Trait will make 4. This additional attack may make use of semi-auto and full-auto fire as normal. An able commander can also increase the effectiveness of Volley Fire by using a Half Action and making a **Challenging (+0) Command Test**. If successful the Horde may make a further 1 ranged attack thus increasing their normal number of ranged attacks by a total of 2.

## WILD HORDE TRAITS

Just as some foes will be well trained warriors, many will be little more than ravening beasts or blood crazy fanatics that fight with little regard for their own safety or no thought of subtle tactics. The galaxy is full of deadly creatures, from the dark forests of feral worlds to the fringes of space where disturbing and bestial xenos creatures lurk among the stars, and in the course of his life a Battle-Brother is likely to encounter many such beings. In combat, a wild Horde is a single mass of surging foes which will press down upon the Battle-Brothers, climbing over their own dead in a frenzied attempt to sink their blades, teeth or claws into the flesh of their foes. They are every bit as deadly as a well trained enemy and should not be underestimated. Tyranid Hormagaunts, Chaos Heretics and Orks are all good examples of wild Hordes.

## Reckless Charge

Many foes will throw themselves into a hail of enemy fire to get to grips with their foes, caring little for casualties or wounds if only they can sink their blades, talons or teeth into warm flesh. This Trait allows a Horde to move more quickly, though at the expense of is defence and some of its number. A Horde with the Reckless Charge Trait can double its move whenever it is in sight of the enemy and ignore reductions to movement from difficult terrain. Each round the Horde uses this increased movement, however, it does so at the expense of some of its number (which are either trampled by their comrades or become entangled in the terrain) and so the Horde automatically loses 1 from its Magnitude. In addition, when using the Reckless Charge Trait, the Horde is easier to hit as its warriors are making little effort to protect themselves from ranged fire. As such, all ranged attacks against the Horde gain a +10 on their rolls to hit.

## Mass Assault

It is difficult for most large groups of foes to effectively focus their efforts onto a single enemy; rather they will attack in a swarm, striking out at anyone in range with equal fury. Some enemies the Battle-Brothers will face, however, are skilled at singling out lone warriors and massing their attacks against them in a brutal display of violence, as dozens of enemies pile over one another to get within arms reach of their target. This Trait increases the Horde's chances of hitting in close combat, reflecting its ability to effectively mass its warriors against individual targets and work together as a single raging foe. A Horde with the Mass Assault Trait may add its Magnitude to its Weapon Skill (to a maximum bonus of +30) when making melee attacks against a single enemy each turn. This bonus only applies to one of the Horde's enemies each turn, though it may change the target of its assault from round to round.

## Dirty Fighters

Many of the most vicious warriors of the 41st Millennium are also the most unscrupulous and will claw, bite and scratch for any advantage they can in combat, often resorting to numerous methods of dirty fighting. This Trait allows a Horde to find weak spots in its enemy's defences and mercilessly exploit them in melee combat. Melee damage inflicted by a Horde with the Dirty Fighters Trait always uses the target's lowest armour rating, regardless of the location the attack actually strikes. In all other respects, the damage is counted against the actual location hit (i.e., arm, head, and so forth) for the purposes of critical hits and any other damage effects.

## Wild Fire

Automatic weapons, especially those with a high rate of fire, are a favourite of less skilled or reckless warriors which enjoy the carnage and collateral damage such weapons can inflict. In their exuberance, however, some warriors, such as Orks, have a habit of firing through their own troops or wildly into melee combat, felling friend and foe alike. This Trait allows a Horde to become more effective with auto-fire weapons, though at the expense of its own safety. A Horde with the Wild Fire Trait gains an additional degree of success whenever it scores a hit with a semi-auto or full-auto burst ranged attack. However, each time the Horde makes a ranged attack and misses with semi-auto or full-auto burst, it has gunned down some of its own warriors and reduces its Magnitude by 1.

## Rampage

Those warriors that favour close quarter fighting in the 41st Millennium usually do so because it is where they excel, and even in an age of lascannons and boltguns there are some foes with the power to literally rip a fully armoured man apart with their bare hands, claws, talons or tentacles. This Trait gives the Horde a chance to inflict additional hits on its enemies in melee combat. When a Horde with the Rampage Trait successfully hits a foe in melee combat, it may immediately make an additional melee attack against the same foe at -10 to hit. If this hit is also successful then it may make another attack at -20, and so on with each additional attack suffering a cumulative -10 penalty. Note that these attacks do not need to inflict any damage to trigger an additional strike, only successfully hit. In all other respects, these attacks are worked out as normal. A Horde wielding two weapons or with either the Swift Attack or Lightning Attack talents may use the Rampage Trait for each attack it makes.

# UNNATURAL HORDE TRAITS

Some foes the Battle-Brothers will face are not wholly of this world; connected to the Immaterium, twisted by strange forces or in the thrall of ancient gods, they possess abilities and powers that defy the natural order. These kinds of foes are among the deadliest that the Kill-team must face, as in large numbers they can exhibit hideous effects on all those around them and can be extremely difficult to destroy with mundane weapons. Unnatural Hordes are also likely to behave differently to more conventional Hordes in combat, using unusual attacks such as psychic powers or innate weaponry rather than simple blades and bullets. Chaos Daemons, Plague Zombies and Tyranid Zoanthropes are all good examples of unnatural Hordes.

## Psychic Shadow

The mere presence of some creatures is enough make a man's skin crawl and his mind seethe with revulsion, and when such foes gather in large numbers, the effects become even more pronounced, pressing in upon the thoughts of all those around them. This Trait affects all those that fight the Horde and makes it harder for them to concentrate as the psychic presence of the Horde scratches and screams in their minds. A Horde with the Psychic Shadow Trait will affect all those within a number of metres from it edges equal to 20 times its Willpower Bonus. Those affected suffer a penalty to all their Willpower tests equal to the Magnitude of the Horde, up to a maximum of -30. In addition, these effects are more pronounced in psykers and whenever a psyker tries to manifest a power within range of the Horde's Psychic Shadow, he reduces his Psy Rating by 1.

## Group Mind

Skilled groups of psykers are sometimes known for manifesting greater powers by combining their abilities in carefully constructed rituals and rites. Some creatures, though, have a natural ability to combine their psychic might, daemons most notably, and enhance their power by mere close proximity. This Trait allows a psychic Horde to enhance it powers, even more so if they can focus their power through a single powerful psyker. A Horde with the Group Mind Trait adds an additional 1 to its Psy Rating as based on its Magnitude. For example, a psychic Horde with a Magnitude of 30 would normally have a Psy Rating of 3, however if the same Horde had the Group Mind Trait it would have a rating of 4. A psychic commander can also take advantage of a Horde with a Group Mind to either enhance his own power or boost theirs, provided he is no further than double his Willpower Bonus in metres from the edge of the Horde. During his turn, such a commander can use the Horde to increase his Psy Rating by 1, though in its next turn the Horde may not use any psychic powers itself. Alternatively he may forgo using psychic powers himself and instead increase the Horde's Psy Rating by 1 (in addition to the +1 from the Group Mind Trait).

## Fanatical Devotion

For many proscribed cults in the Imperium and foul xenos covens, devotion can only be measured in blood, violence and pain. Such crazed individuals have taken their heretical faith beyond that of mere worship or obedience, and revel as much in the wounds they suffer themselves as those they inflict on their foes. Devotees of Khorne are especially well known for this kind of act, though they are far from the only ones to exhibit such behaviour. This Trait makes a Horde more enraged the more wounded it becomes, fighting in a frenzy to the last, just to spill a few more drops of blood. A Horde with the Fanatical Devotion Trait counts has having the Fearless talent (meaning it cannot be broken) if it does not already. In addition, for every 10 Magnitude of damage the Horde suffers it gains an extra melee attack and a +2 to all melee damage rolls, to a maximum of 3 extra attacks and +6 melee damage. Such is the madness of the Horde that they almost throw themselves on the weapons of their foes, and all damage dealt to them in melee combat reduces their Magnitude by an additional 1 point.

## Relentless

While Battle-Brothers may often face fearless foes, driven forward by alien masters heedless of the casualties inflicted upon them, they may also find themselves facing enemies without the wit or mind to care about death. These kinds of mindless foes, such as plague zombies or mind-controlled thralls, will keep coming regardless of the damage they suffer and the scores of their brethren which fall around them, pressing forward with missing limbs and fatal wounds if it means getting to grips with the Kill-team. This Trait makes a Horde nigh unstoppable and heedless of wounds, though not particularly fast. A Horde with the Relentless Trait counts as having the Fearless talent if it does not already have it (meaning it cannot be broken in combat by suffering 25% or 50% casualties and need never take a Willpower Test to avoid being broken). Such a Horde is slow, either by the nature of the sorceries which animate it (such as the case with plague zombies) or the ungainly gate of those possessed by mind control, and so may never Run or Charge. Relentless Hordes are nevertheless extremely difficulty to stop with missile fire, and so only ever suffers 1 point of Magnitude damage from ranged attacks, including those from weapons with the Blast quality. Melee attacks and attacks by weapons with the Flame quality damage the Horde as normal.

## Spawn

The galaxy is full of alien horrors and strange, bizarre creatures of all shapes and sizes. Amongst these are things which are not even remotely humanoid, or come from environments so alien to man as to be difficult for his mind of understand. Many daemons too defy the natural laws of the universe and behave in ways that are unexpected and alarming, warping or changing shape on the battlefield as they fight or as damage is dealt against them. This Trait allows a particularly unnatural or alien Horde to increase it Magnitude when it takes damage as its members split or spawn more warriors from their own bodies. A Horde with the Spawn Trait can make a **Challenging (+0) Toughness Test** whenever it suffers at least 1 point of damage to its Magnitude in a turn. If successful, it increases it Magnitude by 1 as new warriors are spawned. If the Horde suffers more than 5 Magnitude in a single turn and passes it Toughness Test then the Magnitude increase becomes 1d5 rather than 1, and if it suffers 10 or more to its Magnitude, this further increases to 1d10. A Horde may increase its Magnitude above its starting amount though the use of this Trait.

# Massed Battles

*"Guns, steel, fire and blood! My heart sings to the sounds of war and my fangs ache for the flesh of my enemies! For the Emperor!"*

–Kyrir Icefang of the Space Wolves, Battle of Broken Plains

The Adeptus Astartes were created for one purpose and one purpose alone: the destruction of the Emperor's foes. Across the vast stretches of the galaxy and over the long bloody millennia, they have fulfilled this purpose with brutal efficiency, taking the fight to the Imperium's enemies wherever they may be found and wherever they threaten human worlds. Some of these conflicts have been truly epic indeed, such as the Tyranid invasion of the Ultramarines home world of Macragge or the battle for Armageddon which involved thousands of Space Marines from many different Chapters. No strangers to total warfare or massive military engagements, Battle-Brothers are just as likely to find themselves in the midst of a major conflict as they are special operations, and as such train extensively for both. Such massed battles present their own unique environment, changing the way in which the Battle-Brother must operate, the weapons they use and the objectives they are issued by their commanders. One thing that is likely to remain the same, however, is that they are sure to be outnumbered, though this has never been a problem for Space Marines and is an expected aspect of war for these elite warriors.

The Deathwatch, made up from members of the Adeptus Astartes, operates in a similar way to the Chapters and though they are an elite formation used primarily as a surgical strike force against carefully chosen targets, they are often dutifully part of larger Imperial operations. These can include anything from planetary invasions to space battles, where they will find themselves fighting alongside hundreds or even thousands of allied troops supported by armour, artillery, air support and other elite commanders and combat specialists. In such instances the Kill-team can coordinate with its allies and combine its efforts to complete common Imperial objectives, adding their skill and expertise to the greater efforts of the force. In such battles the Kill-team often focuses its attentions on the greatest foes or deadly leaders and overlords while the "rank and file" or support troops deal with the vast numbers of lesser foes.

In games of **Deathwatch,** the Kill-team usually works alone. Even though they are generally outnumbered and may face vast numbers of enemies at any one time, they do not normally need to coordinate with allies and the GM need only ever concern himself with dealing with attacks against and from the player characters. The rules for Massed Battles presented here cover situations when the players will be fighting as part of a larger Imperial effort or when they have substantial numbers of allies on their sides. They are intended to allow the GM to quickly and easily deal with such large combats while not taking away the focus from the Battle-Brothers and their own efforts. This section provides both the GM and players with some rules and guidelines for commanding massed battles, allowing the players to control the efforts of their troops and allies in a leadership role.

# RUNNING MASSED BATTLES

A massed battle can be defined as any combat in which the players are part of a larger fighting force, and usually in which there is a significant amount of "off camera" action going on. For combats in which the players are facing vast numbers of foes, the GM can simply use the Horde rules (see page 359 in the DEATHWATCH Rulebook), amalgamating these enemies into vast mobs which the characters can face in much the same way as individual warriors. However, things can get tricky when the PCs find themselves fighting Hordes, numerous vehicles or enemy support weapons (such as long range artillery or ground attack aircraft), while they themselves are supported by friendly Hordes, tanks, aircraft and the like.

Needless to say, running such a huge combat could be a nightmare for the GM as he makes attacks from one Horde against another or plays out aerial dogfights or long range artillery duels, all of which only indirectly affects the characters and which they have no direct control over. Of course, such exciting and bloody conflicts are an intrinsic part of the 41st Millennium and it is likely that the Kill-team will eventually find itself in such a situation and the GM will want to include them in his games. Presented below are two different methods for dealing with massed battles, each with its own differing degrees of detail depending on the tastes of the GM, and each one allowing the GM to capture the chaos and carnage of a massed battle, while giving the players the chance to feel they are making a difference without excessive dice rolling or complex choices on the part of their characters.

## ABSTRACT METHOD

The easiest way for the GM to run a massed battle is by handling it as a narrative. This means that the GM simply describes the action as it unfolds around the PCs and only makes rolls for attacks against or from the Kill-team. The GM then uses his judgement, depending on the strength or number of allies and enemies (or as determined by the course of the plot) to work out victors and losers. This method also allows the GM to take into account things such as morale, environmental effects or the special abilities of commanders, without the need to assign additional Talents or Traits to combatants. If the GM feels an Imperial Guard regiment is of poor quality, or suffering from weeks of reduced rations and tainted water, he can have them fare badly in battle. Equally, if facing a looted Ork tank, the GM could have it break down or malfunction intermittently, describing the Grots crawling over its hull, hammering it with wrenches, in a vain effort to get it moving again.

If the GM wants to add a bit more randomness to this method, he can make dice rolls, usually a single dice to keep things quick, to determine the outcome of events. For example, he may decide that a company of Imperial Guardsmen will hold if they can roll equal to or less than their Willpower. The same Imperial Guard company may come under fire from aerial bombardment, at which point the GM could roll a dice against their Toughness and have them destroyed if they fail. Just as with results the GM creates using purely his own judgement, this kind of quick random outcome should only be used for action between allies and foes, not for direct attacks from or against the PCs.

## EXAMPLE

*The Kill-team is in the vanguard of an Imperial attack against an island held by Tau forces. Riding in on Valkyries, with a company of Storm Troopers, they must make a beach landing under fire. Deciding to run the battle as a narrative, the GM describes the flight of Valkyries coming in low over the ocean as anti-aircraft fire blazes around them from Tau emplacements on the cliffs above the beach, even having one or two of the Valkyries burst into flames and crash into the surf. The GM only makes rolls to hit the Valkyrie with the Kill-team inside, however. When they reach the beach and jump out onto the sand, they then immediately come under fire from several companies of Fire Warriors (represented as Hordes) supported by Battlesuits. Once again the GM describes Storm Troopers being gunned down and blown apart as they rush up the beach but only rolls for attacks directed at the Kill-team and only works out damage against the Tau from their attacks. After a few rounds of furious combat, the GM then decides that the Storm Troopers have broken through, though they have taken heavy casualties (this equates to reducing the Storm Troopers by half and having the Tau Fire Warrior Hordes retreat along with their Battlesuit support). The Imperial forces, led by the Kill-team then move off inland after the Tau.*

## EYE OF THE STORM

Regardless of the style of massed battle the GM chooses, he should never forget that the game is all about the players and the actions and choices they make. As exciting as a massed battle may be, it can quickly become boring for the players if they are merely spectating, or if all the best action is taking place between powerful NPCs or epic war machines over which they have no control. The GM should also remember that when running a massed battle, the Kill-team will effectively be in the "Eye of the Storm" surrounded by the swirling chaos of war but ultimately only really witness to their isolated section of events. This means that while they may be aware that overhead a grand fleet battle is taking place, exploding torpedoes and vivid lance strikes lighting up the sky, the GM doesn't need to worry about the exact details. As a general rule, the GM should only ever make rolls for friends or foes if the outcome will immediately and directly affect the PCs. In all other cases, the fog of war can swallow up the results and he can determine them 'off camera'. The GM can also use this to his advantage, such as in the case of the space battle above, the Space Marines might see a flame trail burst into the atmosphere indicating a falling crippled cruiser, though have no idea to which side it belongs...

## COMMAND AND CONTROL

Leadership and command can play a large role in massed battles, especially if the GM wants to allow the players to control some or all of their allies. In these instances the GM can have a commander make a **Challenging (+0) Command Test** whenever he wants to get his troops to do anything which is not either firing at the nearest obvious enemy (or firing back at a foe which has just fired at them), or falling back (most troops need little prompting to retreat). Advancing under fire or targeting specific enemies or taking specific locations all require solid leadership. The GM can then add bonuses or penalties to such Command tests depending on the nature of the situation, the foes or the quality of the troops themselves.

If the GM is using the abstract method for massed battles, he can even have allied NPC commanders or the players make opposed Command skill tests with enemy commanders to determine the outcome of combats, where the quality of leadership counts more than the troops involved. This is a quick way of resolving such combats, allowing you to work out the victor and have the loser's forces defeated (though it might play out over a number of rounds). For a little more detail, the loser's forces could instead suffer 1d10 damage to its wounds or Magnitude (plus an additional 1d10 for each degree of success by which the winner wins the opposed test).

## DETAILED METHOD

This method is slightly more involved than the abstract method, though it aims to keep things simple and fast to run and allows the GM to keep the action moving along at a good pace. The detailed method assigns each enemy or ally Horde, Elite warrior, Master warrior (see page 358 in the **DEATHWATCH** Rulebook), or vehicle, with an Attack Value (AV) and Defence Value (DV) based on the damage they can inflict and the wounds, armour or Magnitude they have. To work out these values use the following guidelines:

### Working out Attack Value

- Add 1 point for each dice of damage the unit inflicts with its weapons (if the unit is armed with multiple weapons use the weapon which deals the most damage)
- Add 1 point for every attack beyond the first (additional weapons and twin-linked weapons count as extra attacks)
- Add 1 point if it is using a semi-auto weapon
- Add 2 points if it is using a full-auto weapon

### EXAMPLE

*A Horde of Imperial Guardsman is armed with lasguns and has a Magnitude of 40. The damage from a lasgun is 1d10+3 (adding 1 to the Attack Value for the one dice of damage). Because of its Magnitude of 40, the Guardsman Horde inflicts an additional 2d10 damage on all its hits, adding another 2 to its Attack value. Also as a result of its Magnitude of 40, the Horde can make 3 ranged attacks (2 extra beyond the first) adding another 2. Finally a Lasgun can fire on semi-auto adding another 1. This gives the Guardsman Horde an Attack Value of 6 (3 of for the number of its damage dice, 2 more for its extra attacks and 1 for being able to fire semi-auto).*

## Working out Defence Value

- Defence is the first digit of the Horde, vehicle's or warrior's wounds or Magnitude (use the highest value if the unit has multiple values). For Magnitude or wound values of less than 10 (i.e. scores of 1-9) the Defence Value counts as 0.
- If the unit has armour points, add another 1 to its Defence Value for each full 4 armour points it possesses.
- If the unit or Horde has force fields (a very rare occurrence!), add another 1 to its Defence Value for each full 10 points of the Force Field's rating (see page 166 in the **DEATHWATCH** Rulebook).

## TACTICAL DISPLAYS

Massed battles can become very complicated depending on the number of units involved and the nature of the battlefield. In these instances the GM can find it useful to create a tactical display for his players to show them where units are in relation to one another and perhaps the fighting strength or condition of these units. This can be as simple as making some marks on a piece of paper or using a collection of markers, coins or other counters to provide an overview of the battle at a glance. If the GM wishes to add more detail he could use a grid or hex map to help define distances and include the fog of war so that enemy units (or even friendly ones) disappear and reappear on the map as they fall in and out of vox or visual contact. GMs should also note that creating a tactical display is different from using a tactical map (see DEATHWATCH page 245) as it is intended to give a broad view of a battle, like that which an actual commander might have, rather than an exact representation of the location of the characters and each individual enemy.

## EXAMPLE

*A Magnitude 30 Horde of Imperial Guardsmen is wearing flak armour which provides 4 Armour Points. The Guardsmen use the first digit of their Magnitude to work out the Defence value giving them a DV of 3. They then add another point as they have 4 points of armour giving them a final DV of 4.*

When running a combat between foes and allies, the GM rolls 1d10 and adds the unit's Attack Value, which he then compares to the target's Defence Value, every point over this inflicting a wound or a point of Magnitude. PCs always use their own characteristics (they never use the Attack value and Defence value method) when attacking foes, and foes always use their normal characteristics when attacking the PCs.

## EXAMPLE

*Using the same example as above, the Kill-team are part of an assault on a Tau held island. When the Storm Troopers (AV 6 and DV 5) hit the beach the GM plays out the combat between them, the Fire Warriors (AV 7 and DV 5) and the Battlesuits (each with AV 5 and DV 5). Using all the normal rules for initiative and weapon ranges he begins with the Fire Warriors firing into the Storm Troopers rolling 1d10 and adding their AV of 7, getting a total score of 13. The GM then compares this to the Storm Troopers DV of 5 reducing their Magnitude of 40 by 8 to 32 (the amount over their DV). The Storm Troopers then return fire (after reducing their AV by 1 to take into account the extra ranged attack lost by their reduced Magnitude) concentrating on the Battlesuits. They roll and inflict 7 wounds which are applied to one Battlesuit. Finally the Battle-Brothers make their attacks using their normal profiles against the Battlesuits, using the Tau's normal characteristics, inflicting another 25 wounds, which in addition to the 7 wounds caused by the Storm Troopers destroys a Battlesuit.*

## WHICH METHOD?

Either of the two methods presented here can be used equally well to represent massed battles, and it is completely up to the GM and his own preferred style of play as to which method he chooses. However, GMs may discover that mixing and matching the two methods can be advantageous, depending on the kind of massed combat they are running. While the detailed method is still quicker and simpler than playing out the combat normally, it may be too time consuming or exact for combats which have more to do with the plot than the actions of the Battle-Brothers or their individual prowess in combat. In these cases the GM may wish to use the abstract method at times when he wants to keep the action going at a quick pace, simply describing the chaos of war as the players press on to larger or more important encounters. The abstract method can also be very useful if the GM wants to ensure a particular outcome to keep the plot moving, such as having an Imperial Guard armoured company come crashing though enemy defences just at the right moment, to allow the Kill-team a clear path to their target or a timely airstrike which destroys a nigh unassailable bunker standing in the PC's way. Equally, when fighting important villains or for climatic battles, the GM may wish to switch to the detailed method making the outcome more tense and the combats more desperate.

## VERY DETAILED METHOD

Sometimes the GM may want to map out everything (or almost everything) that happens in a massed battle. This could be because he feels that the players are facing an important or unique foe which would feel too easy if reduced to simplified characteristics, or because the quality of their allies is particularly high or low and could seriously influence the outcome. In these case the GM might want to run the massed battle using all the normal rules for combat, having Hordes fighting Hordes and vehicles blasting away at each other with the full range of their weapons and special rules. Guidelines and rules for pitting Hordes against each other can be found on page 132.

If the GM does chose to play out a massed battle using the complete combat rules, he should remember that the focus should still remain on the characters. Unless a combat between Hordes or vehicles directly involves or affects them, he should not waste excessive time making rolls and marking up wounds and critical effects which only serve to slow down the game and take focus away from the actions of the Battle-Brothers.

# TURNING POINTS

*"Battles can balance on the blade of a knife, equally matched foes locked in combat, their fates determined by the slightest winds of chance; one strong gust and it can all be over..."*

–Master Tactician Hadros

Battles are seldom fought to the last man and in many cases the victor is determined not by size, strength or skill of a force, or even the stalwart leadership of its commanders, but by fate and a few chance encounters and actions amidst a much larger engagement. These key moments in a battle are sometimes known as turning points, and can influence the entire outcome of a combat. The GM can use turning points in his games to map the course of very large battles involving the players, or even entire campaigns or wars, the result of each one affecting an entire stage of the conflict as its ripples spread out to spell victory or defeat for those involved. Turning points are also a way of making massed battles more exciting and interesting, rather than becoming tedious exercises in dice rolling which go back and forth between combatants. They also give the players something very tangible to strive for beyond simply killing their foes, and allow them to come up with interesting tactics or plans to counter an unusual development.

## USING TURNING POINTS

The purpose of turning points is to create some key encounters and actions in larger conflicts which can be used to determine the tide of battle, and whether it is flowing against or with the Battle-Brothers. It is also a useful tool for the GM to make his combats more interesting and give them a more military feel, while also keeping them quick and easy to run. In this way, turning points can work with either the abstract or detailed methods (or very detailed method) of running massed battles above. When creating a battlefield encounter, the GM should choose a number of turning points based on the nature of the conflict and the enemies involved. This can range from one or two to half a dozen or more, with the more turning points involved, the more complex and difficult the encounter for the players. During the course of the battle, the GM then presents the PCs with the turning points (in any order he decides) and they must overcome each one to score a point for their side. If at the end of the battle, if they have won more turning points than they have lost, then the battle is considered to have gone their way and their side is victorious.

Turning points are generally only used in large scale actions where there are lots of other battles going on "off camera" or if the effects of the PCs' actions have far reaching effects. They can, also be used in smaller engagements if the GM wants to add some interesting developments, though as a general rule, if the Battle-Brothers vanquish all their foes then they should win the battle regardless of the outcome of the turning points.

*The GM is running a planetary invasion of an Ork-held world, in which the Kill-team is involved. Rather than playing out each stage of the combat between the Imperial forces and the Orks, he creates a number of turning points. During the first battle of the campaign, the PCs land, along with a regiment of Imperial Guard and an Inquisitor and his retinue, in an Ork-held spaceport. While the GM plays out the battle using the mass battle rules he creates three turning points for the battle, involving destroying the Orks AA batteries, stopping a surprise attack by a mob of Lootas during the battle and successfully killing the Ork Warboss before he can escape. If the Kill-team can win at least two of the three turning points, then the GM rules that the Imperial forces have gained a toehold on the world and can move on to ground operations, if not then they must make another landing somewhere else.*

# EXAMPLE TURNING POINTS

Presented here are a number of example turning points which the GM can adapt for his own massed battles. The GM is encouraged to develop further turning points tailored to his own encounters and which capture the nature of the massed battles he wants to run.

## BIG GUNS

Heavy weapons, whether they are in the form of massive guns, powerful vehicles or even orbital support, can wreak a terrible toll on a force and taking them out can not only save countless lives but also boost morale immeasurably. As a turning point, defeating big guns means destroying them or negating their effectiveness. At its most simple this can be killing the crew or smashing the machine itself, but it could also involve killing forward spotters, activating a jamming device that blocks targeting sensors or raising a shield over friendly troops.

## CUT OFF THE HEAD

Good commanders can turn even the most questionable troops into a serious fighting force and their presence on the battlefield can boost morale and drive warriors to great feats of courage and duty. Needless to say, killing such commanders can significantly reduce a foe's fighting effectiveness. As a turning point, killing an enemy commander usually means just that: finding them on the battlefield and putting a bolt shell between their eyes. Of course leadership comes in many forms and the same effect can be achieved by bringing down the enemy communications network or spreading propaganda among enemy troops to reduce their faith in their commanders.

## TAKE THE HIGH GROUND

Terrain can play a vital role in a battle and a force which makes good use of it can greatly increase its fighting ability. As a turning point, terrain can play numerous roles within a battle, such as covering defended positions, high ground or positions which offer good lines of sight for heavy weapons. In addition to the Battle-Brothers taking a good position themselves, Take the High Ground could also cover situations in which a foe or ally seeks favoured terrain, such as scouts hiding in woods or a sniper setting up in a bell tower, and the PCs must make every effort to either stop enemies or aid allies trying to claim these locations.

## UNEXPECTED ENEMIES

A surprise attack, especially from the flanks or rear, can throw a combat force into disarray as they scramble to reorganise and are stricken with confusion. This alone can be enough to end a battle and turn it into a massacre as troops lose their resolve and turn to flight. As a turning point, an unexpected attack can come in many forms, such as jump pack troops striking from on high, stealthy enemies lying in wait until their foes have passed them by, or even warriors emerging from below the ground. Surprise attacks can also be represented by situations where a fighting force must face extreme and unusual foes, such as the appearance of a Tyranid Hive Tyrant from among a swarm of lesser creatures or having a Daemon Prince burst from the body of a hapless cultist.

## BROKEN SPIRIT

Morale is as vital to a warrior as his weapons and the support of his comrades, and when morale is lost it can make a force run or surrender to a much smaller foe. As a turning point, morale can play any number of roles in a battle, the most common being the instance of a battered, isolated or green unit ordered to hang on against the odds. In these cases it falls to commanders, or the Battle-Brothers, to step in and boost courage by leading by example, giving stirring speeches or making heinous threats. Morale can also affect commanders, even those far from the battlefield offering indirect support such as void ship commanders or artillery captains, if they feel the battle is lost. In these cases it falls to those closer to the action to get them back into the fight via vox.

## A SHOW OF COURAGE

Sometimes a foe will try to intimidate his enemies or boost the morale of his own men by making a display of courage, issuing a challenge to enemy heroes or striding out onto the battlefield to take on vastly superior numbers. In all these cases, such an act can have serious effects on a force and drive them into a frenzy of duty or devotion as they surge forward to emulate their commander's courage. As a turning point, it falls to the Battle-Brothers to either make these acts of courage themselves or crush ones made by their foes, proving to their enemies the misplaced faith they have in such commanders by hacking them down in short order.

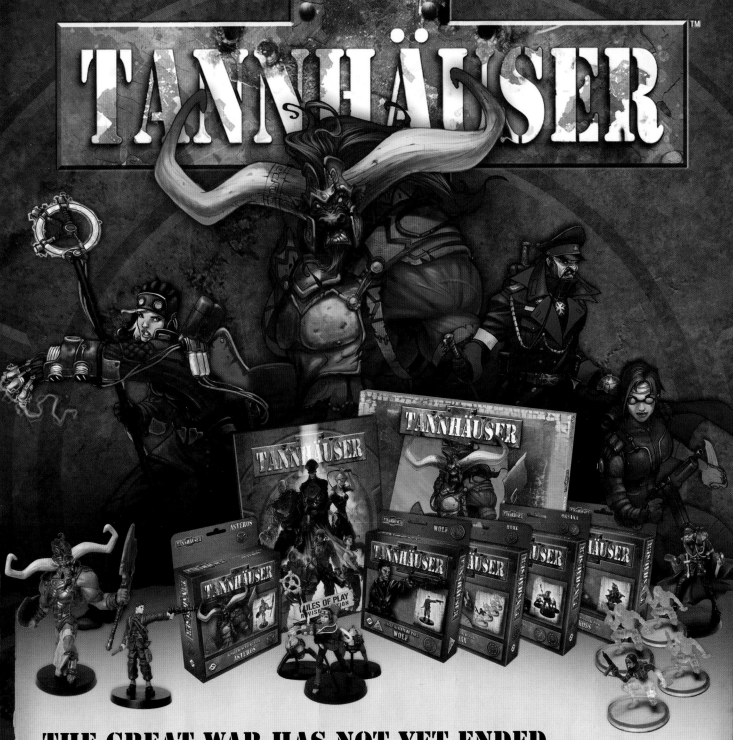